To my anchors: Brian, Ellen, and Bill
And to George, whose early editorial
generosity helped me stay afloat

*A study of animal communities
has this advantage: they are merely
what they are, for anyone to see
who will and can look clearly;
they cannot complicate the picture
by worked idealisms, by saying
one thing and being another;
here the struggle is unmasked
and the beauty is unmasked.*

—ED RICKETTS,
as quoted in
THE OUTER SHORES,
BY JOEL HEDGPETH

*It is advisable to look from the
tide pool to the stars and then
back to the tide pool again.*

—JOHN STEINBECK AND
ED RICKETTS,
THE LOG FROM THE SEA OF CORTEZ

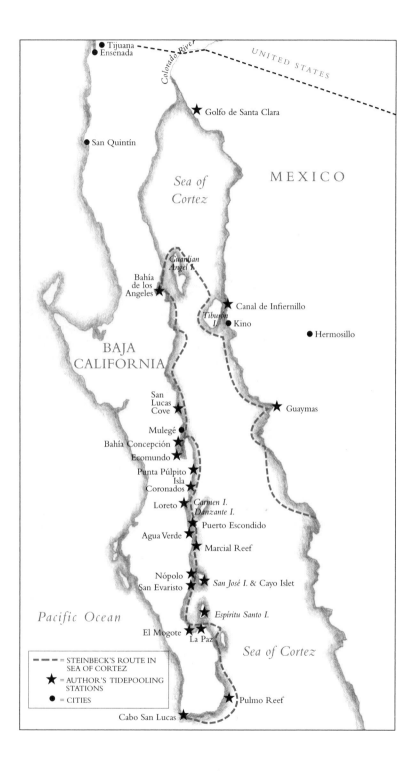

Tijuana
Ensenada
Colorado River
UNITED STATES

Golfo de Santa Clara

San Quintín

Sea of
Cortez

MEXICO

Guardian
Angel I.

Bahía
de los
Angeles

Canal de Infiernillo

Tiburón
I.
Kino

Hermosillo

BAJA
CALIFORNIA

San
Lucas
Cove

Guaymas

Mulegé
Bahía Concepción
Ecomundo

Punta Púlpito
Isla
Coronados

Loreto   Carmen I.
Danzante I.

Puerto Escondido

Agua Verde

Marcial Reef

Nópolo
San Evaristo

San José I. & Cayo Islet

Espíritu Santo I.

Pacific Ocean

El Mogote
La Paz

Sea of Cortez

Pulmo Reef

Cabo San Lucas

= STEINBECK'S ROUTE IN
  SEA OF CORTEZ
= AUTHOR'S TIDEPOOLING
  STATIONS
= CITIES

CONTENTS

Prologue:

A MAKESHIFT EXPEDITION

Spring, 1940. Farmers greeted the season of birds and flowers by blanketing their fields with the new miracle pesticide DDT. Housewives welcomed the introduction of precooked chicken fricassee—the world's first frozen dinner. RCA Laboratories unveiled the electron microscope. The Nazis swept into Denmark undeterred. And eager to be away from it all, to consider the world's future and his own, author John Steinbeck made a trip into the Sea of Cortez.

The world's pace was quickening that spring, but Steinbeck elected to slow his own life to an introspective drift. With his closest friend, biologist Ed Ricketts, he fled to Baja California's desert coast. They traveled aboard an off-duty fishing boat called the *Western Flyer.* Ricketts, owner of a biological supply company in Monterey, California, stalked the tide-pools for hundreds of specimens to pickle and sell. Steinbeck stalked the same habitats for ideas. Both came away changed: shaken and reawakened to the wonders of the world.

For six weeks, the two men cruised the arid coast gathering marine organisms, their lives governed by mechanical failures, an occasionally ornery crew, sexual tension, and the tides. One day, they stood calf-deep in the Sea of Cortez. Their arms were dusty pink from the brine and the sun. Steinbeck was a meaty man—broad shoulders, prominent ears, brooding blue eyes. Ricketts looked elegant next to him, with his boylike face and slender build. Both men hunched over the water, their faces angled toward their feet, eyes squinting into the diamond-splashed brilliance of the tropical shallows.

Small Mexican boys appeared, silent as coyotes. They carried little iron harpoons for spearing fish. They kicked through the seaweed and tossed a few stones into the water. They studied the two strange American men, who did not study them back.

Finally, one of the boys—magnetized by the men's postures, by the intensity of their downward stares and the delicacy of their probing fingers—summoned the courage to approach.

"What did you lose?" the boy asked.

"Nothing," one of the Americans answered.

The boy persevered.

"Then what do you search for?"

It was an embarrassing question, Steinbeck and Ricketts thought.

The two men answered it later in print—not for the boys, but for themselves, and for all wanderers who seek solace in the natural world: "We search for something that will seem like truth to us; we search for understanding; we search for that principle which keys us deeply into the pattern of all life."

If looking for life's answers in the plankton-rich broth of a desert tidepool sounds peculiar now, it was even stranger then. Macho travel writers were expected to slay lions and fight bulls in those days. Other earnest young men were beginning to contemplate the battlefields of Europe. It was the dawn of a dark era, and Steinbeck and Ricketts met the coming storm by mucking about in briny puddles. They spent their days scooping up warty sea cucumbers and sedating writhing brittlestars. They laughed a lot. They discussed *Faust,* the poet Li Po, and Hitler. And they drank. You had to wonder what they were up to. People, myself included, are still trying to figure it out. Like the Mexican boy on the beach, we want to know what Steinbeck and Ricketts were really looking for in a tidepool. We want to know if they found it, and whether we might find it, too.

Those questions were enough to draw me, my husband Brian, and our two young children into a burnt wilderness for two months, following in the *Western Flyer*'s wake. Hundreds of strange sea creatures were the most tangible of our quarries. Two dead men were our guides. One living (though occasionally vegetative) man was our captain, until briefly, but memorably, he lost the will to live. Then we were on our own.

We laughed some and drank a little—probably not nearly enough, because we were too distracted by each day's perils to risk much joyful inebriation. Though Steinbeck and Ricketts counseled against seeking adventure of any sort, adventures often snuck up on us just the same.

Our goal—truth, understanding, some principle that would key us "deeply into the pattern of all life"—proved maddeningly elusive. Along Baja's desert coast, every answer led to a new question, and every shimmering tidepool seemed to reflect how little we knew about anything at all.

"We made a trip into the Gulf; sometimes we dignified it by calling it an expedition," wrote John Steinbeck and Edward F. Ricketts in *Sea of Cortez: A Leisurely Journal of Travel and Research.* (It was later issued in abbreviated form, minus a three-hundred-page scientific appendix, as *The Log from the Sea of Cortez.*) The 1940 Steinbeck and Ricketts expedition was a marine organism collecting trip. But it was much more than that, and the hybrid *Log* is not just a book of science but a book of observation, escapade, and the kind of half-brilliant, half-addled philosophy that long days at sea, plus lots of Carta Blanca beer, sometimes inspire.

In Europe, bombs were falling. On Monterey's Cannery Row, the sardine plants still whistled, and America had not yet entered the world war. But other forms of hatred filled the void. Steinbeck had received the first of many death threats for *The Grapes of Wrath,* a controversial best-seller that would earn him a Pulitzer Prize and a reputation as an atheistic, communist rabble-rouser. In his lifetime, he would see his writings publicly burned. Even in his hometown of Salinas, California, the censorious bonfires blazed. Those who admired Steinbeck wanted his time. Those who envied him—including one woman who slapped him with a paternity suit, later dismissed—wanted his money or his fame. Those who despised him wanted him dead.

Writing *The Grapes of Wrath* and enduring its subsequent notoriety drained Steinbeck. He wanted a break from writing fiction. He wrote to his friend Carlton Sheffield, "I've worked the novel—I know it as far as I can take it. I never did think much of it—a clumsy vehicle at best. And I don't know the form of the new but I know there is a new which will be adequate and shaped by my new thinking. Anyway, there is a picture of my confusion."

Steinbeck longed to hide away—from the war he knew was coming, from politics and literary criticism, and from his own marriage troubles.

The Sea of Cortez, an eight-hundred-mile-long gulf bordered by mostly unpeopled desert, was the perfect place to hide.

Ricketts also knew a thing or two about escape. The need to flee a romantic entanglement, a recurring theme in his life, once prompted him to tramp solo through Indiana, Kentucky, and Georgia. But this time around, Ed wasn't running. Unlike Steinbeck, he wasn't desperate or haunted. In fact, in 1940, Ricketts was in his intellectual and emotional prime.

The biologist had celebrated recently the publication of his magnum opus, a guide to invertebrate tidal life called *Between Pacific Tides*. Even more significantly, Ricketts had completed three important essays that summarized his philosophical views, including one on what he called non-teleology—a rejection of cause-and-effect thinking in favor of a Taoism-inspired acceptance for "what is."

It was a surprise to humble Ed—if to no one else—that popular American magazines had little interest in publishing this essay on abstract philosophy. But his enthusiasm did not flag. Ricketts was flooded with ideas, though he had no audience except for that circle of sympathetic readers who were his friends. As for Steinbeck, his intellect and spirit were dry. He had all the audience in the world but little he wished to say. The two men formed a symbiotic union.

They cruised south in a sardine seiner, assisted by Sicilian-American deckhands who were more interested in Baja's whorehouses than in its flora and fauna. Ricketts kept a journal of their scientific findings and recorded many colorful trip anecdotes. Steinbeck—hard to believe—kept no journal at all.

When it came time to commit the travelogue to paper, Steinbeck included many of his own memories, insights, and flashes of humor. Despite the use of a narrative "We," his voice is so strong in the *Log* that for years reviewers believed it was his book alone, a misconception that still lingers because modern paperback editions trumpet him as the primary author. In fact, Steinbeck relied heavily on Ricketts's trip journal, importing entire thoughts, stories, and one long lecture nearly verbatim. Ricketts was thrilled. "It's so damn beautiful . . . ," he wrote a girlfriend after reading the first parts of an early draft. "He takes my words and gives them a little twist, and puts in some of his own beauty of concept and expression and the whole thing is so lovely you can't stand it."

Sometimes, Steinbeck and Ricketts agreed so seamlessly that they couldn't remember who initiated a given thought. More often, they traded ideas without truly understanding each other's finest points. They both adored Bach, and their late-night rambles often resembled counterpoint in classical music: two parallel motifs on a common theme, weaving but never blending.

Yet other times, as when he penned the *Log,* Steinbeck seemed to enjoy disappearing into his friend's ideas, even when they conflicted with his own. It was like diving into the deep, dark waters of another's mind. The challenge was to make it look easy: to dive smoothly, and leave no ripples.

My husband, Brian, is an environmental educator with an undergraduate degree in biology. He dropped out of graduate school to teach children about the northern woods. He is short, dark, and fearless, always willing to poke his fingers beneath shadowy boulders where fingers do not belong. He is endlessly obliging—agreeing, for example, that he will not swim or hike too far unescorted, or reach for things that bite or sting, when we both know very well that he will. And he is also kind. Some years ago, during our honeymoon in the Caribbean, when I was too paralyzed with fear of man-eating sharks to snorkel at the reef within view of our rental bungalow, Brian's loyalties were stretched thin. There was the enormous fringing reef on one side—barracudas and sea turtles and gumball-bright fishes. And there was me on the other, swimming timidly within the dock's shadow. His fidelity was tested, but did not snap. We enjoyed our waist-deep-and-no-further vacation. I've owed him ever since.

In spite of—perhaps because of—my own abyssal terror, I studied fisheries. I earned a graduate degree in marine management, then promptly fled academia to become a journalist and writer.

Our much-consulted copy of the *Log,* purchased the year we started dating and thumbed through every year since, has been horribly abused. It has been defaced with asterisks and blurry notations, including the passage we asked our Conservative rabbi to read during our marriage ceremony. The passage was about religious feeling—about how it can be found in ecological connections, in the mysterious web of life that prompts us to stare into the tidepools, up at the stars, and back down into the tidepools again. "I don't get any of this," the rabbi deadpanned to a formally attired audience. "But maybe some of you do."

Our *Log* has been dunked countless times in saltwater and rescued to dry as a bloated accordion of salt-stained pages. It won't fit properly on any bookshelf. It can't be shoved or stacked. The yellow pages have worn to a velvety softness. The cover did not so much rip, finally, as dissolve. Ten years and two kids after we first read it, we considered buying a new paperback edition. But then, we thought, why just read it? When will we choose, instead, to live it?

We wanted to follow in the wake of the original *Western Flyer* voyage, stopping at the same villages and towns, the same tidepool collecting stations (a fancy term for shoreline stops in the middle of nowhere), to re-create the trip as faithfully as possible.

We wanted to know more about John Steinbeck, winner of both the Pulitzer and Nobel Prizes. And more about Ricketts, who both was and wasn't *Cannery Row*'s "Doc": a sweet, soft-spoken man loved by children and dogs, a man who detested mysticism but embraced mystery, a lover of truth who surrounded himself with yarn-spinners like Steinbeck. He spent his life serving science, but he also revered Lao Tsu, the ancient Chinese scholar who said, "Give up learning, and put an end to your troubles." Ricketts was paradox made flesh. Steinbeck loved that about his friend, and so did we.

We also wanted to compare the Sea of Cortez of yesterday and today, using Ricketts's copious notes and Steinbeck's impressions as an informal biological baseline. The *Log*, we hoped, would prove to be an invaluable scientific resource. The novelist and the biologist recorded in great detail what animals they encountered, and where. Both men were environmentalists ahead of their time and ecologists before *ecology* was a household word. Their concern about overfishing and the plight of marine creatures resounds today.

There is no other body of water like the Sea of Cortez (also known, less romantically, as the Gulf of California). So near the United States, it remains relatively unstudied and unspoiled. We'd traveled there several times, but the most recent trip was five years earlier, and pessimistic reports about the sea's health made us want to hurry back all the more. The endangered vaquita—a small porpoise that is one of the world's rarest cetaceans—lives there. So do several endangered species of sea turtles, over nine hundred species of fish, and more than twice that many species of marine invertebrates. The gulf's islands, inhabited by rare birds and reptiles, are evolutionary models, like a less-known Galápagos at America's doorstep. Tourists have flooded Cabo San Lucas and discovered a few other ports—La Paz, Loreto, San Felipe. But the Sea of Cortez has hundreds of miles of coastline without cities, without even sizable fishing camps or regular sources of water. The harshness of the land and the terrible roads have hidden and preserved many of the sea's treasures.

It was an amazing place in Steinbeck's time, over sixty years ago: sharp-ribbed mountains slanting down to a sandy, cactus-studded shore, and then into pristine azure waters boiling with fish. It is an amazing place, still. Those were our more tangible reasons, literary and scientific, for planning a trip.

Then there was the matter of expectations: how we would shape and record our Mexican journey. At first we considered being formal and rigorous, with an ironclad itinerary and regimented plans for the book that I—the family scribe—would subsequently write. We dashed such militaristic thoughts and took inspiration from the *Log*'s authors:

"We have a book to write about the Gulf of California. We could do one of several things about its design. But we have decided to let it form itself: its boundaries a boat and a sea; its duration a six weeks' charter time; its subject everything we could see and think and even imagine; its limits—our own without reservation."

Yes, yes, we thought.

"And so," as Steinbeck and Ricketts wrote, "we went."

PART ONE

*In
the
Garden*

ZUIVA

"My God, this is small."

How would a real estate agent put a positive spin on it? *Not small. Cozy.*

I reached out for one of *Zuiva's* dark wood countertops to balance myself. I was reeling—not only from the light rocking of the afternoon waves, but from all the travel that had finally gotten us to this little boat, anchored in this little bay, about two-thirds of the way south along Baja's Sea of Cortez coast.

There was no response from Captain Doug, whose six-foot-tall frame made the *Zuiva* look even more Lilliputian. When he bent forward to clear the entryway, his long black hair nearly swept the ground.

Brian crowded into the aisle behind us. "Where's the head?"

"You're looking at it," the captain answered nonchalantly.

"I knew we had to use a bucket," I said. "But I thought there was a closet or something for privacy."

"Guess not," Doug said.

But he had known it to be so. He had visited the boat months ahead of us, and hadn't ever thought to mention it, though we'd plied him for details during our many long-distance phone calls.

All five of us, including the children, had paddled out to the boat this calm afternoon: three in the folding kayak and two in the inflatable rowboat, a cheap model that wallowed in the waves like a drunken manatee. Now we all stood in the *Zuiva's* main cabin, in a one-foot by four-foot aisle flanked by two narrow, foam-covered bed platforms. The children pressed into the beds' corners. Tziporah lunged for me nervously whenever I passed, wanting to be carried. She reminded me of a cat forced into a car for a visit to the vet; the strange motions alone told her that something was not right and she pawed desperately, seeking stability. Aryeh shifted his weight from foot to foot, unable to contain his excitement. Any movement threatened to topple piles of coiled rope or stiffly folded sails.

"Can't we get this stuff put away somewhere?" I asked.

"Sure, go ahead," Doug said.

But when I went to push various items into various holds and hatches, he frequently stepped in, moving the item back to its original position or to another corner of the packed cabin. He'd only slept aboard the *Zuiva* a handful of nights, but he'd already appropriated the boat as his own kind of nautical bachelor pad. While Brian and I spent our first two Baja nights camped on shore, assembling our kayak and recovering from travel-induced exhaustion, Doug had spent his time aboard the sailboat, claiming the better of the two cots and jamming his clothing and tools into the stuff-holes lining the boat's starboard side.

At the head of each skinny bed was a small cupboard. One cupboard's lid lifted to reveal a hatch brimming with old jars, miscellaneous boat papers, and receipts dating from 1976. The other cupboard was topped by a recessed sink, now filled with Doug's vitamin bottles, all-natural toothpaste, garlic cloves, and onion skins. There were no water taps or pipes in sight. Under the useless sink sat ancient spices left by the boat's original owners: scentless basil leaves, and dried Chinese mustard from the Watergate era. Papery wasp nests plugged dark corners.

A tea tin hammered to the wall held an old stash of bone-dry pens. Next to it, a weathered postcard was decorated with one of Hokusai's famous prints: the terrifying image of a spiky, many-toothed wave dwarfing the lean prow of a Japanese boat.

The whole place was a mess—something I'd never imagined possible in the sailing world. In a harbor where I once worked as a fuel jockey, yachties had paid me to wipe the faintest shoe scuff-marks off their gleaming white-decked boats. I'd visited cruising boats this size and smaller—marvels of miniature efficiency, with dining tables that doubled as cots, and padded seats that doubled as storage areas. But this spare model had no seating or tables of any kind. Nor did it have any doors or curtains, except for a scarf-sized strip of floral cloth covering one scratched window, opaque with age. An ancient row of flip-switches and a disconnected depth sounder attested to the boat's former days of electronic, well-lighted glory.

Forward of the main cabin was a low-ceilinged, V-shaped berth—hardly more than a claustrophobic crawl space, painted swimming-pool blue. At the point of the V, rusty lengths of chain coiled just inches from where Brian, Tziporah, and I would lay our heads. Our feet would lie propped atop bags of luggage, our knees pulled into our chests. Aryeh would sleep in the skinny bunk opposite Doug's.

"There's one thing I still don't get," I told Doug, "This long pole thing here . . ."

"The spar."

"Okay, the spar . . ." At least I had discovered how to get his attention, by using a non-nautical term that he could not bear to let linger in the air, uncorrected. "Why is it taking up the whole aisle?"

"Nowhere else to put it."

The thick, metal bar was to be used only occasionally to support a light-wind sail. If it had been only as long as the aisle, it would have posed a hazard for feet in space that was already narrow and short. But it was longer than that. To fit it, Doug had wedged the spar diagonally, so that it blocked the middle of the cabin and extended into the V-berth.

"But this can't be right. Where does it normally go?"

He brusquely ticked off where it *couldn't* go: on the decks, or anywhere outside, where it might get in the way once we were under sail.

"But can't we experiment? Try lashing it along the sides or up the mast or something? I'll help you."

The suggestion seemed only to annoy him, even though the present arrangement was untenable. It was our first clue: The captain was just as bewildered by all this as we were. He'd been familiar with the one boat he'd briefly owned—a boat even smaller than this one, set up for easy solo handling. He knew the lingo; what ropes (sorry, *sheets*) would loosen or tighten (I mean, *trim*) the sails. But even he didn't know where half of the equipment should be stored, how to make this rattrap look and function like the seaworthy boat it once was. We'd already deferred to him on certain points: that we didn't need the electronics anyway; that a simple lead line would suffice in place of a depth sounder, and that all the other gizmos were unnecessary in a place without fog or much sailing traffic. But when we pressed him on key matters—here, in Baja California, in person, on a breezeless and gnat-filled day—he barely responded. We proclaimed our ignorance openly. He muttered and stewed.

Stuffing the children back into the life jackets and harnesses they'd just shed, we squeezed back outside the cabin. The stern of the boat was taken up by a square, open-air cockpit—rear hatch space, two benches, and a long tiller that took up most of the space between. Netting would be added to partially enclose this outer deck, one of a dozen chores to fill the weeks ahead. But the space would never be child-friendly. Under sail, the person operating the tiller and tending the sails would need to shift from side to side, commandeering most of the space. The swinging boom that supported the base of the main sail would pose an additional hazard. For now, though, we all crowded out onto the stern deck, clinging to each other and the lifelines as we negotiated these unfamiliar spaces.

"Did you see the wooden rail around the boat?" I whispered to Brian. "What about it?"

"It looks like it would fall right off if you hit it with something. Guess it's just as well we didn't bring a bottle of champagne."

Except for a raised eyebrow, Brian's expression hardly changed. He was not unworried—he'd developed an anxious stomachache while packing in Alaska that was only now, nearly a week later, fading into resigned, low-grade nausea. But he was too distracted by more pressing mechanical matters to react with any vigor. Never mind that the peeling gunwales looked like cracked porcelain, or that the name *Zuiva* on the boat's stern had faded to illegibility. There was a more serious matter to consider: the boat's motor. It didn't work.

Here, at least, we were in good historic company. The *Western Flyer*'s skiff had a motor that didn't work either.

"We come now to a piece of equipment which still brings anger to our hearts and, we hope, some venom to our pen," the *Log*'s authors wrote about the Hansen Sea Cow. This small outboard motor was supposed to help them zip in their skiff between the *Western Flyer* and the nooks and crannies of the Baja coast. But the Sea Cow was devious. It ran in spurts—just enough to keep the crew hoping. It quit as soon as it was truly needed. When it seized up entirely, the crew was forced to row to tidepooling locations. Even though Tex, the engineer, spent most of the trip taking apart, cleaning, and reassembling the motor, it continued to act like a machine bewitched. Steinbeck—and surely this was Steinbeck, not Ricketts—kept returning to the subject of the Sea Cow as a humorous running gag.

Having our own Sea Cow might have been a comical device—funny after the trip, if not in the middle of it. But humor was the farthest thing from our minds. The Sea Cow was an accessory—the skiff's motor, not the *Western Flyer's* motor. Steinbeck and Ricketts had seethed when forced to row in order to get from their mother ship to their destination ashore. Our bad motor, on the other hand, was our only motor.

"It's a sailboat. So sail it," a purist would have said. And one purist— our captain—surely did say that, along with a few four-letter words. But Brian and I had traveled this coast years before. In kayaks, we had wallowed within inches of wave-battered cliffs. We had walked narrow cliff ledges and explored niches filled with ancient-looking bones. We did not want to add our remains to the piles.

All boats have personalities, Steinbeck believed. Some seem irritable and swing defiantly off course. Some respond sluggishly after a storm. A few have been thought to shudder before striking a rock—perhaps even to cry out. No other inanimate object comes so close to being alive. This is not mysticism, the *Log's* authors wrote, but identification. The sailor pours his soul into the boat, trusts himself to it, and projects his feelings onto it.

The *Zuiva*, a twenty-four-foot Columbia sailboat, was no different. She had feelings, too. She hated us. Or maybe she was simply afraid.

Our sailing trip began in April. But our expedition—all the grandiose planning and fretting and organizing that any voyage requires—had begun many months earlier. First we had to find a boat. Just after an old friend and expatriate Baja businessman named Roy agreed to loan her to us, *Zuiva* slipped from her anchorage and nearly collided with Isla San Ramón, one of several guano-stained desert islands dotting a protected corner of a long Baja bay, Bahía Concepción. We'd never even met her, and already *Zuiva* was trying to get away from us.

"Not too impressive," Roy wrote me from Mexico after the incident. He must have been rusty on Steinbeckian boat psychoanalysis, because he blamed the slip not on *Zuiva's* own skittishness, but on improper anchoring by our newly appointed captain. Over the winter preceding our trip, Captain Doug had commuted between his home in northern California and *Zuiva's* anchorage on the Baja Peninsula to start preparing the sailboat for our spring voyage.

I wrote back from my home in distant Alaska, reassuring Roy that it wouldn't happen again. But already I could see the lines of tension forming: between the boat's owner, who happened also to be an old friend, and the boat's captain, who happened also to be the new husband of my sister, and the boat herself, who happened to be about twenty feet shorter than we all would have liked.

Beggars can't be choosers, though, and we were bold beggars indeed. The boating part of our budget was five thousand dollars for an entire two-month trip. Yacht charters in Baja run about ten thousand dollars *a week*. Chartering a commercial fishing or research vessel in Steinbeck's day cost him twenty-five hundred dollars, plus salary for a full crew—captain, engineer, and two seamen. Today, it would cost six figures. Just the thought of all those zeros started me thinking of alternative forms of transportation. An old canoe, say. Or feet.

Steinbeck and Ricketts had difficulty securing a vessel for their trip, too. First, they considered traveling by truck. Then they discovered what we also knew: that much of the Baja coast is sheer cliffs and roadless, spiny desert. None of the driving is easy. Some of it is impossible. Out of range of any car or truck, there are islands: more than one hundred of them in the narrow gulf. Steinbeck and Ricketts adapted quickly to the idea of traveling by sea, but few boat owners wanted to have anything to do with them. Ricketts was an okay guy, the Monterey fishermen agreed, but Steinbeck wore bohemian turtlenecks and involved himself in controversial union politics. Besides, the Gulf of California was a dangerous place. One Monterey boat owner negotiated a charter, only to raise his asking price, effectively bolting from the deal. Only the *Western Flyer*'s master, Tony Berry, acquiesced after nearly every other boat owner declined.

The *Zuiva*, our pint-sized version of the seventy-six-foot *Western Flyer,* was an eleventh-hour offering as well. We had spent a long winter hunting for a cheap but seaworthy boat and self-sacrificing crew without finding any leads. Projecting our quest onto the Internet succeeded only in attracting lots of spam. ("Girls! Girls! Girls!" every junk email subject line seemed to say. *Yes,* I thought. *But can they tack?*) We wrote to friends, acquaintances, and myriad organizations. Jacques Cousteau didn't return our phone calls. "Jacques Cousteau is dead," a friend later told me. "Well," I said, "that explains it."

Hiring a large vessel would have been more historically fitting, but a small, economical sailboat seemed our only hope. There was irony in this, considering that even Steinbeck and Ricketts, in 1940, considered a sailboat too antiquated for their needs. They were nostalgic for the ways of the nineteenth-century naturalists—the "slow heave of a sailing ship, and the patience of waiting for the tide." But they appreciated diesel nearly as much as they appreciated Darwin. "We can look with longing back to Charles Darwin, staring into the water over the side of the sailing ship," the *Log*'s authors wrote, "but for us to attempt to imitate that procedure would be romantic and silly."

When Roy informed me that he had an old sailboat anchored south of Mulegé, which he had bought reluctantly for a pittance from cash-hungry acquaintances and rarely used himself, we uncorked the wine and kept it flowing for a weekend. Never mind that we'd never even seen a photo of *Zuiva*. In parts of the world, marriages have been arranged with less information.

Later, it would occur to us to ask what the boat's name (pronounced *zwee-vah*) actually meant. "An Indian word, I think," Roy said. "Something to do with luck."

"Would that be good luck, or bad?" I asked him.

"I don't know."

Steinbeck and Ricketts started their trip in California and had to endure a long open-water trip in the Pacific before they could commence their study of tidepools, at Baja's southern tip. We had the advantage of knowing we'd board a boat already anchored in the more sheltered Sea of Cortez. The *Zuiva* was a humble craft, but without her, we might not have traveled Baja's coast at all. And this way was better, we told ourselves. Who wants to spend all day listening to the clang and chug of a big fishing vessel when one could have the silent, clean slice of a petite sailboat?

Friends warned us: A sailboat is a hole you pour money into. We laughed politely, and thought, *A prissy yacht maybe, but our little Zuiva is a workhorse.* That's how Roy described her in his emails: bare-bones, nothing fancy, without refrigeration or a stove or electronics of any kind. Roy wouldn't charge us to use her, but we'd have to drain our entire budget just getting her into operable condition.

More advice from the sidelines: Sailing brings out the worst in people. Two separate female friends tactfully offered this opinion, dredging up memories of domineering fathers and finicky equipment and snappy commands. Still we paid no heed. Pessimism, just like a seventy-six-foot purse seiner, was an extravagance we couldn't afford.

Some people sail for pleasure. We couldn't help fantasizing, of course—about shirtless days and tanned toes and the inevitable pod of dolphins leaping alongside our bow. But sailing for us was a means to an end. We wanted to see a remote coast, much of it unreachable by road. The *Zuiva*, we hoped, would take us there, and if she did not, we would not be romantic. We would not let our means be confused with our end: to search for marine invertebrates and maybe for ghosts, to find answers on that fine edge where desert and ocean meet.

Our choice of captain, like our choice of vessel, required compromise. Captain Doug, a small-scale organic farmer by trade, didn't join our expedition out of affection or loyalty. Family ties aside, I'd met him only once, and only briefly. I recalled a tall, long-haired, taciturn man, smiling across a picnic table and stooping into the rustic shack he shared with my sister, then disappearing among rows of herbs and fruit trees once family obligations had been met. He'd never traveled outside the United States. He'd never sailed outside of Humboldt Bay, his home port in the heart of the California redwood country.

Doug agreed to join our cause because he wanted to gain sailing experience and access to a boat he might borrow again once we all chipped in to spruce it up. We would have preferred a captain with more experience, but we got what we paid for: basically, nothing. No, that's not fair. Doug was a whiz at mending and splicing—pre-trip essentials—as long as he was alone and unpressured. He, no doubt, would have favored a crew that knew how to trim the sails and anchor. At the very least, he would have appreciated a crew that didn't whine or wear diapers. Our son, Aryeh, was five. Tziporah, our daughter, was almost two. We all made concessions.

All winter I traded more emails with Roy and long-distance phone calls with Captain Doug in northern California. I made checklists for everything: medicines to bring, and clothes, various boating and fishing licenses, and scientific equipment—a lofty term for what amounted to fishing gear, one hand-net, a kid's waterproof microscope, and a bunch of Tupperware. We didn't intend to keep or kill any organisms, only to observe and record them. That plan saved us from needing expensive aquariums and difficult-to-acquire Mexican collecting permits.

We ordered dozens of books. Modern technology made it easy. In Steinbeck's day one might have heard of some singular, technical volume by word of mouth, then gone searching dusty bookstores up and down the Pacific coast. Now we simply needed to log on, point, and click. The boxes from various dot-com warehouses arrived days later, full of naturalists' guides and Baja memoirs and nautical manuals and desert encyclopedias and kids' picture books in Spanish. A few of the books were wonderful. The rest were garbage: self-published, disappointingly thin, terribly written. We hadn't been choosy enough, after all. We'd never held each book in our hands, ruffled the pages, scanned sample paragraphs. We'd simply bought. In the end, we returned a few and shelved others mostly unread. I could imagine Steinbeck sifting through our book boxes with a pencil behind his ear, lips pursed, reddened bulbous nose wagging.

We knew that keeping our children safe would be a challenge, but photos in family-oriented sailing books reassured us. They showed toddlers wearing harnesses, strung to safety lines, and babies playing on deck, naked and blissful. Experts reassured us: Sailboats are small, but children love small spaces. One photo showed an infant tucked into a flat net pocket along a sailboat's interior wall, using a space no larger than a briefcase as bassinet, playpen, and fort.

We made a preliminary trip, well ahead of our Baja departure, to libraries and museums in northern California, searching for biographical material on John Steinbeck. We worked and played as a family. We watched our children bloom. Aryeh dragged us away from the glass-and-chrome perfection of the Monterey Bay Aquarium to go to the real beach, just in time for low tide. We watched the surf send rivers of current into the Great Tidepool—one of Steinbeck's and Ricketts's favorite spots, where the latter man's ashes were ultimately scattered—on a stretch of coast in Pacific Grove, north of Monterey. Tziporah spent a trancelike afternoon at Point Lobos beach, repeatedly burying and recovering a mango. We all visited Cannery Row: the old Chinese grocery store that John Steinbeck wrote about, and Ed Ricketts's real lab, now a gentlemen's club. If we were disappointed at all, it was by the fact that we could not feel the spirit of either man among Cannery Row's T-shirt shops and bric-a-brac. But no matter. We knew where their ghosts really lurked: farther south, where we'd be heading soon. In Baja.

Over the winter, in Alaska, we bought thousands of dollars of sailing and safety gear for a boat we'd never seen, read as many of the manuals and watched as many sailing videos as we could stomach. Tying bowlines in front of the television set during a long northern winter felt like some sort of post-lobotomy therapy: soothing, no doubt, but perhaps not adequate preparation for a maritime voyage. Brian and I were just as busy with the science end of things: trying to learn about bivalves and gastropods and echinoderms, cramming our heads full of both scientific jargon and Spanish. At the same time, we both had to work extra hours at our paying jobs to fund this voyage. Doug traveled hundreds of miles to completely replace the boat's wire rigging, then returned to his California farm.

Ten days before we were supposed to hop a red-eye flight from our home in Anchorage to San Diego, to rendezvous with Doug and load no fewer than fifteen bags and boxes on a bus bound for Baja, he called us.

"I can't do this," he said.

I protested, hoping this was just a case of travel jitters. I pleaded. Then I asked Doug to hand the phone to my sister Eliza. "Do you realize how much we've already spent?" I asked, not wanting to involve her, but desperate all the same. "We've been dreaming of this trip for ten years."

She reiterated his concerns about sailing an unfamiliar coast, with unfamiliar people. An angry male voice boomed in the background. Eliza and I said our good-byes quickly.

After hanging up, Brian and I sat on our kitchen floor with our heads in our hands, trying to brainstorm a list of names to replace Doug. Qualifications: must be ready to leave the country in less than two weeks and share a bathtub-sized berth with two other adults and two young children for two months. Our list was short.

After an hour, Doug called back, sounding sheepish. "Never mind," he said, and the trip was back on.

CAST AND CREW

In 1940 Monterey, the *Western Flyer's* crew was assembling under a similar thundercloud of excitement and trepidation. An official charter was signed. Last-minute permits were obtained. Fine camera equipment, including an eight-millimeter movie camera with light meters and a tripod, was procured to document the trip. (To the crew's consternation, the filming was a complete bust and no footage turned out.) Cases of spaghetti, canned fruit, whole cheeses, and gallons of olive oil were stuffed into cupboards and hatches. A fifteen-gallon barrel of formaldehyde for preserving specimens was lashed to the boat's rails, where the crew prayed it would not burst.

"Toward the end of the preparation, a small hysteria began to build in ourselves and our friends," John Steinbeck and Ed Ricketts wrote in the *Log*. "There were hundreds of unnecessary trips back and forth. Some materials were stowed on board with such cleverness that we never found them again."

The purse seiner, only a year old and still shipyard-shiny, would be home to seven people. Ed was forty-two years old, a father of three, separated from his first wife, Nan. He had delicate features and dark eyes. Though he'd spent much of his life knee-deep in water, he had a strong aversion to getting his head wet and usually kept it covered. When he did remove his hat, a loose forelock of reddish brown hair would fall over his eyes. He'd brush it back with a grin, the smile lines around his eyes crinkling.

When Ed talked, it was with a clear, high-timbered, professorial voice. But he was also a good listener. He expressed authentic wonder at other people's ideas and opinions. He made the people around him feel intelligent. He didn't speak down to anyone, not even the neighborhood prostitutes who visited his lab for discreet counsel. He'd take a break from filling the veins of cadaver cats with blue plastic so that he could attend more fully to the details of a local girl's latest heartbreak. They repaid him—it has been rumored—with the products of their miscarriages. No local biologist had a better collection of embryology slides and glass-jar fetuses than Ricketts. Everyone trusted Ed. The main difference between Ed and John, a friend of both men once suggested, was that Ed didn't know how to tell a lie and John didn't know how to tell the truth.

Though friends called him Doc, Ricketts had no Ph.D. In fact, because he'd neglected some graduation requirements at the University of Chicago, where he pursued a bachelor's degree, Ricketts didn't even have an undergraduate diploma. Nonetheless he contributed greatly, through his writings and ideas, to the development of ecological thought. He knew how to observe, how to reflect, how to think of animal behavior—including human behavior—in new and interesting ways.

John was thirty-eight. He was a large and clumsy man—prominent forehead, receding hairline, a thin caterpillar of a mustache. He'd spent his childhood as a loner, roaming the fertile Salinas Valley on a red pony. He sought out bubbling creeks where he could perch along the banks in contemplation. In adolescence he towered above the other boys and had trouble attracting girls.

Years before he met Ricketts, Steinbeck enrolled in courses in zoology and tidepool fishes at Hopkins Marine Station, in Pacific Grove, California. He frequently helped Ricketts collect specimens and owned a share in his friend's scientific supply company. But his expertise stopped there. What intrigued Steinbeck was not so much the technical rigors of biology as much as the grand paradigms, the potential for metaphors. A biologist carefully observes life, asks questions, finds connections. Doesn't a good writer do the same thing? Steinbeck later veered away from science, into fiction. But he never forgot his early inspiration. Once, a young woman accosted the famous writer at a party. "What do you do for a living?" the uninformed lady asked. "Well," Steinbeck answered, "You might say I am a sort of biologist."

John had always been a little uncomfortable in his own skin. Success, which had come to him only in the previous five years, helped him stand a little straighter. But he still ducked behind his companions when a newspaper photographer appeared to see the *Western Flyer* shove off. Steinbeck's voice was husky. His laugh was a low rumble. He dressed sloppily in jeans or baggy corduroys, old sweaters, and a sheepskin coat. In Baja, he'd wear a horizontally striped shirt—almost a parody of the natty nautical look—that matched the shirt his wife often wore.

Aah, the wife. Carol. Just the mention of her name made the crew raise their eyebrows in mock alarm. One of them—Tiny or Sparky or Tex—whistled through his clenched teeth. Captain Tony Berry shot back a stern look. Carol was coming on the trip—they were all surprised to hear it—but there was nothing that could be done. At *least we'll have someone to do the cooking,* Sparky said. But he was dubious. Carol hadn't warmed to any of the crew. Even around Steinbeck, she appeared aloof. Though she had promised to keep the crew well fed with chicken cacciatore and fresh-baked bread, those meals never materialized. Sparky was named galley chef in her place, leaving Carol with no defined role on the *Western Flyer.*

No one could know this yet, of course, but Carol would not be mentioned in *The Log from the Sea of Cortez.* Her presence would be excised from the travel narrative, her entire silhouette snipped out, the mysterious hole in a post-divorce photograph. Steinbeck would cut her out so cleanly that very few readers would ever notice that something or someone is missing. "It's okay to lie to others," Steinbeck told Ricketts on more than one occasion. "Just as long as you don't lie to yourself." But it's hard to do one without the other. The memories make the story. The story reshapes the memories.

Captain Berry was a sober and well-respected man who kept his purse seiner in fine repair. He hired his brother-in-law, Sparky Enea, as one of the crew. Wherever Sparky went, so did Tiny Colletto, his friend since childhood. Both Sparky and Tiny were Italian-American, and bantamweight: five-foot-one or five-foot-two, and all the more feisty for their diminutive stature. The two men had spent most of their childhood days roughhousing with other neighborhood toughs. Finally, at the age of eleven, they decided to make some money from it. A 1920 photo in a memoir by Sparky shows two cherubic, olive-skinned waifs in the ring, gloves poised for action, while a paying audience of knickered boys and bow-tied gents looks on, smiling.

Hall "Tex" Travis, who towered a full head and beefy neck above Sparky and Tiny, signed on as the boat's engineer. He planned to marry after the Cortez trip. Sparky and Tiny would seek temptation and trouble in Baja. Tex would try to avoid it.

The entire crew thus gathered: a biologist, a famous writer, an alienated and soon-to-be-invisible literary wife, plus four hardy Monterey men accustomed to fish guts and engine oil beneath their fingernails. Lots of diversity there. Or, looking at it from the Ricketts perspective—the biological perspective—one might say no diversity at all. For on this trip to the Sea of Cortez, Steinbeck and Ricketts were straining to shed their human-centered perspectives and see into a broader, dazzling realm of life, ancient and future.

In that larger realm, the seven humans aboard the *Western Flyer* were practically homogenous members of a single species, just one among the earth's nearly two million taxonomically described organisms. And those are just the ones we know. Every year, in the Sea of Cortez alone, new species are found and named. Noah's ark emptied long ago and we still don't have anything close to an accurate passenger list.

Lump *Homo sapiens* together with all the other vertebrates and the group represents a mere 3 percent of known animal species. We share this narrow wedge of the evolution pie with fish, whales, dinosaurs—anything that has backbones. We're biased of course, thinking that our little slice of life is the *crème de la crème*. When we want to insult someone, what do we call him? Spineless.

But actually, the invertebrates—boneless creatures from bugs to worms to sea stars to jellyfish—are the rulers of our wet and creeping world. God liked humans, so the Bible says. But he or she certainly lavished more time on the spineless beasts. In addition to having an "inordinate fondness for beetles" (in the words of English geneticist J. B. S. Haldane), the creator seems to adore marine invertebrates—the little critters that Steinbeck and Ricketts slogged through tidepools to find.

There are about five thousand species of marine sponges and an equal number of echinoderms—spiny-skinned creatures that include sea stars and sea urchins. There are three thousand species of marine flatworms, and well over fifty thousand species of mollusks—a class of soft-bodied animals that includes oysters, octopuses, and snails. Some sixty-five thousand crustacean species belong to Arthropoda, the phylum that also includes terrestrial insects and is the most abundant animal group on earth, both in total number and in number of species.

Humans are an oddity, an aberration. Invertebrates, on the other hand, blanket the earth. In many places, they *are* the earth. The pyramids of

Egypt, the smooth limestone of fancy buildings, the sedimentary rock of some bluffy shores, and the very bottom of the ocean are made of compacted layers of fossilized invertebrate material: shelled creatures, and even simpler protozoans.

As Steinbeck and Ricketts packed for their trip—perfecting the stowage of scientific equipment so fancy that it would never be used, and dipping into their "medicinal" whiskey well before the boat left dock—they talked, with the giddiness of schoolboys, of all the wonders they'd soon see.

AGUA BUENA, AGUA MALA

Ed Ricketts had two recurring dreams: one hot, one cool. The hot dream involved fire, the all-consuming hunger of a blaze. Four years before his Sea of Cortez trip, his home and laboratory on Cannery Row went up in flames when a power surge pulsed through the cannery next door. Ricketts barely escaped with his life, plus "one white flannel shirt, one pair of trousers, one pair of rayon shorts," and a much-loved typewriter with all the specialized symbols and foreign accent marks a worldly naturalist requires. He managed to drive his car out of the garage before the whole structure came crashing down. He later rescued a safe in which he'd stored some gorgonzola cheese, miraculously unmelted: "Still delicious," he marveled. But nearly everything else he owned—a large scientific library, microscopes, his phonograph, irreplaceable notebooks and files, family heirlooms—was lost. Ricketts never felt safe in the lab after that day, and the event returned to him again and again, in vivid dreams.

Baja California is itself a land afire. Night is different—almost lunar in its cold, dry stillness. But just after dawn in late spring or summer, the swelter builds so quickly, especially in a tent or in the airless bowels of a boat, that your body is forced to wake up while the mind lags behind. Flies buzz in heat-drunk circles and land in awkward places, attracted to the sweat trickling down an ear or behind a knee. You twitch and moan, only semiconscious. The sun streams in, the air warms, all the previous night's desert coolness is sucked out and the dreamer is left gasping. The brain is still cycling through one last phase of sleep while the body boils. It would be easy to find your dreams invaded by leaping flames. Finally you wake, confused, irritable, and damp. Only after thrusting aside the tent flap, or stumbling onto the boat's cool outer decks, can you inhale the day's first, full, fresh breath. Waking in the Baja desert is like that: like escaping from a blaze, or like being born again.

The Cannery Row fire deprived Ricketts of many of his material possessions and family mementos, and left him only with his ideas. The biologist's other recurring vision, a simple daydream, was an antidote to that feverish disappointment. He dreamed about waking next to a cool, life-filled sea.

For more than a week we worked on the *Zuiva,* preparing the boat and ourselves for departure. But every night Brian, the children, and I returned to our base camp on the shore. We slept in a tent just above the high-tide line, where all night we could listen to the waves massaging the sand. One morning, wakened early by the intense dawn heat, I crawled out of the steamy tent, leaving my family in twitching sleep, and stumbled toward the water's edge. There, mirror-calm, was Ricketts's dream, and my own. The Sea of Cortez was just as I'd remembered it from years past, cradled within the desert's rocky arms. It was as if the world's greatest meteor crater had been filled with turquoise-tinted mercury. The gently rippling waterline divided worlds: smooth and rough, glittering and matte, refreshingly cool and fatally parched.

Seeing the gulf at this quiet, solitary hour reminded me why I'd fallen in love with this place, why Steinbeck and Ricketts had loved this place, why we were all here. Where the outgoing tide whispered along the shore, the sand was damp and fine and full of quarter-sized holes, the burrows of tiny crabs. Just feet back from the water's edge, the desert began in earnest: rocky, dry, every inch covered with burrs and boulders and ancient sun-bleached clamshells. Cardón cactuses, taller than men, stood guard among the rubble, their fleshy arms pointing to even drier places upland, where the mountains climbed, steep and red. A dove's soft cooing echoed from the slopes.

I walked along the shore. Between two clumps of mangroves, the only dash of electric green along an otherwise tawny beach, a white egret stalked the tideflats. Its slim beak hovered over the glassy bay, ready to spear fish. It stepped and paused, stepped and paused, its dark stiltlike legs piercing the water without a ripple.

Just below the tide line, a hot spring bubbled up between the mangroves, trapped by a man-made ring of large stones that just broke the water's surface. There was a Grecian stateliness to the scene. The perfection of that stone ring, between those two columnlike mangrove clumps, seemed to magnify the bay's stillness. Even Highway 1, the slim, winding ribbon of asphalt that had delivered us overnight from Tijuana to this southern Baja beach, was silent.

Finally the egret swung its head and gave me an exasperated look— *You thought I didn't see you there?*—before flapping away. But the bird's disappearance didn't spoil the scene. Now the two clumps of mangroves seemed like a portal, through which I saw for the first time the world awaiting us: the deeper blue of the waters beyond, and the far side of Bahía Concepción, rising up in the form of hazy ochre mountains, painted with chalk-colored streaks. *Zuiva* bobbed in the distant center of the inner bay, looking innocent and even regal at such a distance—a white hull and single mast swaying to some inaudible tune.

The sky was cloudless, a pale double of the sea. And the sea itself was a dozen shades, from baby blue and transparent jade to navy, darker the farther one looked, so that each deepening shade drew the eye with a sense of mystery and promise. Out there: torpedo-shaped tuna and bucktoothed triggerfish. Out there: white, eye-dazzling sand flats undulating with stingrays and shadowy seaweed forests. Out there: ebony depths stitched with phosphorescent light. Out there: life, and life, and life.

Steinbeck began his love affair with the ocean early. His parents owned a cottage in Pacific Grove, within a short walk of tidepools and the whistling buoy at Cabrillo Point. The writer spent his boyhood summers at the ocean's edge, finding footholds in the slippery surf-battered rock. Those memories never left him. In *Travels with Charley,* the travel book he wrote near the end of his life, Steinbeck describes feeling pulled toward his "home ocean," the Pacific:

"I knew it first, grew up on its shore, collected marine animals along the coast. I know its moods, its color, its nature. It was very far inland that I caught the first smell of the Pacific."

He continues, "I believe I smelled the sea rocks and the kelp and the excitement of churning sea water, the sharpness of iodine and the under odor of washed and ground calcareous shells. Such a far-off and remembered odor comes subtly so that one does not consciously smell it, but rather an electric excitement is released—a kind of boisterous joy."

Ricketts, on the other hand, was born and raised in Chicago, over a thousand miles from the sea. He first saw marine creatures in a book given to him by his uncle. That stimulated his interest, but didn't really explain it. Perhaps he was drawn to marine biology, Ricketts himself once theorized, because he had a terrible aversion to milk, related to some pre-memory infant shock. No marine organisms give milk, except for the marine mammals, which would also explain why Ricketts shunned whales though he loved nearly everything else oceanic. It's a preposterous theory that sums up Ricketts quite nicely: one part logical scientist, one part screwball philosopher.

But a seaside childhood is not required to create an ocean-loving adult. I knew that from my own experience. I didn't glimpse the ocean until I was thirteen. I didn't encounter the Sea of Cortez until a half-dozen years later. I was just out of college, not sure what to do with my life, and recently heartbroken. Even now I remember that first pain, which seemed to signify that the world was no longer a hopeful and wondrous place and never would be again. It hurt just to breathe.

I hitchhiked across Mexico with my sister Eliza, trying to put miles between me and the boy who had wrung my heart. Three weeks riding in the back of pickup trucks, inhaling dust and straw, going town to town across the Mexican interior, helped a little. I took my first sips of tequila in the night desert and joined some locals driving in crazy circles, chasing jackrabbits. I began to feel stronger, but in a world-weary way. And I was about three decades too young to be world-weary.

Then, as one last excursion before heading home, Eliza and I boarded a ferry bound for Baja California. In San Francisco, my older sister had professionally massaged the injured back of a middle-aged traveler named Dean who now lived under a thatched roof in a Baja fishing camp. He had invited her to drop in sometime—not an easy task, because the camp was separated from Baja's main highway by several miles of hard-to-cross desert. Carrying plastic water bottles and our backpacks, Eliza and I staggered one afternoon out of the shimmering desert heat and into the camp. Dean was stunned. He'd told plenty of people to visit him over the years, but few had.

I was stunned, too. I'd never visited a seasonal fishing camp or anything like it. Mahogany-haired women giggled from behind the walls of one communal hut. Unmarried fishermen occupied their own thatched dwellings and ate together at a bachelors' table. Dean's hut was similar to the others, with hammocks strung from the wall posts, and scorpions lurking in the dusty corners. But it also had shelves crammed with books on anthropology and the works of desert gadfly Edward Abbey. A day's bus ride from San Diego, this camp had an exotic quality that made me think of more distant places, like Fiji. But Dean had been to the South Pacific. The two places weren't anything the same, he told us. He preferred Baja.

What amazed me more than all this, though, was the sight of blue-green water glistening beyond the sand dunes. Perhaps it was because I'd spent an afternoon walking the desert. I was dehydrated. Even my retinas felt baked. The dazzling light beyond the dunes, and the promise of coolness, had the quality of an illusion.

Eliza and I made our way to the water's edge and then strode tentatively in, up to our chests. The sea wasn't a mirage. It still seemed hallucinatory, though: What were those translucent strings swimming through the water? And what were those electric-blue sequins? The sea wasn't clear or sterile—nothing at all like a pool, or a lake, or even the Mediterranean, which I'd swum in once. This was a glittering soup. Staring downward for several minutes at one small square of complicated, life-filled sea, I attracted the attention of a local fisherman, who had accompanied us to the beach.

"Is she okay?" the fisherman asked my sister. In my stupefaction, I must have looked ready to pass out.

"I'm fine, I'm fine."

"A little sad, maybe," the fisherman said.

And that's when I noticed: For the first time in a long time, I *wasn't*. But any catharsis was cut short. Suddenly, my legs and back began to sting.

"Do you feel that?" I asked Eliza. She was beginning to shift her weight side-to-side, too. Before she could answer we were both running out of the water, our skin lashed by a passing cloud of jellyfish. There were no immediate marks on our skin, only the hot, prickly sensation of a searing burn.

"*Agua mala,*" the fisherman explained. Bad water.

A lesson: The sea that soothes can also bite. But I was still smitten.

LEAVE-TAKING

Now, all these years later, I wanted to be smitten again. But there was no time for rapture, only for work.

A string of simple vacation homes lined one end of the sandy beach. The Ecomundo campground's cluster of thatched huts, used by back-packers, kayakers, and college students, lined the other end. Roy, Ecomundo's proprietor and our generous host, allowed us to use one of his guest huts, which served as part of our base camp. Next to the hut, our mound of expedition gear occupied a chunk of prime beachfront space, prompting even Roy to look skyward and mutter—amiably, I hoped—each time he passed. But we weren't ready to leave anytime soon.

Packing doesn't happen once on a long trip; it happens again and again, and never seems to get any easier, especially when you're changing forms of transportation. Bribes had helped us get this far, greasing our cargo into Mexican buses from Tijuana south, despite luggage restrictions. But no wad of pesos would help us now. What could be stuffed into a bus resisted fitting into a dinghy or kayak. What could be lashed atop a kayak wouldn't fit on a sailboat's clutter-free deck.

The trip had barely begun, and already my camera's shutter had stopped working, rendering obsolete a brand-new macro lens and endless plastic baggies of film. Doug discovered that his expensive fishing rod wasn't transferred between buses; he'd never see *that* again. We eyed the complete contents of each other's boxes for the first time. Me: "That's a lot of dried apples." Him, eyeing our hundreds of pounds of books: "Geez. Look at all that shit."

"That's why we came, remember," I said. "They're reference books. We need them."

"Oh, right," he sulked. "For studying bugs."

Whoever was not on kid duty—Brian and Doug, or Doug and I— spent each day paddling back and forth from *Zuiva*'s anchorage, hauling away garbage and incrementally substituting new cargo for old. From

Doug's perspective, he was doing twice as much boat work as either Brian or I could do singly. From our perspective as parents accustomed to laboring as a silent split-shift team, his work day lasted eight hours or so, with carefree breaks at siesta time and at sundown, while ours lasted sixteen. But for now, this difference in perceptions didn't matter. We were all pitching in, and the boat was looking less like a floating junk heap and more like something that might possibly sail off into the sunset some day.

Aryeh adapted best of all to our new surroundings. Since crossing the border, he'd greeted every dark-skinned stranger with *Hola*. He was also linguistically prepared to answer *Sí, me gusta helado*—"Yes, I like ice cream." No one had asked, but it paid to be ready.

Aryeh was so taken with the Mexican desert that he adopted a new identity. *Me llamo Saguaro,* he said to anyone who would listen, renaming himself after his favorite type of Sonoran cactus.

At Ecomundo, his enthusiasm stayed in high gear. He quickly made a friend. Unlike adults, who require a long warm-up period—*Where are you from? What do you do?*—Aryeh and Ellis sized each other up immediately and disappeared down the beach: two freckled, spectacle-wearing kindergartners wading shin-deep after fish and clams.

Ellis's parents had recently bought a new house on the bay, in an enclave of expatriate Americans. They allowed their son to wander freely along this roadside beach, since the water was warm and shallow—essentially a football field–sized wading pool. Brian and I spent the first few days attempting to monitor our son's whereabouts obsessively, trailing after both boys with squeeze-tubes of sunscreen and water bottles and admonitions about staying within an adult's sight. Only exhaustion helped us loosen our grip. It is hard, after all, to keep on the heels of two five-year-old boys scampering among crab holes and mangroves. Being the worrywart guardian was a thankless job, especially in such a tame, paradisiacal environment. After a day or so we gave up and merely scanned the horizon every ten minutes or so for distant matchstick silhouettes: small, narrow, white bodies, topped by speck-sized mops of brown hair.

Watching the boys having a blast, I felt relieved. But I also felt envy. We grownups were doing all the work. No time for *us* to lounge or fish or poke through the rocks as long as the *Zuiva* was in such bad shape. And while Brian and I scrubbed decks and hauled garbage, Aryeh was getting to know this beach and all its invertebrate residents.

"What do you call this little guy?" I asked him one afternoon in our hut, as he endured a few moments of restful shade in order to bring me a tiny crab he'd caught. The sandy beach here was infested with them: nickel-sized bodies with comically mismatched claws. When agitated, the tiny crab brandished its singular oversized claw high in the air, its long stalk eyes peering over the enormous pincer.

"Fiddler crab," Aryeh said. We thumbed through a few guidebooks. Fiddler crab, indeed.

"Lucky guess," I said.

Later, he brought me a different kind with even, slender claws, elegantly folded in front of its small lacquered body. "And this one?"

"Elbow crab," he said.

"Now how do you know that?"

This time, Aryeh wouldn't even hang around while I looked it up. Smarty-pants. Once he learned Latin he'd be insufferable.

In contrast with our son, who was reveling in newfound freedom, Tziporah was miserable. She suffered through diarrhea and had to be coddled endlessly. Her eyes were pink and runny with infection. Her skin blazed spotty red from sunburn and fifty no-see-um bites, trophies from our first few nights camped near mangroves. "Eyes!" she'd shout whenever a ray of sun brushed her face—her abbreviated request for her favorite pair of blue sunglasses. "Hat! Hat!" she'd moan, pulling the brim down as low as it would go. We knew she'd acclimate to tropical travel in a week or so, but in the meanwhile, she was a dripping, clingy mess. The only thing that cheered her was a visit from Eco, the black-haired, free-ranging mutt who was the campground mascot. Tziporah would relinquish her sweaty spot on my lap to run after the dog. He'd respond by gnawing on her chubby, sunburnt arm.

Between bouts of protecting the dog from the baby and the baby from the dog and scanning the horizon for small boys, we slashed open boxes, untangled bungees and ropes, and tried to make sense of piles of canned food, carabiners, buckets, dry-sacks, fuel, and water bottles. We chased after stray plastic bags and flapping bits of tape. On *Zuiva*'s decks we scrubbed away rust stains and stowed water bags and hoisted new sails.

Brian spent an afternoon snorkeling underneath the anchored boat, scraping away barnacles and other organisms that had settled on the keel, until his hands were bloody. When I paddled out with both children to check on him, he looked woozy but enraptured. The keel had been a death scene, he said. The barnacles, pried free by the scraper, had faced their imminent demise by squirting clouds of sperm in the water. Through the milky haze, he'd spied other creatures fastened to the hull: two species of coral, a sponge, a brittlestar bigger than his hand, a three-inch-long octopus. As he chipped and scraped, yellow-striped sergeant major fish had gathered in schools all around him, feeding on the falling detritus.

"I felt terrible," Brian said, the red welts around his face proof that he'd worn his snorkel mask too long. "It was an entire ecosystem down there. I felt like I was destroying a coral reef."

So far, on this ecologically motivated voyage to investigate the coast, we'd seen little, studied even less, and recorded nothing. But we had managed to slaughter a few dozen creatures.

Doug, who glowered in the cramped quarters of the sailboat, was a different man ashore. He accepted the dinners we cooked for him with genuine thankfulness and responded with friendly, if still reserved, chatter. He shared his private cache of pistachio nuts with Aryeh. We, in turn, tried to mask our horrified expressions as the captain taught our son to fling each empty shell behind the mangrove bushes, in flagrant violation of leave-no-trace camping guidelines. We picked up the shells, but otherwise bit our tongues.

At siesta time, Doug lolled in one of the hut's two hammocks, casting a benevolent eye toward Tziporah. When our daughter lovingly called out "Ug, Ug," to get his attention, he'd grin back shyly, his features softening. The single eyebrow mounted over his dark eyes—a potentially menacing brow—looked less stern when his heavily lashed eyes were twinkling. During happy moments, he looked more like a long-haired, carefree boy than a man.

Each day, longing for the deep blue ocean beyond Bahía Concepción, Brian and I tried to question our captain about the master plan: What chores should we do next? Do we need to fix anything else? We were eager and willing laborers—in fact, mindless cleaning and organizing helped allay our anxieties. It felt good to end the day with chapped hands and sun-reddened cheeks. But Doug didn't know how to delegate or collaborate. He was a solitary tinkerer, not a master planner. Prior to the trip, we'd suggested coordinating all our meals, but he demurred, and in the end, we all packed our own edibles. Now, on a shoreside afternoon when

I consulted him about water supplies, he shrugged his shoulders. No opinion.

I did the math: "We'll hit a town every five to seven days. One gallon per person per day. Kids could get by on half, but we should bring extra to be safe. We're up to forty or so. Can't go long without water."

Correction. We—Brian, the kids, and I—couldn't. Once, Doug had gone several days without water, he told us in a rare, relaxed moment of siesta-time camaraderie. He'd abstained from libations of any kind on purpose. As a sort of vision quest, he said. Which worked. Wasn't even that hard to do. Doug told us this and there was a calm, satisfied look in his eye—the look of a guy who finds comfort in fasting, deprivation, and hallucination. Why didn't I want to know this private fact about the man who would pilot us along a desert coast?

The days passed slowly, with every roadside beach emptying as cabana-renting tourists packed up and headed north to escape the mounting late-spring heat. We ordered a new motor from distant La Paz. Waiting for it to arrive, we stared out to sea, watching *Zuiva* strain against her anchor chain like a dog refusing to heel. Every thatch-rattling breeze seemed wasted.

The *Western Flyer*'s crew had marked their own imminent departure by attending the annual Monterey sardine festival: a barbecue, a boat parade, empty beer cans tinkling against the *Western Flyer*'s hull "like little bells." With time to kill, we found our own festival: Mulegé's annual *Corriendo de Los Cerdos,* the Running of the Pigs—a nod to the better-known running of the bulls in Pamplona, Spain.

Mulegé sprawls alongside a muddy estuarial river. The afternoon of the charity festival, a jungly humidity cloaked the village. We'd hoped to mix with local native Bajacalifornios, but the crowd consisted mostly of American expatriates who hadn't fled the region's escalating heat. The women wore sarongs or thigh-high shirtdresses with knotted fringes. The men wore T-shirts and tank tops that stretched to cover *cerveza* paunches. Most of the hundred or so folks gathered looked like they'd just rolled out of bed or in from the beach. Maybe it was just the plastic flip-flops many of them were wearing. It is impossible to stride purposefully in flip-flops; one can only shuffle. Nearly everyone was tan—not just bronzed, but thoroughly roasted, with shoulders and necks the color of beef jerky. I made a mental note to use more sunscreen.

By the time the races were due to start, it was difficult to breathe. Tziporah lay flushed and sweaty in my arms, looking like a victim of dengue fever. A volunteer from the local Rotary Club raffled off items one could only hope not to win. When an olive-green afghan was awarded to another ticket-holder, we exhaled, grateful that the gods had passed up this opportunity to torment us.

The Running of the Pigs had sounded like dangerous fun. Didn't at least one tourist die every year in Pamplona? Pigs were smaller than bulls, but still, pigs could be ornery. "She went to shit and the hogs ate her," my stepfather used to cackle, whenever we asked him where someone had gone.

Just off the main plaza, some burlap sacks were heaped next to a chain-link fence, in the shade of a few wilting trees. The sacks were tautly filled but small. And they were moving. Suckling pigs, one per bag, lay in the sacks, panting from the extreme heat.

By now we'd started getting wise. We noticed the stakes in the dirt, perhaps fifty feet apart, strung together with wire lines. There would be no running of the swine through the streets. No Pamplona-style theatrics. No children risking life or limb to stay ahead of angry sows. There would only be a fifty-foot tethered baby-pig dash.

"We used to do it with burros, but then things got too rough," one of the event organizers told me.

The pigs hardly ran at all. They strained left and right, trying to pull away from the guide wires, or stopped in their tracks until someone clapped or stomped behind them. At least we attended a party, we told ourselves during the taxi ride back to Ecomundo. But deep down, we were disappointed. More than anything, we simply wanted to be on our way, out to sea. It should have been a warning: Follow in someone else's footsteps too closely, try to re-create artificial exuberance, and you'll never find your own travel rhythms.

Later we found out that even Steinbeck hadn't attended the festival he wrote about so nostalgically. "We asked John to come to it, but he never made it," recalled crewman Sparky Enea in his own memoir of the trip. "I was surprised he wrote about it. Anyway in *The Log from the Sea of Cortez* he got some of the facts wrong. I guess sometimes he was still writing fiction."

Perhaps we weren't out of sync with Steinbeck after all. All of us had the idea of a perfect trip, the way things should begin, the way that life should proceed logically from desire to fulfillment, as perfect and as satisfying as a novel.

The following evening, Roy invited us to the cafe. Doug decided to skip the festivities. "That's too bad," said Roy, who had gone through the trouble of finding and chilling bottles of champagne. He looked a little wounded.

Until this point we had not seen much of Roy. Or rather, the Roy we saw for a few minutes here or there was not the old friend we had remembered from years past.

He'd seemed stressed and distracted, dubious about our plans to sail with young children, suspicious of our fickle-tempered captain, concerned about the fate of the not-quite-shipshape *Zuiva*. In addition to all this, he had little positive to say about the Sea of Cortez. There were fewer whales coming into Bahía Concepción these days, he told us when pressed. And fewer dolphins. Butter clams were just sustaining their numbers. Hachas—a type of scallop—were down. There were no sardines. He hadn't seen any boobies, a type of seabird, this year at all; the booby was Roy's personal barometer for the state of the local fisheries.

This was precisely the kind of information we'd be seeking on our trip, to get a sense of how the sea had changed since Steinbeck's day. But I wasn't sure what to make of it. Were our friend's impressions accurate? Was Roy depressed about the sea's faltering health? Or was he just depressed, period?

"When's the last time you got out for a paddle?" I asked him. He exhaled through pursed lips, his voice lowered to a baritone mumble. "Dunno. Not for a while."

On this night, though, analysis and anxiety were set aside, and it was the old Roy who saw us off. He refilled bubbling glasses and regaled us with stories. When he laughed, his deep voice filled the cafe and rolled out across the quiet waters. I'm sure everyone on the bay could hear it. I half-suspected the entire shoreline community to materialize along the margins of the cafe's pool of light, attracted the way fish are attracted at night to a flashlight hung over a boat's rails.

Our imminent departure brought out the warmth of this moment, and the joy of it almost made us wish we weren't departing. Steinbeck and Ricketts said it best: "It would be good to live in a perpetual state of leave-taking, never to go nor to stay, but to remain suspended in that golden emotion of love and longing; to be missed without being gone; to be loved without satiety. How beautiful one is and how desirable; for in a few moments one will have ceased to exist."

After we drained our glasses, we thanked Roy for all he'd done and begged him not to worry. Brian, the kids, and I—with Tziporah in my lap—piled into our triple-seat kayak and followed a beam of reflected moonlight across the shallow bay, to *Zuiva*'s anchorage. Every paddle stroke left a trail of sparks in the water. No, it wasn't too much champagne. The bay was glowing with natural phosphorescence.

We tied up alongside the sailboat, hoisted the children over our heads—up and over the netting and lifelines—and climbed aboard. It was never an easy task from the kayak, which rested low in the water. Doug was waiting inside. We lit some kerosene lanterns. From the *Zuiva*'s open cockpit door, we looked out over the black silk of the bay's smooth surface and watched the few house lights winking along the desert shore. The lamps filled the cabin with an oily warmth and a comforting scent I've always associated with the backcountry travel of olden days, before folks learned to pack light and travel fast.

Zuiva no longer looked cramped and slovenly. My eyes had adjusted to her architecture. Before, where I'd seen a confusing nexus of lines and slopes, I now saw *boat*, a purity of purpose. Aryeh and Tziporah settled quickly into their spaces. We all went to sleep listening to the gentle slosh of water against the hull, ready to lift anchor at dawn.

RISING CURTAIN

"Ready about?" Doug called as we steered into the wind. He stood in the cockpit, hand on the tiller, long black hair flying in snaky coils.

I scrambled to uncleat the main sheet behind him. "Ready!"

"Hard-alee!"

I let the sheet out from one direction, dashed to the other side of the boat, and prepared to pull the corresponding sheet in from the other side. But I was overstoked on adrenaline. The sail flapped angrily, stalling midtack. I'd made the shift too soon. I should have waited for the wind to grab the sail and ease us into the new direction. My heart throbbed in my throat. Doug glared at me.

Swiftly he dropped his head to avoid the confused swing of the boom and hurried to reclaim control of the boat. I trimmed—tightened—the jib, to help this small sail catch the wind again.

"Do it again," Doug demanded, steering back into a tacking position. "Ready about?"

"Ready?" Now my own response sounded like a question. Which way were we going now? *Hard-a-what?* The noises were deafening: all that metal against metal, and the *whap-whap* of the sails, like some giant golem beating the dust out of gargantuan carpets.

"Now what are you supposed to do?" Doug quizzed me. My mind had wandered. In the cabin below, I could hear cupboards flying open and pans rattling up and down the aisle. Aryeh was shrieking. Or was that Tziporah? Brian was taking care of them both while he simultaneously searched for a missing chart and stooped to catch the vegetable cans rolling down the aisle. More thunks and rattles. It felt like the boat was heeling far to one side, like its port side was ready to splash down into the drink at any moment.

"Are we leaning too far?" I asked. "It really feels like we're leaning too far."

"No, it's good. Get ready."

"Ready? Ready for what? For tacking again?" I prepared to let go of the main sheet, but it was no use—I hadn't uncleated it behind me.

"Ah, shit." That was Doug, noticing my error. Should I stay ready, uncleat the sheet, make it tighter to fight the confused flutter of the sail, or just get out of his way? Or maybe he was cursing something else. A metal cup that had been resting on the cockpit bench, near the tiller, rolled in the captain's direction. He snagged it angrily and chucked it into the cabin without seeing who or what it might hit. A spoon followed. Then a handheld compass.

"Ready about?"

Not that again. It had seemed so easy before. We'd rehearsed this maneuver a dozen times, zigzagging across the inner bay in small, measured tacks. But now I was nervous and couldn't think at all. We were heading north, to an anchorage at the mouth of Bahía Concepción. The red cliffs on the bay's east side faded to pale pink—*had we sailed that far away from them?* The bay's western beaches looked darker yellow as we approached. It was hard to judge distance on a desert coast that had no trees or houses to provide visual context. *Weren't there shoals in this area? Why was he taking us so close?*

"Just tell me what to do now in plain language and I'll do it," I said to the captain.

"You should know. I already told you twice."

"Tell me again. I'm learning."

"Go ahead, learn," he said, gesturing to the flapping sails.

"But I can't," I said. "You're making me nervous."

"I'm not making you nervous. *You* are making you nervous."

"No," I said. "I'm pretty sure. It's an objective fact. *You're* the one making me nervous."

After several more tacks, I called Brian to take my place. He was better at tacking, and better at keeping his mouth shut. I ducked into the cabin to see how Aryeh and Tziporah were doing. We'd lifted anchor at dawn in a hurry, without eating breakfast. Now I wedged my body between the cupboards and hurried to make them peanut butter and jelly sandwiches.

Tziporah ate hers and immediately vomited it back up. The mess covered the bunks, the floor, my shirt, and all her clothes. Brian fished a bucket out of the hold. He filled it with saltwater and passed the sloshing container to me in the cabin. I tried to strip Tziporah clean, wash her clothes with one hand, and sop up the vomit without falling on the slippery floor. The boat continued to sway as we tacked relentlessly across the bay's broad, foam-specked waters.

Twenty minutes later, I'd managed to wring the clothes. I'd swabbed the stinking cabin aisle. Aryeh had finally stopped shrieking in disgust. Tziporah felt well enough to ask for food. I held her limp, sweating body in my lap and fed her a piece of cheese. She vomited again.

About seasickness, a naturalist once wrote: "In first place the misery is excessive, and far exceeds what a person would suppose who had never been at sea more than a few days.... I often said before starting that I had no doubt I should frequently repent of the whole undertaking. Little did I think with what fervor I should do so. I can scarcely conceive any more miserable state than when such dark and gloomy thoughts are haunting the mind as have today pursued me."

That wasn't Ricketts, it was Charles Darwin. He'd been at sea aboard the *Beagle* for only three days and already he was wishing he'd stayed in England.

Dark and gloomy thoughts were haunting me, too. With Tziporah's vomit still coating my hands, I railed out loud: "This isn't any fun!"

As if in answer to that complaint, dolphins suddenly appeared. A large pod of them intersected our path, heading into the bay while we struggled to sail out. Dozens of battleship gray fins sliced through the choppy waves. Shining rounded humps arched through the water, disappeared, and then emerged again. Doug loosened his grip on the tiller and we slowed to a lurching bob. I clipped Aryeh's safety harness onto a cockpit U-bolt so he could dangle his arms over the lifelines and watch the great pod swim by. I stood in the cockpit doorway and held Tziporah high. For a few moments her eyes brightened.

We tried to capture the pod on video camera—one of the few times we'd bring out the camera at all—but quickly gave up. Through the viewfinder, the fins and waves melded into a confusing blur of spray and glinting triangles. All the water around us was churning with wind, with life. It was better simply to look and to marvel. Then, almost as quickly as they'd appeared, the dolphins were gone.

The *Western Flyer* cruised along the cool, foggy Pacific coast for seven days. Except for a stop at San Diego, they ran nearly day and night. Their plan was to motor directly to Cabo San Lucas, where they'd begin tidepooling, then follow the Sea of Cortez north as long as the tides would allow them—to the Midriffs, about two-thirds of the way north along the peninsula coast. Near Isla Angel de la Guarda, they would fight racing currents and cross the narrow gulf, and continue south along Mexico's more-developed mainland shore. They'd stop in Guaymas, a city even then, and explore shallow lagoons to the south, before crossing back to Baja. The circle completed, they would round the peninsula's southern tip and head home.

We hoped to cover the same ground, but—because *Zuiva*'s home anchorage gave us our starting and ending points—in a different order. Our starting point, near Mulegé, was close to their midway point. We planned to sail south first, toward the peninsula's tip. Eliza would meet us for a week in La Paz, as a break from her farming—and our sailing—routine. Then, after she headed home, we'd backtrack north, continuing as far as we could manage, given the tide's increasingly powerful flow north of Bahía Concepción. We did not look forward to crossing the gulf, or navigating the mainland's treacherous lagoons, but we hoped to see those areas, too, completing our own Cortez circle.

All day we sailed past steep beaches backed by wrinkled, rust-red hills. We saw no signs of life on the bay's eastern side, and only a few buildings on the bay's road-accessible western side. But these looked rustic and vulnerable, dwarfed by the mountains rising behind. Just north of Ecomundo, the glint of distant road traffic faded as the highway headed inland, through treeless mountain passes.

Twenty-two miles long and from two to five miles wide, Bahía Concepción is eastern Baja's most sheltered body of water. It only takes a day to drive here from the U.S. border. But proximity alone scarcely matters where there is little to drink, and hardly a scrap of shade in hundreds of scorched square miles. Southeast and across the gulf, in mainland Mexico, the Spanish conquistador Hernán Cortés managed to topple the sophisticated Aztec empire. But he and his minions failed miserably here in Baja against an aboriginal people who roamed mostly naked, who lived without shelter, who ate rats and snakes when other game was scarce. The desert rewards those who live simply, even if it does not reward them with much.

From Ecomundo north to the mouth of Bahía Concepción, there are a few RV-accessible beaches, but no hotels and not a single harbor or marina. Imagine California's San Francisco Bay, only six miles longer than Bahía Concepción, with one-thousandth the population and not a single dock. Most of the peninsula is desert, receiving less than ten inches of rain a year. Most of the land is steep and bare, a thinly inhabited spine twice the length of Florida, formed by four major and many lesser mountain ranges. In some places, the mountains are knife-edged and sheer, dropping directly into the blue gulf. Elsewhere they are worn and rolling, eroded by infrequent desert downpours. From afar, the desert hills can look seductively soft, like gently folded pleats of brown suede. But up close, the suede reveals its prickly nature. Hikers who wander inland find themselves slipping along flood-cut arroyos of sharp-edged scree and struggling through thorny scrub patches.

At the end of our first sailing day, we pulled into Bahía Santo Domingo, a cove that was little more than a dip in the tawny shoreline. Nausea had knotted our stomachs all day. Now, giddy anxiety took its place. Doug was happy to stay aboard, to be alone on a still and silent boat, but the rest of us couldn't wait to go ashore and explore our first tidepools. For the first time, we would walk where the *Western Flyer's* crew had walked and do what they had done.

Darkness would fall in three hours. We stuffed dry-sacks with everything we could imagine needing: journals, identification guides, the *Log* itself, artists' pencils, sketchbooks. Then we thought of the children, and packed more: water bottles and snacks, extra clothes in case we got soaked and chilled, a first-aid kit because accidents happened only when we didn't have one at hand. Doug watched us with a bachelor's amusement, puzzled by all the fuss.

Steinbeck and Ricketts described rounding a point, Punta Concepción, from the open gulf and collecting specimens along Bahía Concepción's eastern shore. Bahía Santo Domingo offers the only good anchorage for miles, and the cove itself is small, bordered by ochre bluffs to the north and gray bluffs to the south. It was the only logical place we could imagine them having stopped.

Kayaking to land from the sailboat, we surveyed the shoreline, trying to guess exactly where they would have beached their dinghy. Nature lent our act of landing a sense of timelessness. The same wavelets that might have carried Steinbeck and Ricketts now, in recycled form, carried us the last few feet to shore. The patterns visible on the beach were enduring patterns. Sloping sheets of hard, red rock underlay the shallows, followed by cobblestones, followed by rippling sand, followed by a seven-foot-wide strip of large sun-bleached shells, well above the high-tide line.

To our satisfaction, the land looked just as the *Log*'s authors had described: "Behind the beach there was a little level land, sandy and dry and covered with cactus and thick brush. And behind that, the rising dry hills. Now again the wild doves were calling among the hills with their song of homesickness." Sixty years later, the doves still cooed from their perches atop cardón cacti. The breathy song sounded cool and dry—like dusk itself.

If the land looked and sounded just as it had when Steinbeck and Ricketts were here, the tidepools reflected the passage of years in more complex terms. The *Western Flyer*'s crew reported finding beautiful pink-and-white murex shells, which Sparky collected by the washtubful to bring back to his friends in Monterey. We couldn't have filled a tub, but we did find a handful of specimens, as well as other shell-fancier's favorites, like olive and tulip shells. They reported finding hachas (also called pen shells). We didn't find living species, but above the tide line, we sifted through all kinds of empty bivalve shells, including the hachas, and also clams and cockles. The vast number of empty shells suggested that this place had been rich with shellfish, and that people had partaken—perhaps too enthusiastically—in this richness. We had heard of snorkelers finding great shell middens underwater, smothering other seafloor species.

Steinbeck and Ricketts found a sandy seafloor strewn with sand dollars. We didn't see a single one. Below the high-tide line, we didn't even find much sand. Our tidepools were rocky tidepools—hard red ledges washed by gentle waves. Balancing on great slats of dimpled, quartz-veined rock, we spotted dozens of sulfur sea cucumbers. We sidestepped crusty mats of barnacles, each one of the volcano-shaped bumps no bigger than an earring stud and just as sharp.

We carefully lifted brittlestars out of rocky crevices. The slender sea-star cousins have small dark bodies and five thin arms that whip around in a fire-hose frenzy. The central body disk looks innocent—like the gently rounded, unseeing button eye of a teddy bear. But the thrashing legs look evil and alien. Shifting the writhing brittlestars from palm to palm was mesmerizing, like playing with a Slinky. Both Tziporah and Aryeh insisted on holding each one and took turns replacing every star to the place where it had been found.

We found hermit crabs, a moon snail, a colonial tunicate, and some polychaete worms. We watched several species of small, bright tropical fish, including the ubiquitous yellow- and black-barred sergeant majors, swim between our ankles. And we saw lots of stuff we couldn't name: purplish lumps and jellied masses that might have been tunicates or someone's lost lunch—it was too hard to call. Every new species we spotted felt like a hurried introduction: *Sorry, I've always been bad with names, but I'm sure we'll be seeing lots of each other in weeks to come.*

To the west, a copper haze settled over the bay as evening approached, but we had no desire to leave the beach. We had poked around the water's edge, never wading more than knee-deep, for three hours. The whole time it felt like a scavenger hunt: on to the next ledge; look under the next cobblestone; careful not to slip on the razor-edged barnacles; maybe a few inches deeper. The children didn't pause or flag once—not to ask for dinner, not to ask when or whether we would return to the boat. Only when it was so dark that we couldn't see from one end of the beach to the other did we sit above the tide line and scrounge through our dry-sacks, pulling out bags of crackers and shivering as we hurried to make notes and sketch some rough shapes.

Unlike Steinbeck and Ricketts, we weren't gathering specimens, only looking—and yet our task still felt urgent and acquisitive. What did we expect to show for it at day's end, in addition to abraded fingertips and sore backs? What did we expect to show for it at the end of fifty such days? We didn't know, but the not-knowing fueled us, too.

Some of the species we saw matched those noted by Steinbeck and Ricketts. But other prominent features—like the red ledges of rock—didn't match what they described at all. The *Log* itself was vague about station locations. Only later, studying the original captain's log kept by Tony Berry, would we understand our error. On our very first attempt to beachcomb in their footsteps, we had overshot Steinbeck and Ricketts's tidepooling spot by ten miles.

Our biggest concern had been that we might find a sterile, lifeless beach, stripped by visitors, pollution, or some other twenty-first-century hobgoblin. Instead we found more creatures than we could count or name. Sunset and the upward surge of the tides had limited us to a three-hour search, but always there would be the next tidepooling station, as Steinbeck and Ricketts called the twenty-three collecting stops they made.

At subsequent stops, we'd choose our anchorages more carefully. But finding the same shore explored by our predecessors would never be easy. A beach, we were reminded time after time, doesn't look the same from one hour to the next. We had arrived at the middle of the day's tidal cycle. The day's lowest tide had already passed, and now the water was rising, creeping imperceptibly up the shore. Each day's lows and highs were like a curtain rising and falling on a stage, and even the stages themselves—sea bottoms shallow or sloped, muddy or sandy or rocky—would change all along our route. No two places and no two moments could ever be identical.

Tidal ranges vary by location, by moon phase, and by season. At the northern end of the Sea of Cortez the tides are, at greater than thirty feet, among the world's highest. Farther south, they are less substantial. Even so, on a single beach in the middle Cortez, full- and new-moon tides can rise several feet over a few hours. But at quarter phases, when the moon and sun are exerting less combined gravitational pull on the earth's envelope of water, they may rise just a few inches. With the aid of computer-generated tide tables we could aim to hit a low tide on the same beach that the *Log*'s authors had explored at low tide. But depending on the day they visited, their low tide might have been inches or feet lower than ours—meaning they might have walked or waded several more yards farther from shore.

Even if we knew precisely when and where they started collecting, this snapshot of a place would be imperfect. Because even as Steinbeck and Ricketts collected, the water rose or fell. Over hours of collecting, they would have shuffled forward or back to keep ahead of the waves, just as we did. There was no red X or modern quadrat on the ocean floor to show where our Monterey duo had found every sand dollar or sea anemone. Without that X—without replicable conditions—we could not claim to be modern empirical scientists, and did not want to be. At best, we might claim to be amateur naturalists, in league with a long tradition of curious bunglers. Maybe we were nothing more than wide-eyed travelers.

FISH BOIL

The next day was almost windless. The water was pearly flat and the sky shimmered in it. We did not move fast or far. But over the course of a drowsy day, we nonetheless managed to proceed steadily south, heading deeper into a scorched wilderness.

Doug hung out the drifter sail—a large, puff-catching sail meant for days like this. The light breeze came from just off to one side, so we did not need to tack. We sailed a slow, straight line, parallel to land. The boat sloshed but did not rock: mild headaches and general malaise below decks, but no vomit today. The open coast beyond Bahía Concepción unrolled before us like a royal carpet woven with the colors of the desert: mustard, ochre, chalk white. One person alone could handle the tiller, watch the compass, and stare at the coast as it slid by, shimmering through a veil of heat. Doug's expertise was not required. He was free to nap on his narrow bunk—long, thin body laid out like a vampire in its coffin—peeling open one dark eye to make sure Brian and I hadn't assaulted the sails' dignity.

It was my kind of day. I liked standing in the cockpit by myself, one sun-glazed arm steadying the tiller, making minute adjustments. Those gentle oscillations, so rhythmic and pregnant with purpose, were immensely satisfying. The boat could have been drydocked and still I would have stood at the tiller, pulling gently and with great hope.

We were navigating from one distant headland to the next along a scalloped coastline, far enough offshore that we couldn't see vegetation, or roads or trails if there were any. At such a distance, the mountains looked small and smooth and brown, like little cups of flan. The horizon changed so slowly you could not be sure it changed at all. But still you had to pay attention. Though it felt like we weren't moving, we were in fact catching the wind. When I let my attention waver to study a chart for less than a minute, the boat turned thirty degrees, angling landward.

At one point in the day, we were moving so sluggishly that Doug decided to go for a swim. He stripped off his clothes, put on his life jacket and harness, and jumped off the stern. Attached to the sailboat by a rope (as was our kayak, towed behind us), the captain carved a substantial whitewater plume. Even a few knots was quite a speed to be dragged, as demonstrated by the way Doug's body flailed and twisted in the boat's wake. For a brief moment, a thought bubbled to the surface: *What if we couldn't get him back aboard?* But Doug was strong and able. Even without a ladder, he managed to haul himself back into the boat, flashing a wide smile.

"Thank you for inviting me to come along on this trip," he said, smiling as he squeezed the salty water from his long hair. His gratitude caught us off guard. Brian and I exchanged grins. We were touched.

Doug returned belowdecks, and I stayed at the tiller. A squadron of pelicans skimmed low over the smooth sea. In the far distance, a whale's rounded slate-gray back parted the water, then vanished. Even farther—so far on the watery horizon that one imagined the earth curving where the sky touched the sea—we occasionally saw small patches of boiling water.

The first time Brian and I read about this phenomenon, in a classic angling book by Baja veteran Ray Cannon, we dismissed it as hyperbole. But we have seen it several times since, and it is true. Small fish school near the surface, and larger fish gather to eat them, and larger ones yet enter the fray. Before you know it, the water is shimmering and churning, with a flash of silver each time a fish clears the surface in its frantic effort to escape. That quick flash burns an image onto the mind's eye long after the waters open to reclaim the fish itself. In the water, he is one of a school. But in the air, alone, he becomes a defiant hero, and we root for him to escape the predator's jaws—unless, of course, those jaws are our own.

In past years, Brian and I had towed a fishing line through Baja boils and hauled up dinner: a roosterfish, once, and a prehistoric-looking needlefish, and a barracuda whose muscular thrashing left steel-colored scales on everything it touched. On this day, though, the boils were too far away. We towed a flashing lure behind the boat all afternoon and only managed to catch our own motor's propeller.

A good travel writer travels first and writes only later. But still, I couldn't help but notice that a day like this—hot, still, with smooth and dreamy seas—would never spawn any best-seller. Forget *The Perfect Storm*. We were sailing into *The Perfect Lull*.

Steinbeck had similar thoughts about his own trip. He told his agent that few people would be interested in this Baja trip—a concept that perversely pleased him, coming on the heels of *The Grapes of Wrath*'s best-sellerdom. He was adamant that his publisher not misrepresent the *Log* to the public as an adventure yarn. And in the *Log*'s first pages, Steinbeck and Ricketts said directly to their readers: "We had no urge toward adventure. We planned to collect marine animals in a remote place on certain days and at certain hours indicated on the tide charts. To do this we had, in so far as we were able, to avoid adventure."

In place of thrills, Steinbeck and Ricketts offered ideas. That was their greatest joy on the Cortez trip: letting time and thought unspool like a slowly trolled fishing line. Maybe everything they thought and said wasn't brilliant or even true. But that didn't matter. They were just fishing: putting out a long line into the dreamy current, to see what might bite.

In the *Log*'s rigorous index, under the heading "Speculations on," there are these subjects: aphrodisiacs, biologists, boats, cannibalism, capitalism, collecting, collectivism, communism, dominance, drinking, ethics, Fascism, fish schools, hope, knowledge, law, laziness, leadership, leave-taking, memory, Mexican Indians, military mind, mutation, "over-production," place names, reality, religion, scientific writing, steering, taxonomic methods, technological progress, teleology, time-sense, unemployment, vulgarity, waste.

The romantic, reading a love story about Paris, goes there and stands under the Eiffel Tower's shadow, expecting to find passion. If he does not, he feels cheated. The Sahara enthusiast, raised on reams of forlorn desert literature, travels thousands of miles to Africa and is surprised if she does not find mystery or alienation among the endless dunes.

Sixty years later, we moved slowly south along the blue gulf, half-expecting life's mysteries—or at least oddities—to reveal themselves, as they apparently had to Steinbeck and Ricketts. Occasionally, inspiration struck us. But more often, we pulled up an empty line, and Brian and I

looked at each other quizzically, with little to say. It became a running
joke: "When are we going to have Big Thoughts?"

On shore, the sea life of the tidepools dazzled us and sent our minds
straining in all directions, trying to identify and understand. But there
was something about being on board the *Zuiva* in those first days that
mentally anesthetized us. Tropical heat and seasickness didn't help. Never
in my life have I felt so unable to think, to learn, to talk about anything
of importance, to write, even to read.

All of us except the captain, whose stomach had been trained on a
sailboat even smaller than this one, longed for each day to end so that we
could anchor and kiss *terra firma*. I told Aryeh and Tziporah that the nausea would go away, that we would get our sea legs and adjust, but we
never did. It was surprising to us, because we were a seagoing family,
accustomed not only to ocean paddling, but northern ferryboat and fishing trips. But the skinny, mountain-flanked Sea of Cortez has its own
rhythms. At times there is no wind at all. Then, it looks like a mirror, or a
shimmering mirage. With the first stirring breezes, it quickly becomes a
choppy gulf, with box-shaped waves. There are no trade winds and none
of the ocean's tall, rolling swells.

The *Zuiva* was too big to dance with the sea, as a kayak does, and too
small to ride above it well. Belowdecks, the lurching and sloshing never
ceased. The air grew stale. When we propped open the ventilation hatch
in the forward berth, Doug growled "Close it!" because ropes dangling
from the sails inevitably snagged the open hatch cover. We told Aryeh to
come to the cockpit doorway, to breathe fresh air and orient himself to
the horizon line. Already woozy, he hated the intense sunlight and the
constraints on his movement. To sit outside, he had to be jacketed and
harnessed and shackled in place, and he could not stray or shift an inch.

Nausea was not enough to explain our lack of philosophical inspiration
at sea, though. Surely, Steinbeck and Ricketts must have looked green on
choppy days. Worse yet, they were hungover much of the time. Still, didn't
they manage to joke and ponder, to talk about everything from aphrodisiacs to St. Augustine? Yes. But surely not as much as they'd have us believe.

Steinbeck didn't manage to write anything during his Baja trip, even
though he promised his agent he'd write articles along the way. There simply wasn't enough time. In Baja he found himself surprisingly busy just
keeping up with each day: watching the wheel, collecting and preserving

specimens, conversing with his travel partners, making sense of a new place. According to his biographers, Steinbeck didn't even keep a journal on the trip.

Many of the *Log*'s philosophical asides are reworked reflections that Ricketts or Steinbeck wrote well before their trip. The *Log* was not necessarily the birthing place for these ideas, it was simply a catchall. Steinbeck's genius was in his sense of architecture: He saw the whole trip as a home for these orphaned musings. But new ideas were not so quickly and easily spawned. And yet Steinbeck, hoping to walk in the immortal shoes of other Big Thinkers, wanted to believe it was so.

Charles Darwin's *Origin of Species* "flashed complete in one second," Steinbeck wrote in his novel *Sweet Thursday*. But no, that wasn't true either: Darwin's complete theory was the result not only of a long and difficult and nauseating voyage, but also of five years of contemplation back in England. Darwin wasn't able to identify many of the specimens he bagged during the famous expedition aboard the *Beagle*. He hadn't even labeled them adequately. Not understanding the full significance of the various species of finches at the time he collected them, Darwin stored his specimens randomly, with no reference to each bird's island of origin. If not for the more meticulously labeled collection of a lower-ranked shipmate, this historic piece of evidence would have been omitted from the theory of natural selection.

More than a century later, we project our own desires and expectations on what was actually months of haphazard collecting, followed by years of intellectual stewing. Steinbeck was wrong about Darwin's "flash," and Brian and I were misguided even when we joked about craving flashes of our own. Steinbeck was no Darwin, just as I was no Steinbeck. But we all wished that experience would lead quickly and directly to epiphany. We all wished that our minds would encounter the intellectual equivalent of a fish boil: light and life everywhere, small ideas attracting bigger ones, everything astir. Inspiration and creative energy aren't quite that easily summoned, however. And enlightenment—a kind of transcendent flash following prolonged contemplation—is another thing altogether. Ricketts knew that best of all, since enlightenment—"breaking through," he called it—both preoccupied and eluded him. Steinbeck described it this way in his loving memorial essay, *About Ed Ricketts,* which became a preface for the 1951 edition of the *Log:*

"He was walled off a little, so that he worked at his philosophy of 'breaking through,' of coming out through the back of the mirror into some kind of reality which would make the day world dreamlike. This thought obsessed him. He found the symbols of 'breaking through' in *Faust,* in Gregorian music, and in the sad, drunken poetry of Li Po. Of the *Art of the Fugue* he would say, 'Bach nearly made it. Hear now how close he comes, and hear his anger when he cannot. Every time I hear it I believe that this time he will come crashing through into the light. And he never does—not quite.'"

THE TIDEPOOL'S WAY

When we first studied the *Western Flyer*'s route, it had seemed a perfect thing. We convinced ourselves that they had stopped at all the best tide-pooling places and skipped any place that was ugly or buggy or lifeless. We had forgotten that none of the *Western Flyer*'s crew knew the coast well. Only Cabo Pulmo, La Paz, and Bahía de los Angeles were on their must-see list. They stopped where their hunches guided them, and where they had time and energy to collect.

Our second night's anchorage revealed how much they had missed. Punta Púlpito (Pulpit Point) is a high, obsidian-veined outcropping flanking the northern end of a soft-sand beach. This dark headland stands near the halfway point between Mulegé and Loreto. The cove just inside the point is inviting, well-protected, and ecologically rich. It was not one of the *Western Flyer*'s stops, though logically it should have been.

But on the day they motored past, they were tired. They had been in the Sea of Cortez for ten days and had already collected and preserved in great quantity. "The eyes grow weary with looking at new things," they said, and on this day they chose to stay aboard and fish, cruising far off-shore with lines set to catch tuna.

Behind the Púlpito beach rose a sheer, crumbly bluff. To the south, the beach curved to a second, smaller headland, where smoothly sculpted caves and shelves of rounded sandstone jutted above the water. Large Sally Lightfoot crabs with red cloisonné carapaces skittered over the ledges in response to any shadow or vibration. Approaching them, we heard the *click-click-click* of their spiny legs, tapping nervously at the rock.

Wherever the sandstone was pockmarked and worn, the holes had filled with seawater, creating perfect, sheltered pools. Every dime-sized dimple in the shelf was home to a tiny sea urchin, whose black spines just fit the edges of the dimple. The fit was too snug to be a matter of chance. Sure enough, the urchins excavate these rounded depressions, which provide them some protection from the pull of waves and the probing beaks of predatory birds.

Larger sandstone holes—one, as large as a wading pool, filled with sparkling-clear water—looked like aquarium tanks. Rainbow wrasses and large semitranslucent shrimp shared one pool. A slim, pinkie-sized fish called the blenny rested on the pool's rocky bottom, swimming forward in jarring little leaps, like a bulldog testing its leash.

Steinbeck and Ricketts brought a blenny like this one aboard their boat in Bahía Concepción, just up the coast. Though only four inches long, it had needlelike teeth and viciously attacked the fingers of anyone who molested it. Officially tagged *Hypsoblennius gentilis,* they referred to it in the scientific appendix as "the-fish-that-bit-Carol." Omitted from every page of the *Log*, Carol survives in this one mention only.

We left the blenny and wandered to another Púlpito pool, where a spotted stingray, as big and round as a pie tin, stared up at us with black ball-bearing eyes. The brown-mottled creature had glided into this dead end when the tide was high, overflowing the hole. Since then, the water had receded. There was no way out until the tide returned. We watched the ray swim around the pool, the edges of its cartilaginous body undulating like the bottom of a ballroom-dancer's skirt. Finally the stingray gave up on escape and settled to the bottom of the pool, burrowing under a fine layer of sand. When camouflaged this way, only its spiracles—gill-like flaps on either side of its eyes—were visible, pulsing with slow, underwater breaths.

On an extremely flat beach, one can watch the tides race in, forcing a beachcomber to retreat in a matter of minutes. But on steeper shores such as this one, where the water moves slowly, it can be hard to measure a rising tide's progress. I remember a beach I visited with Aryeh in Alaska, when he was two. We planted a stick in the sand, at the water's foaming edge. A few hours later we returned. The stick was out of our reach, still erect, but far out in the water, surrounded by gray waves. "You moved the stick," my son said. "I didn't," I told him. "The water moved." But he didn't believe me. He could understand the crash of a wave, but not the whole ocean creeping back and forward in silent measured breaths, like a giant's heaving chest.

Now, though, he believed and understood. The jutting sandstone shelf made a vertical yardstick. The stingray inside the pool was proof. The tide had brought it in. And the tide, we hoped, would get it out. We checked back every hour or so, fearful that the warming, deoxygenated water in the pool would hasten the ray's demise. We even tried to shepherd the ray to a possible exit, but that didn't work, and we stopped intervening. This was nature's drama. Only the rising tide—slowly bubbling up and over the sandstone shelf's rounded edge like a rescuer scaling Rapunzel's hair—could grant the stingray its freedom.

This cove was exceptional. Tidepools are rarely so pool-like. More often in the Cortez, they are puddles ringed by cobblestones, or damp spots beneath boulders. The crusty top of a reef, just peeking above the sea's surface, creates tidepools with as many nooks and crannies as an English muffin. Lava rock ledges have their own cranny-pattern. Every hole where an ancient air bubble popped makes the perfect home for an anemone or crab. The uppermost part of a beach may receive spray only a few times each year, during the highest spring tides, but this arid strip is part of the littoral—or tide-washed shore zone—too.

Soupy seawater can collect between ripples of beach sand, making protected water holes where some critters thrive. In the fine sand itself, pinholes attest to crabs, clams, and other burrowers hiding a few inches down. And at the microscopic level, there is life even in the interstices between sand grains. But often the beach that is best for sunbathing—flour-soft, unblemished—is the worst for tidepooling. One day you find yourself stepping out of a dinghy onto a white-sand crescent, cursing the absence of coarse, skin-shredding rocks, and you know you have evolved from empty-headed sun worshiper into tidepool savant.

The tidepools we saw were not merely random aggregations of sliming, swimming, creeping life. They were organized into parallel strips or zones—snails and barnacles here, then limpets and chitons, maybe some sea urchins and sea stars next, and in deepest water, some living seaweed, sponges, and coral heads—like a garden that has grown just a little shaggy. Borders overlapped, interlopers crawled or swam from one strip to the next, and the lines were not straight or even. Like terraced Indonesian rice paddies, the littoral zones were a truce between mathematical perfection and the irregularities of climate and landscape. Nonetheless, there was a high degree of order in the shore design, the kind of order that prompts some to see God's hand in the work, and others to sing hosannas to science.

Each tidal zone represents a different set of mixed conditions, suitable only to some kinds of marine organisms: a range of ecological niches waiting to be filled. The highest zone spends most of the time uncovered by saltwater. Invertebrates here are preyed upon by terrestrial animals and exposed to the withering sun. This zone is often dressed with a garland of dead, wave-tossed algae, or seaweed, which ferments in the heat and provides smelly shelter to whole ghettos of amphipods (sand fleas) and bug-like isopods, which we called rock roaches. Some of the creatures in this mostly dry zone may be on their way elsewhere, slowly evolving into terrestrial organisms. Periwinkles need to dampen their gills occasionally, but they will drown if kept submersed in saltwater for very long.

The lowest parts of the shore are almost always flooded. There, invertebrates are preyed upon by larger fish, and by each other. In between, the midtidal zone might seem the happy medium, the safest place for a critter to hang out, but this zone experiences the most changes of all, even if those fluctuations aren't long-lasting. The organisms there have adapted to the constant flux; some even require it. If the high littoral zone is Minnesota—exposed to the elements, but otherwise dull—then the midlittoral is San Francisco. You live there because you need a little action in your life.

Usually the middle part of the shore is covered and uncovered twice a day. Even when covered, though, the water is always changing. In shallow areas, temperature can skyrocket under a broiling afternoon sun. Salinity increases, too. Where seawater moves sluggishly, oxygen is quickly depleted and waste products accumulate. The rising tide is a rebirth, flushing away carbon dioxide, bringing coolness and moisture and nutrients to desiccated animals and plants, stirring the tidepools back into life. But the rebirth comes too late for some.

We worried that the stingray, left unassisted to fate and the tides, might die. But we also that knew that death is the tidepool's way. Along the shore, creatures expire all the time, in excruciating fashion. Snails and many of their mollusk cousins are armed with a radula, a tongue studded with file-like teeth. Some snails use this radula to mow rocks, scraping an edible, microscopic layer of detritus and plant material. But this tidy vegetarianism doesn't suit all the snails. Fiercer species use their mouthparts to drill holes through the shells of fellow mollusks and suck out the victims' soft body parts.

Radula aside, teeth aren't common among soft intertidal beasts, so gastric juices often must deliver the killing blow. There's more lethal spit in a tidepool than in a whole year of sci-fi films.

When a sea star wants to eat a mussel, it clamps onto the shelled creature with its puckered arms. Slowly, patiently, the sea star exerts a terrible pull, until the mussel's tightlipped seal breaks and the bivalve falls open. But the agony does not end there. The sea star ejects its own stomach through the aperture of its tiny mouth and injects that stomach into the mussel shell, where it digests a still-pulsing meal.

The sea anemone's dining habits are just as startling. When the tide is out, anemones draw their tentacles inward and collapse onto themselves. Clamped onto a dry rock, these sedentary, saclike cnidarians look like nothing more than shiny pillows of mucus. But the pillows are really ferocious carnivores that make the moving, breathing sea their accomplice. Underwater, sea anemones wave their pretty, translucent tentacles in the current. They look as innocent as flowers. Food walks or floats by and the anemone fires off spring-coiled barbs, topped with stinging cells. The stunned victim is pulled toward the oral disk—a mouthlike hole between the "flower petals" or tentacles—and digested.

In a tidepool you can see murder, birth, starvation, decay, cooperation, ingratitude, ancestor worship, courtship, and sabotage—but only if you look closely. That's easier said than done. It's one thing to talk about the digestive antics of snails, sea stars, and anemones, and another thing to catch them in action. Life is nothing like a television nature-documentary, where the videographer seems to arrive at just the right moment, where editors cut away dull hours of tape, and where telephoto lenses bring us effortlessly close. In real life, it is hard just to spot some marine organisms—they tend to be most colorful when underwater, and conveniently drab when exposed to predators and to the air. It is harder yet to understand what those organisms are doing.

Aryeh and Tziporah were our best tidepoolers by far, because their brains were uncluttered with bias and expectation. If they saw a gob of spit on the sand, they did not dismiss it as a gob of spit. They leaned closer and saw it was, indeed, a cnidarian. I walked too fast, with my eyes too far off the ground. They stayed bent over all the time, like a miser searching out his lost nickel, and didn't count the number of rocks they had to turn to find a new species. I saw a slimy ball of string attached to the underside of a rock and dismissed it: "Just some worms." But for Aryeh and Tziporah, there was no "just" as far as worms were concerned. To them, every living string was sacred.

In the evening, we kayaked from the beach back to the sailboat. The trip took only minutes, but we towed a fishing line behind us, just in case. Paddling around our previous anchorage the night before, we'd hauled up a skinny, inedible lizardfish, but nothing nibbled this time. When we arrived at the sailboat, we didn't want to get out of the kayak yet—the bay at sunset was shimmering with liquid gold, and the children were quiet, murmuring appreciatively at the water all around us. In the far distance, we could make out two Mexicans in a *panga,* a motorized fishing skiff, lifting nets from the water off Punta Púlpito. Except for one other sailboat, this was the only other human activity we'd seen in three days.

"Maybe we could buy fish from those men," I said to Brian.

"Really?" he said, sizing up the distance. "You don't mind?"

We forgot about the line trailing passively in the water behind us until, halfway to the panga, the kayak jerked and we all heard splashes. Brian hauled in the trembling line while Aryeh shrieked and twisted in the middle kayak seat. The fish was still fighting in the water while Aryeh begged, "Let me see, let me see; bring it in!" In his giddy squirming, I was sure he would tip the boat. Tziporah was asleep in my lap, while the whole rear of the kayak bounced and swayed with Brian's and Aryeh's happiness.

Finally, back at the sailboat, we all had a good look at the fish. It was a streamlined beauty. It had the bullet-shaped body of a speedy pelagic with a ridge of nine sawtooth finlets or spines on both top and bottom, like a row of zipper teeth, between its rear fins and tail. Its iridescent silver-blue skin was spattered with bright yellow dots. Racing stripes shimmered along its sides. We guessed—and our fish book confirmed—that this was a sierra, in the same family as tuna and mackerel. A sierra! It was an omen. On board the boat, we took turns holding it and passing it around tenderly, like a newborn child. Then we fried it in chunks, with garlic, olive oil, and citrus-flavored spices, and we ate it.

Catching the sierra pleased us greatly. It reminded us of something we regularly forgot and had to relearn, day after day, whenever we worried about our own inadequacies and the makeshift nature of our small expedition. Early in their book, Steinbeck and Ricketts had chosen the sierra to illustrate this point.

"The Mexican sierra has 'XVII-15-IX' spines in the dorsal fin," they wrote, speaking in ichthyological code. "These can easily be counted. But if the sierra strikes hard on the line so that our hands are burned, if the fish sounds and nearly escapes and finally comes in over the rail, his colors pulsing and his tail beating the air, a whole new relational externality has come into being—an entity which is more than the sum of the fish plus the fisherman. The only way to count the spines of the sierra unaffected by this second relational reality is to sit in a laboratory, open an evil-smelling jar, remove a stiff colorless fish from formalin solution, count the spines, and write the truth 'D. XVII-15-IX.' There you have recorded a reality which cannot be assailed—probably the least important reality concerning either the fish or yourself.

"It is good to know what you are doing. The man with his pickled fish has set down one truth and has recorded in his experience many lies. The fish is not that color, that texture, that dead, nor does he smell that way."

Do not, the *Log*'s authors were saying, *limit yourself to a pickled-science view of the world.* It is only one truth of many, perhaps not even the most important one. There is more to this world than spine-counting, just as there is more to this world than bean-counting and widget-making.

If we'd wanted to know everything about the life cycle of sea stars—and nothing else—we could have observed them better in a tank, in a building, hundreds of miles from here. If we'd wanted to learn about the periwinkle, we could have done a master's thesis on that dingy snail and nothing else. But that was not our mission here. We watched a stingray for hours until the tide rose and the stingray scooted away. We spent a whole day experiencing the sea in all its sun-drenched, wave-tossed messiness; and finally, we tasted it. Then we fell asleep with smiles on our faces.

But even while we smiled at the words of Steinbeck and Ricketts, we still had a bit of the pickled scientist in us. After all, we had counted the sierra's spines. We had noted its size and markings. We had consulted our guidebook to find out the fish's full pedigree, thumbing pages frantically even as the garlicky oil smoked in the frying pan. Did the fish taste any better as *Scomberomorus sierra*? No. But even the narrowest scientific truths were new and thrilling to us. We didn't feel ready to graduate beyond them.

The following day we nervously petitioned Captain Doug to stay longer at this spot. "This is why we came," we said. For once, even he was impressed by the life under our boat and on the shore. We laid over for an extra day, swimming and laughing and walking the beach, and never regretted it, knowing the next day's long sail would be a return to nautical hell.

A PREMATURE EPITAPH

In our rapture over all the animals we'd so far seen, from dolphins and whales to crabs and chitons, we'd almost forgotten that we were traveling a "ruined" sea. That is how many popular authors and journalists had characterized the Sea of Cortez.

In an award-winning 1995 newspaper series called "A Dying Sea," journalist Tom Knudson of the *Sacramento Bee* summarized the gulf's problems as basic: "overfishing, aided by greed, corruption, poverty, and lawlessness." He quoted environmental groups who estimate that most edible fish populations have decreased 30 to 70 percent in the last ten years. This great, "amniotic" sea, he said, was being destroyed. "If major steps aren't taken soon, you can kiss it all goodbye."

Some environmental groups have elegized the gulf, adopting the kind of morbidly poetic fervor that Steinbeck himself might have used in his fictional work—when he wasn't feeling skeptical, or listening to cool, rational Ed. "Then the birds began to disappear, for there was nothing to drive the bait fish to the surface," lamented one organization's web page, summarizing the sea's decline in recent decades. "The sky became as empty as the sea. The unimaginable had occurred: the Sea of Cortez had become a barren hunting ground; it had become a place of silent emptiness. Perhaps forever."

Well-intentioned organizations, usually based in California and Arizona, make loose claims: that manta rays are nearly extinct, or that seabirds don't flock to the Cortez anymore, or that the whole region north of Loreto is one vast lifeless bolt of blue silk—pretty water, sure, but nothing in it. Every time we passed dolphins and rays, or paddled past rafts of birds, or dined on fresh-caught fish, it was hard not to think of those claims and wonder: Did the person who wrote that brochure or created that web page ever travel more than a few dozen miles of Cortez coastline?

It was hard not to become contrary, or at least confused. But maybe the confusion was good. It helped us to pay attention to what was in front of our eyes: instead of black and white, a hundred shades of gray; instead of a dying sea, a thousand living invertebrates that didn't realize their coastal homelands were already silent, barren, evidently beyond hope.

The word *overfished* so commonly precedes the gulf's name in print that it seems part of the name itself, just as the adjective *fertile* was attached to the gulf's name years ago, and *dangerous* years before that. Journalists and travel writers are little different from schooling fish, following the lead and lingo of those who have gone before.

This is not to say that the Sea of Cortez is not dangerous *and* fertile *and* overfished, only that adjectives come easier than information. In-depth, long-term studies on gulf fisheries—better yet, on the ecosystem as a whole—simply do not exist. The official catch data that are available have more holes than a fisherman's net. Little of it is reputable, given the wishful thinking and chronic corruption that plagues Mexican government.

North of the border, the Cortez has been the subject of hundreds of scientific papers. But aside from some jargon-free publications on seabirds and island biogeography, studies of the gulf tend to be limited and esoteric: "Pterobothrioides, a new genus of tapeworms," or "Isolation and characterization of heterotrophic aerobic thermophilic bacteria from three geographically separated deep-sea hydrothermal vents." The puzzle pieces are agonizingly small. Assembly of a big picture is many years away.

The seas that merit the most political and academic attention are ones—like the Red Sea or Mediterranean—that share multiple national borders. A shared ocean is a scrutinized ocean, and usually a heavily harvested one as well. Each country wants to know precisely how many edible organisms lurk on every bank and reef, what catches are made, and whether it is getting its fair share. Competition between nations fills data banks and fisheries journals, even while it ignites wars.

The Sea of Cortez has been spared both the tragic conflict and the helpful scrutiny. Until the twentieth century, Mexico disregarded its patrimonial sea almost completely. Mexico has Latin America's longest coastline, but the Mexicans are not a coastal people. A mere one-twentieth of the Mexican population lives on the coast, compared to four times that percentage in Chile and eight times that percentage in Argentina.

This inland orientation began with the Aztecs, who anchored their empire in the heart of the Valley of Mexico, in Tenochtitlan. Without any great rivers upon which to stage civilization, the indigenous peoples of Mexico concentrated their activities on lakes, like the shallow, brackish Lake Texcoco. Gold and silver, the booty that attracted Spanish conquest, were found inland. Agrarian activities in the valley were more important than aquatic activities on the coast. In fact, from the coast came only things that were little desired: tropical diseases, a hot and humid climate, and intruders. The bias remains.

Today, Mexico City is the world's largest urban center. Ringed by mountains and nearly two hundred miles from the coast, it is positioned almost equidistant from the Gulf of Mexico to the east and the Pacific Ocean to the west.

Environmental groups in Mexico City try their best to keep an eye on the distant Cortez, but the problems of a quiet, desert sea pale next to other national ecological crises: acid rain and oil-industry pollution in the Gulf of Mexico, hazardous waste along the U.S. border, deforestation rates that rival those in Asia or South America, armed conflicts caused by natural resource shortages, and in Mexico City itself, the world's most toxic air, tainted not only by industrial emissions and car exhaust but also by airborne fecal dust. Compared to all that, why worry about a few less fish or mollusks on a scarcely populated frontier?

Science arrived late in Baja; regular monitoring and enforcement, even later. Fisheries agents in Baja are like Wild West sheriffs. Their jurisdictions are impossibly huge and inaccessible, their budgets are paltry or nonexistent. If an agent isn't corrupt himself—an easy thing to be, when your boss is thousands of miles away on the mainland—then he is often hamstrung by corruption.

Until recently, most local small-scale fishermen simply didn't report their catches. At times they have caught enough to wreak havoc, though; the sea turtle and the totoaba fish, in particular, were harvested nearly to extinction. Larger operators, who frequently unload their catches on the gulf's mainland shore, are supervised more directly, but their larger size and deeper pockets make them hard to control. That this area has been tragically overfished is an *assumption,* albeit a reasonable one. Whether the sea may also be remarkably resilient or even rebounding is anyone's guess.

Doomsday scenarios aside, the Cortez is *not* like Europe's North Sea, or the Mediterranean, or any other sea plagued by the double whammy of coastal development and the environmentalist's conundrum of "too many boats and too few fish." Isolation has achieved what federal management usually cannot. Some fisheries have been heavily tapped, but other problems common to coastal zones, like pollution, are remarkably absent. Except in the far north delta, wholesale habitat destruction is practically unknown.

The Baja desert's relative lack of roads and human settlements—everything about this coast that intimidates travelers—makes it a friendlier place for marine life. Even the tides, which foil many boaters' plans, are part of a grand and life-giving design. Extreme tides and strong currents draw nutrient-rich water from the gulf's cool and prodigious depths, turbocharging the marine food chain. That food chain includes not only marlin and dorado and tuna—top predators—but also some five thousand humbler species.

How are those creatures doing—and *why?* We, too, wanted to know. And any time we encountered a Mexican fisherman or scientist, I planned to ask. But in the meanwhile, we were overtaxed simply asking *what.* What is that porous, purple Nerf ball squashed beneath the rock? What is that wad of rubber-band-colored tentacles?

Every night, Brian turned to his own water-stained diary, where he was attempting to transcribe the names and descriptions of every species that Steinbeck and Ricketts had seen, correlated to each of their tidal stations. They had listed their species taxonomically. He was trying to reorganize them in more user-friendly fashion, correlated geographically to each of the tidal stations.

"I should have done this earlier," he berated himself. "How was I supposed to know it would take weeks?" The worms alone were killing him: nematodes and annelids and sipunculids and echiurids. Even in a termite-sized scrawl, the species lists filled pages. We were too busy simply tallying the meek to know yet what kind of Earth—rich or ruined— they might be poised to inherit.

MELT

Traveling north from Baja's southern tip, the *Western Flyer*'s crew began to get their travel legs, gaining familiarity with the tidepools and with each other. The deckhands hadn't trusted Steinbeck when he was a famous name in Monterey, but his earthy humor won them over in Mexico. Captain Tony was impressed by the author's competence in general. Steinbeck knew the compass and the stars, he knew how to steer, and he cared enough about the trip's collecting mission to make sure everyone woke and worked on time. This discipline was a departure from his younger days. As a dreamy paperboy, John had been known to fall asleep on neighbors' lawns when he was supposed to be delivering morning copies of the *Salinas Index*.

Ricketts was another matter. The biologist had been easy to like in California, where he was a Cannery Row fixture. But he was hard to fathom here in Baja, in close quarters, his high voice quivering with excitement about the exotic species they saw each day, doing his little "tippie-toe mouse dance" when he'd had a few too many beers. Ricketts knew and loved the tidepools best of all, but he wasn't always the first to slog into them, primed for hard, hot-weather work. He spent two to three hours at a time in a bathtub on the deck. He drank prodigiously. Ricketts acted, Captain Tony noted with contempt, as if this six-week trip was his own private, tropical vacation.

Brian and I recognized the tension between crew members. But the notion of this trip as a vacation for anyone was utterly alien. We weren't bronzed, we were burnt. We didn't feel lean and strong, we felt sore and perennially hungry. Our backs ached; our toes and fingers were rubbed raw. Hygiene: unmentionable. Sex lives: nonexistent.

At seventy-six feet long, the *Western Flyer* had enough space for deception and intrigue—Carol flirting with Ricketts and Tiny; Steinbeck snooping through portholes. But on the *Zuiva*, asexual exhaustion ruled the day. There was no privacy for any kind of amorous coupling. No time

or energy, either. Brian and I were getting along well, but we spoke surprisingly little. Nearly every waking moment was spent in split-shift
work, sailing, studying, and tending children.

Brian and I had never spent so much time so close together, with so
little personal interaction. We did not chat idly; there was always the
sense of Doug scowling and moping, just inches away. At night, we did
not so much fall asleep as pass out, our legs propped up by piles of luggage, with Tziporah between us. Our identities seemed to be fusing not
because we were lost, romantically, in each other, but only because we
were lost in the work at hand. One of the *Log*'s literary underpinnings—
the fact that it is written as "We" in a combined Steinbeck and Ricketts
voice—seemed less gimmicky and more understandable now. Whether
desert sun or boating life itself was to blame, identities did seem to
change on a tropical sea voyage. To merge, or simply to melt down.

One morning on the sailboat's deck, Doug saw a flash of light. It caught
the corner of his eye—winking, then disappearing, like a flicker of something silver slipping off the boat and into the water. He mentioned it
repeatedly throughout the day. "Did you see it?" he asked Brian and me.

"No," we said.

"What do you think it was?"

"We don't know."

He persevered, his large eyes dark and wide, his furry brow lifted
quizzically.

"It was metal," he said. "Like a tool."

Doug developed this theory, completely hypothetical: If someone had
borrowed one of his tools, without asking, and left it lying on the boat's
bow until we lifted anchor and started sailing, then the tool could have
been jarred from its resting place until it slipped into the water. Sounded
like something a kid would do, Doug theorized.

The captain called to Aryeh menacingly, drawing out each syllable of
his name. Aryeh came to the cockpit and responded to Doug's questioning. Their conversation was muffled, but by the end, I could hear Aryeh
saying "maybe" to Doug's terse suggestions.

When Aryeh crawled back into the cabin, baring his teeth in a forced, stressed smile, I tried to ask him about the exchange. "Did you take his tool?"

"No," Aryeh said.

"Were you out on the bow today?"

"No."

"So why did you say 'maybe' to him?"

"I don't know." And there was the nervous smile again, confused and eager to please.

In the cockpit, Doug was stammering to himself: *I knew it! I knew it!*

"Wait a minute," I called to him through the cabin door. "Are you sure you're missing something?"

"No."

"Then why are you blaming Aryeh?"

"Because it seems like something he'd do. It's the only thing that makes sense."

"He's only five, Doug. Kindergartners are suggestible. Say it enough times and you'll convince him that he *did* do it."

But Aryeh had said "maybe" to him, and that was enough. "I saw the flash," the captain said several more times that day, with a half-satisfied, delusional smile.

Our daughter, Tziporah, had developed a toddler's crush on Doug. Unlike the many adults who reached out to pinch her cheeks and comb her hair, he played hard-to-get, and she found that irresistible. But she, like Aryeh, frequently fell from his good graces. Tziporah had the disconcerting habit of crying at least once each day, especially when the boat shifted suddenly, causing her to knock her head against the wall, or whenever some projectile launched by Doug ("Get this goddamn thing out of here!") came flying into the cabin and whacked some part of her body.

"Why is she doing that?" Doug would snap in response to her caterwauling, lowering his head to glare at us through the cabin door. He seemed aggravated, but also truly puzzled.

"She's a baby, Doug," I said. "When she's hurt, she cries. It's normal."

But her pain evoked no sympathy from him. There *were* things that received his compassion, however; objects mostly. The poop bucket, in particular, seemed to bring out his nurturing instincts. To use it, one squatted in the narrow aisle of the cabin, with no more dignity than a barnyard animal. Then you dropped the bucket over the side of the boat, attached to a rope. It was important to let the lip of the bucket reach into the current, to give the soiled container a good washing. But if you let the bucket fill with too much water, it would drag violently as the boat sailed ahead, straining the bucket's handle. We'd lost one bucket already, and though we still had a replacement, Doug paled at the thought of losing or damaging another. "Be gentle with that thing!" he admonished us more than once.

"I wish he could show as much concern for the kids," I muttered to Brian.

As the trip progressed, Doug began to seem mildly, but cumulatively, unstable. On good, bright, windy days, he donned his formal sailing costume: surprisingly preppie, chino-style pants; a white-hooded cotton shirt that covered his tattooed torso; brown-leather deck shoes; a canvas hat that he tied tautly under his chin; and some serious sailing gloves that looked more suited to East Coast yacht racing than to Cortez cruising. Minus thirty inches of hair, he could have come from Harvard.

The gloves were absolutely necessary, he assured me. "Really?" I'd asked. I told him I wished he had advised us to bring sailing gloves when we'd discussed our packing lists together. But he'd never mentioned them. Now, he had several pairs along.

"Should I borrow your gloves when it's my turn to sail?" I asked, still thinking in those early days that this was a somewhat normal, friendly kind of trip.

"No," he said. "Don't touch them."

As the trip wore on, Doug's costume deteriorated. The same was true for Steinbeck and Ricketts, who began to look more relaxed and ragged with each day's passage. It was also true for me, Brian, and the children: Our skin darkened, we swapped protective pants for shorts, and short-sleeved shirts for sleeveless ones, and finally gave up on our salt-encrusted surf shoes and walked around the boat in bare feet.

But Doug's clothing changes were erratic and counterintuitive. He quit the chinos and went back to his hippie-style Guatemalan shorts. When the wind stopped blowing, he sulked and removed his shirt, even if it meant his chest and back would burn. Even on a glaring day, he might stow the hat and bake his skull. His gloves said the most: When he wore them, it meant he was in a nautical mood, ready for the slap of the sails. When he stuffed them into the holes next to his bunk, watch out; his hopes had crumbled, and he might spend a whole afternoon without saying a word.

His appetites were similarly mood-driven. When he was perturbed, he would not eat, and not eating seemed to make him only more troubled and slothful. His long, lean body was poorly suited to fasting. He was morose when dehydrated or when his blood-sugar levels were low. His captaining abilities were modest and he had little interest in navigation. I worried about the mistakes he'd make on a completely empty stomach. If and when Doug did fix a snack, it was usually a snack for him alone. But when Brian or I cooked, we cooked for him, because it was in our own best interests to do so.

Days aboard *Zuiva* started when Doug awoke, near dawn. Without a word and without a plan, he'd start pulling up the anchor—a rusty coil inside the compartment where Brian, Tziporah, and I slept; in fact, right next to our heads. The boat would immediately lurch: our wake-up call, if the groaning anchor hadn't already startled us to our feet. It did not matter if this part of the day was calmest. It did not matter that there wasn't enough wind for sailing.

Anxious that an uncontrolled sideways drift might impale us on a coastal rock, Brian and I would yank on clothes. Once there wasn't even time for that, and Brian had to run outside in his open-fly boxers, indecently exposed as he helped unfurl the sails. There was no time for a leisurely pee, or for Brian to swap his early-morning glasses for contact lenses. Tooth-brushing seemed a bourgeois conceit considering the more pressing matter of cliffs looming up on our starboard side. One of us would hurry to join Doug in the cockpit, because sailing this boat was usually a two-person job, especially when we were exiting or entering an anchorage.

Under sail, making coffee was a trial. We didn't have a gimbaled stove; ours was a simple two-burner camping stove balanced atop a cupboard. When the boat bobbed, pans slid and the kettle sloshed. Once I spilled boiling water on my foot, and from then on I tried to cook only when we were sailing in a straight, established line, on even seas. This did not bother Doug: He wasn't a coffee drinker. He was hardly a water drinker. But for Brian and me, it was a subtle torture. As soon as the *Western Flyer* had left Monterey, "from the galley ventilator came the odor of boiling coffee, a smell that never left the boat again while we were on it." We associated the smell of coffee with camaraderie and normalcy, and we could not read those lines from the *Log* without feeling they had enjoyed something that we could not.

Though Doug ate the least, he had brought the most and choicest foods. Here our family had erred gravely. We were accustomed to backpacking and paddling, to packing light, and because we were from Alaska, to avoiding any strong-smelling, wildlife-attracting provisions. In other words, we'd brought along the culinary equivalent of tightly packed sawdust. But on a sailboat, of course, none of this was necessary. While there wasn't enough room for five people, there was enough room for real food.

Doug had brought along big, smelly jars of salmon, about a dozen boxes of fancy-label crackers, heavy cans of organic vegetables, and deluxe stove-top meals. In addition, my sister had sent him with vast quantities of gourmet macaroni and cheese, knowing our kids loved it. The captain did share his food, but every time I opened a package to cook for everyone, I felt I had to grovel. And every time Aryeh or Tziporah emptied a cracker box—one of the only things they could stomach when seasickness struck—Doug's eyebrow compacted. "When those crackers are gone, I'm gone," he said.

As long as he wasn't cooking, Doug figured he didn't need to clean, either. Every day, Brian or I washed a bucketload of dishes. Doug took great care to wash only his spoon and dish, even if we'd blackened several pots making his dinner. This called to mind a scene in the *Log*. The *Western Flyer*'s crew had agreed to take turns washing the dishes, but Tex managed to disappear into the engine room whenever it was his turn. One day the other crew members surrounded him with cold eyes and vengeful hearts.

"My God, are you going to hang me?" Tex asked.

"Tex," Sparky piped up, "you're going to wash 'em or you're going to sleep with 'em."

Tex protested, but the threat was sincere. The crew lifted loads of dirty dishes onto Tex's bunk. Tex resigned himself to washing the dishes, the *Log*'s authors reported. But he never did get the catsup out of his blankets.

On board the *Zuiva,* I recounted the anecdote for Doug. "Funny story," he said. But he never did wash any plate but his own.

We sailed twenty-eight miles from Punta Púlpito to Isla Coronados, the island that was our next tidepooling spot. Strong winds pushed us along at seven knots, a good clip, for part of the day. Doug's mood was buoyant. He wore his gloves for several hours and even chatted a little. Then the wind petered out, and small acts of skipper vengeance took its place. He protested against using the motor. He refused to assist or instruct me when it was my turn at the tiller. It was all dully familiar—evidently linked not to Brian's behavior or mine, but to some internal emotional weather system that we couldn't control any more than we could control the sea. On his own farm in California, Doug might have been moody and fickle—Eliza would later admit, apologetically and to her own regret, that this was so. But on a farm, Doug had acres of unkempt fields in which to hide and mope. On the *Zuiva,* he could not flee. And so the sailboat became his prison, and ours.

By early evening we had bobbed south for over ten hours, instead of the five or six we had hoped to sail swiftly. Now, the hat shape of Isla Coronados was dark and clear, and we could even see a fine rim of white sand and green mangroves where the water met the shore. The lowest tide had come and gone, but the water was still low enough. There was still hope. With efficient anchoring, we might be ready to pile into our kayak and paddle to shore in twenty minutes.

As we approached the island, Doug tacked slowly back and forth under sail, like a day-tripper reluctant to turn home. How anyone could be both stressed by his confinement and, paradoxically, halfhearted about getting to land was beyond my comprehension. As usual he hadn't eaten much all day, which gave me an idea. Wedging myself between the cup-boards, wary of scalding spills, I started preparations for dinner. I boiled water for one of everybody's favorites, noodles with salmon jerky, and told Doug it would be ready at the anchorage. Everyone would benefit: Doug would have an incentive for making good time—he'd get to eat a relaxing dinner instead of choking down food in the cockpit—and we'd get to go ashore before the tide rose any higher.

The next time I glanced out the hatch, we were almost to the beach. Suddenly the boat was leaning away from the island. Doug had tied the tiller to one side, into a makeshift autopilot. The sailboat bobbed in a circle, unmanned. Doug squeezed into the cabin and pressed toward the stove, hovering over me, an empty bowl in his hand. I stared at him, open-mouthed.

"But we're almost there," I stuttered.

"Not really."

"I thought this would give you a reason to get to shore," I said, confessing my whole plan.

"Your plan backfired."

"But don't you want to get to land?" I squeaked.

"Not as much as I want to eat."

He scooped food into his mouth while we watched, helpless. We didn't dare take over the tiller when he was in a mood like this. And approaching a shallow, unfamiliar anchorage without the aid of an electronic depth-sounder was the hardest part of sailing. It required concentration and coordination—one person at the stern, another near the mast, someone swinging a lead line to check the depth of the water. We didn't feel comfortable doing it without him.

After Doug finished his dinner, he started the engine, something he could have done two or three hours earlier. We motored close to shore, anchored, and, minus the captain, paddled the rest of the way by kayak, spilling onto the white-sand beach well past the optimal collecting tide.

BURNED

We were eager to tidepool at Isla Coronados because Steinbeck and Ricketts had described it so oddly. They said it had a "burned quality." On the small, reddish brown isle—a dead volcano, dotted with cactus and scrub—they detected "a resentment of the shore toward animal life, an inhospitable quality in the stones that would make an animal think twice about living there." They went even further, hinting at some invisible element like "radioactivity" (an imprecise synonym in 1940 for the eerie unknowable) to explain the creepiness they felt. They collected some sponges, corals, crabs, and other species, but they did not consider it a rich environment.

Expectation can be a potent force. A mind that has been set to see strangeness or harshness has a hard time rebelling against its own preprogramming. "The things of our minds," the *Log*'s authors wrote, "have for us a greater toughness than external reality." Knowing that, we tried to see Coronados with fresh eyes, tainted neither by preconception nor contrariness.

Along the island's southwestern corner, where we anchored, several habitats existed side by side. A long, low, hook-shaped point reached toward the mainland. Most of the point was rimmed with dazzling sand, so soft it swallowed our feet and made beach hiking surprisingly strenuous. In deeper water, there was a small forest of seaweed, which glinted silver with the swift movements of dozens of fish, hiding beneath the weed's gray-green shadows. In the middle of the point, sand yielded to rocky foreshore. Jumbles of black boulders created their own shallow-water worlds.

We squatted between the barnacle-encrusted boulders, in a protected maze of ankle-deep channels and clear little pools, sifting and probing. There was as much to see in a single square foot as in a square yard: It was the time spent looking, not the distance covered, that decided whether one saw many species or just a few. But like perennially anxious shallow-water crabs, we continually had to adjust our positions—

stepping sideways, finding new footing, clambering backward a few inches at a time with our T-shirt tails dragging in the water—to avoid being toppled by the gently rising tide.

At times during this trip we would see less than Steinbeck and Ricketts saw, but this time we saw far more, even though we'd missed the day's lowest tide. Fastened to rocks we located many tube worms, hidden away in their white or brown chalky casings that resemble knotted pasta. We saw pulpy-soft masses of yellow flatworms that looked like peaches gone bad. Brian picked up several bristle-covered worms, probably the stinging *Eurythoe,* and managed—always lucky—to avoid being stung. We found the ubiquitous, gray-green sea cucumbers living in rocky crevices, and one brown sea cucumber, a less-common creature. There were crabs of all kinds: hermits, and true crabs, including the decorator crab, which disguises itself by planting bits of algae on its hard-shelled back.

By this time, we were questioning the Steinbeck and Ricketts description of the island as relatively lifeless. And still, we weren't done finding new things. There were more species to be spotted and tallied, including many of the softer, brighter, deeper-water invertebrates: reddish cup corals, bright orange and purple sponges, compound tunicates and anemones and bryozoans. Of the sea stars, there were two kinds of brittlestars and a fleshy sunflower star. Of chitons, there were two species also. As always, there were gelatinous masses we couldn't identify at all.

While Brian, Aryeh, and Tziporah continued to tidepool among boulders, I went wading along the sandy intertidal, cooling my legs in the sparkling turquoise shallows. As I walked, I thought about Ricketts and Steinbeck and their casual dismissal of this place. Then I thought about their route. The town of Loreto, which would be our next stop, had been their last. For them, a major port always meant refuge and excess. In other words, inebriation. We'd arrived at Coronados fresh and eager—desperate, in fact, since we'd pined for landfall all day. They'd walked these same shores with hangovers. The island wasn't "burned." *They* were. If pressed, they might have admitted as much, since the subjectivity inherent in all kinds of observation and reflection—journalistic reportage, artistic creation, and science, too—was one of Steinbeck's favorite subjects. Our knowledge of the world, the *Log*'s authors would have maintained, may be built upon foundations that are no more or less stable than the average person's mood.

Mulling over this idea, I spotted what looked like an old shower-curtain ring lodged in the otherwise blemish-free sand. *You never know when you'll need one of these,* I thought, remembering an eccentric Baja beachcomber I'd once met who collected curtain rings by the dozen. Lifting it out of the water, I saw that this ring wasn't made of plastic, but what looked like tightly packed fragments of ivory and yellow sand. It was broken on one side, and pliable. A month earlier, I would have dismissed it as an odd bit of garbage, but now I looked closer and realized I was holding something living in my hand: a moon snail collar.

I recognized it only because I was in a fine mood—content and curious—and because I'd spent an absurd amount of time lately in the steamy bowels of a boat, staring at textbook photos of invertebrates. One antiquarian guide, published in 1936, said that naturalists through the ages had puzzled over and misidentified these sandpaper-textured rings. In fact, a textbook informed me, the moon snail extrudes its fertilized eggs in a continuous mucus-covered sheet, embedded with sand, creating a rubbery natural cement. The sheet wraps around the snail as it is formed, shaped by the snail's enormous fleshy foot. When complete, the snail abandons the collar-shaped egg case. In time, the case crumbles, freeing up to a half-million free-swimming larvae.

So that was what I held in my hand—a half-million baby snails! In that one living shower-curtain ring were nearly as many potential gastropods as there are humans in the state of Alaska (the northern limit of the moon snail's range, by the way). And what does that mean? Nothing, except that even a "burned" beach can be a study in the mysteries of plenitude.

But, it should be noted, not all those snail larvae will survive to adulthood. "There is some poetic justice," wrote Ricketts in *Between Pacific Tides,* "in the assumption that many of the minute larvae will provide food for the mussels, which later on will be eaten by adult moon snails."

From the tidepools, the volcanic profile of Isla Coronados looked like an old fedora, just the sort Ricketts would have worn. Nearly flush to the shore, the 928-foot cinder cone was soft and brown, with a well-worn dent on top, where a 1940s gentleman would have slid his fingers each time he lifted his hat to greet a lady walking down the street. It was a welcoming landmark. We tried to feel the same radioactive creepiness that the *Log*'s authors had reported but couldn't raise a single goose bump.

Perhaps further inland, we thought. Our tidepooling completed, we walked fifty feet from the shore and everything felt different. Away from the water's cool edge, the temperature skyrocketed twenty degrees. The sandy beach ended and we faced a prickly plateau of volcanic rocks and knee-high pitahaya cactus—all sharp edges and thorns and small holes that looked perfect for poisonous snakes and spiders. Each footstep had to be chosen carefully. Just as we relaxed into a natural pace, we were startled by the explosive skitter of a small lizard, bone white and scrawny. It disappeared into the scrub so quickly that we were left with only a flashbulb-quick impression of its ghostly appearance. We felt like we'd glimpsed the last, lone survivor of an apocalypse.

We felt daring as we walked inland, without snacks, water bottles, or our snakebite kit. And we felt a little sneaky. Technically, all Sea of Cortez islands are federally protected wildlife preserves and landing on them is prohibited without a government permit. This regulation has been on the books since 1978. For two decades it was ignored by everyone: local fishermen, ecotourism companies, kayakers, sailboaters, scuba divers. It's still ignored by almost everyone, but that isn't the point. Until recently, most people—including officials in Baja—didn't give the matter much thought. But beginning in the late 1990s, fisheries and conservation agencies began cracking down.

The islands near Loreto are monitored better than most, because they fall within the boundaries of Bahía de Loreto National Marine Park—a park created in 1996 and still working out the kinks in its mandate. If someone is found landing or camping on an island without permission, they can be asked to leave. Does it happen? Only sometimes. But enforcement will almost certainly become more strict.

This was our fourth trip to Baja, but it was the first time we attempted to play by the rules. The only problem was, no one could explain them to us. From home I'd written and emailed Mexican federal agencies to inquire about island permits, but I hadn't received a single response. I wrote them and said I was a tourist. I wrote them and said I was a guide-book author. I wrote them and said I was a journalist. Still no answer.

I phoned the Mexican fisheries office in San Diego, and named the

Sea of Cortez islands we thought we might visit by sailboat. The woman on the phone had never heard of them. In some ways, Baja had entered the twenty-first century: rules, permits, email. In other ways, Baja was as remote and obscure as when the *Western Flyer* visited. "Coronados?" the fisheries woman had said. "Is that near Cancún?"

Now here we were, hiking inland at Coronados under a cloudless sky, feeling thirstier by the minute, tiptoeing between thorny plants, rambling over and around oven-hot rocks since there was no evidence of a footpath. "It's somber here," Brian said, and I did not know if he was echoing my feelings or simply expressing his own unease.

"Burned," Steinbeck and Ricketts had said. Definitely. Very burned. And kind of creepy, too: absolutely silent away from the water's edge. No sounds of surf, no birdsong.

Except for the sun-blanched, almost skeletal lizard, we hadn't seen anything move. This austere volcanic landscape reinforced all the standard desert illusions: that deserts are lifeless, that they are dangerous, that they are wastelands. Why would anyone visit such a harsh place? Why all the fuss about permits? And if visitors did come, what could they possibly do?

"Maybe we should turn around," I finally said to Brian. We'd walked for only five minutes and I was already picturing our family in a *New Yorker*–style cartoon, wearing tattered clothes, dragging ourselves in single file across generic sand dunes toward a shimmering mirage.

We veered back toward the beach and unexpectedly came face-to-face with a sign: *Sendero—La Flora Del Isla Coronados* (Path—The Flora of Coronados Island). It was the first man-made object we'd seen along the coast in four days, since leaving Bahía Concepción. The sign announced that we were on a nature trail sponsored by three groups: the Nature Conservancy, a Mexican environmental agency, and Bahía de Loreto National Marine Park. A sandy, groomed footpath bordered by shells and other scavenged objects meandered ahead of us. An interpretive sign next to a spiky bush with wiry downturned limbs identified it as a *Palo Adán,* or Adam's tree. The little tree looked like a broken-ribbed umbrella turned inside-out by a gust of wind. It had small, flame-red flowers. It was lovely.

Farther along the trail was a short, fat-trunked tree with nubby twigs, identified as a Matacora leatherplant. And there were a few more signs and many more plants: bushes that looked like creosote and ocotillo, and thick, low mats of succulents, not thorny or cactuslike at all. Many of the plants had small waxy leaves that, on close inspection, looked vibrantly green—not burnt at all. Suddenly we felt less thirsty and less endangered. The *New Yorker* cartoon disappeared from my mind, replaced by images of schoolkids on field trips from nearby Loreto, traipsing along a tame and prettified trail.

The sun was dipping below the peninsular mountains now, the jagged coastline west of Isla Coronados softening from sunbaked brown to lavender in the falling light. As the air cooled, a sweet green smell blanketed the island. Lengthening shadows highlighted animal tracks on the sandy path, tracks we hadn't noticed before: skinny, helix-shaped snake tracks; little mice and reptile prints. Several more blanched lizards skittered ahead of us, emboldened by the coming darkness. The first skinny lizard had seemed like a creepy omen, but the next half-dozen seemed comical. So much for the illusion of lifelessness.

We finished the nature trail loop in about fifteen minutes and headed back toward the beach, where we spotted a composting toilet erected by volunteers, and more signs: "Animals and plants living on this island are very sensitive to human presence. Your visit may harm them." And: "Fishermen friends: Don't bring domestic animals or pests here," with explanations about the island's endemic reptiles and prohibitions on cutting cactus, harvesting bird eggs, and disturbing wildlife.

The national marine park director would tell me later that his most successful projects involved eradicating nonnative fauna from the islands—cats and dogs and other domestic animals, usually left here by fishermen. Nearly every island in the gulf, no matter how remote, is visited by thousands of people each year. The problem with these islands is not that they are wild or hostile, but that they are fragile and all too habitable.

Forget "radioactivity." Forget any inhospitable quality that would make an animal think twice about living here, as the *Log*'s authors had suggested with spooky overtones. The only quality that would intimidate a native animal here, the signs suggested, was man's own shortsighted avarice.

We see what we are ready to see: a desert fierce or fragile, tidepools either "burned" or brimming, a shower-curtain ring or the preemie ward for a half-million snails.

Steinbeck and Ricketts were wrong. But that's what a good hangover will do to you.

BOYS OF LORETO

Loreto was enticingly close now. The town is Baja's longest continually occupied settlement, an oasis of civilized pleasures in the shadow of the Sierra de la Giganta's steep flanks. I could feign enthusiasm for its rich missionary history, but what I truly remembered most fondly from previous trips was the sidewalk-*asadero* smell of grilled steaks, and the soothing hiss of air-conditioning on sunburnt skin.

"Are there restaurants there?" Aryeh asked.

"Restaurants, stores, streets, everything," we said.

"I want a hamburger," Aryeh said. Fine, *hamborguesas* for everyone. *Con queso.* Seated next to us, Brian half-collapsed at the mention of cheese, his eyelids fluttering weakly. We didn't have a "Tex" or "Sparky" with us, cooking up weekly washtub-loads of sailor's spaghetti. Judging by the fit of our clothes, Brian and I had lost several pounds each since crossing the border, and the kids were always hungry.

"Milk?" Tziporah asked shyly.

"Cold milk," I said. "In a glass."

"And pop?" Aryeh asked.

Yes.

"Pop! Pop!" the children screamed, dancing on the bunks. Now we'd started it. We had several hours of sailing ahead of us, with the kids squirming and eager, oblivious to Doug's grunts of disapproval.

Loreto was barely five miles from Isla Coronados. The day had dawned calm and surprisingly cool, with no hint of the bad weather to come. The wind sighed into the sails, inspiring only anorexic flutters. Doug clambered to the bow. He fiddled out of view, struggling to replace the jib sail with a lighter, more responsive one we'd never used, while shouting semi-audible directions to Brian—half-dressed, caffeine-deprived—in the helm.

I occupied the cabin aisle belowdecks, trying to contain two crew members who were prematurely ready to race ashore. Telling the children they'd soon be eating glorious junk food had been like telling

Bligh's crew they'd soon be seeing naked, buxom South Pacific women. Appetites roused, they were uncontrollable, more mutinous in their extreme happiness than they'd ever been in their discontent.

At the same time, I scrambled to assemble all the sailing papers we might need in port. The forms, photocopied from nautical guides, asked for our names, ages and ranks or titles. Every person aboard should be described, the directions instructed. It was easy enough to fake the adults' titles—captain, first mate, deckhand. But what to call Aryeh: galley boy, in a boat without a galley? And what to call two-year-old Tziporah: shark bait? It didn't matter, as long as we filled in the blanks.

Confused about port protocol, I prepared for all eventualities—assembling identification cards and ownership papers, studying charts for anchoring hints, and finding a town map to locate the port authority. Doug and Brian struggled to hoist the new sail, a colorful spinnaker. It wasn't coming easily, as judged by Doug's cursing and stomping on the deck, just over my head. From Brian, I could hear only weary, one-syllable questions: "Now?" "This?" "What?" "Doug!?"

In matters of diplomacy, appearance mattered at least as much as paperwork, I presumed, recalling how the *Western Flyer's* crew always hurried to clean and shave before meeting with port officials. I dug a compact mirror out of a duffel and squinted at a swaying reflection I hadn't seen in days. One last detail: I pried a thumb-sized bottle of perfume from a dark corner and dabbed it on my wrists.

While I was busy combing salty dreadlocks from my hair, the formerly calm and windless seas suddenly began to pick up. Even as I yanked a comb through tangles, I had to brace myself between bunks. A gray-green wave slammed the side of the boat hard, darkening the nearly opaque cabin window—more shouts above, and a small splash belowdecks. Ah well, a little too much perfume. Just as well. The perfumed dousing just barely covered up the seaweed smell that had infiltrated my clothes.

Outside, a brewing storm transformed the gulf in a matter of minutes. Irregular waves slammed the boat, tossing Aryeh and Tziporah from side to side in the cabin. A few profound cranium thunks silenced all talk of *hamborguesas*. Suddenly, blush and lip gloss seemed just as irrelevant. The water, glassy when we'd lifted anchor—calm even minutes earlier—was now evenly coated with foaming chop for as far as the eye could see.

Later, Brian would fill me in on what had happened up on deck. The captain's timing had been laughably bad. He'd elected to hoist our light-est-weight sail just as a powerful north wind came blasting through the funnel formed by Isla Coronados and the mainland near Loreto. As soon as the sail had billowed, the steering had gone haywire.

Now, Doug barked commands at Brian to help him bring the sail down while maneuvering through a slalom course of other large, anchored boats—including a few modest cruise ships—on the coastal approach into Loreto. It was yet another display of miserable seamanship, this time with witnesses. The question of whether we had the right to enter Loreto's small-boat harbor became moot. Barely in control of the sail-boat, Brian and Doug tucked into the shelter of the harbor while the wind howled past. Tying up to the pier, they were both visibly shaken.

Pangas lined the inner harbor, with more arriving each minute as fishermen took shelter from the windstorm. Ours was the only sailboat. The depth in the harbor was no more than four feet, with the tide due to drop another foot or so. Our draft was three and a half feet. Good enough, our skipper said, demonstrating either a flexible attitude toward docking or toward math, we couldn't tell which. With a storm blasting and town pleasures calling, we weren't about to disagree with him.

So far on this trip, we hadn't anchored off any town. Even Ecomundo had been nothing more than a string of houses along the shore. We hadn't been required to check in with any port authority, because we hadn't passed any ports. Today was a Saturday. Guidebooks emphasized the need to present oneself to the port captain, but they made no mention of what to do on weekends or holidays.

In Steinbeck's day, when foreign visitors were few, port protocol was strict. "One fine thing about Mexican officials," the *Log*'s authors wrote, "is that they greet a fishing boat with the same serious ceremony they would afford the *Queen Mary,* and the *Queen Mary* would have to wait just as long."

The *Western Flyer*'s crew didn't dare leave their boat. Instead they cleaned and dressed and then waited impatiently, sometimes hours, for the Mexican officials to row out to them in little skiffs:

"Everyone who has or can borrow a uniform comes aboard—the collector of customs in a washed and shiny uniform; the business agent in a business suit having about him what Tiny calls 'a double-breasted look'; then soldiers if there are any; and finally the Indians, who row the boat and rarely have uniforms. They come over the side like ambassadors. We shake hands all around. The galley has been prepared: coffee is ready and perhaps a drop of rum. Cigarettes are presented. . . ."

We doubted if anyone would come aboard our tiny boat, and if so we had little to offer them. Modern health concerns have made old-fashioned hospitality harder to simulate. A pack of cigarettes or box of matches made an easy gift in Steinbeck's day, and even in our own just a decade ago. But in Baja as in lands north, smoking has begun to lose favor. Disease is no laughing matter, but I fondly remember how easy it was, during earlier travels, to ignite an acquaintanceship with the strike of a match. Everything about that ancient ceremony had served the needs of etiquette: the courtesy of the shared pack, the passing of the flame, the first half-lidded puffs that gave strangers a chance to size each other up and to choose their opening words. North American Indians, with their peace pipes, understood this. But we modern hedonists abused tobacco, and now we must give up the cancer sticks altogether.

The only visitors who approached our boat were underage. Instead of rum-laced coffee and cigarettes, we handed out fistfuls of dried fruit and American breakfast cereal. It might not have impressed a customs agent, but the local kids loved it.

We walked several blocks into town, admiring the rose- and lemon-colored stucco buildings. On a pleasurable afternoon like this one, it was possible to forget about the worst of the missionary era—the floggings and disease—and admire instead its art and architecture. The older houses downtown had ornate windows, ironwork gratings, and arched doorways. Potted plants adorned second-story balconies. There was a look of well-tended permanence here, at least in the eyes of unshowered visitors whose shoes and hair were crusted with salt.

The gallery-style tourist shops were full of blue-rimmed margarita glasses and hammered-tin suns and lizards. The downtown shop clerks, unlike their counterparts in some resort-dominated towns, did not pander. Instead of "How much you wanna pay?" one elegant shopkeeper peered over his reading glasses, set aside the English-language novel he was carefully decoding, and asked me, "This word, please: Can you tell me what it means to 'opine'?"

We had a blissful lunch at a sidewalk cafe—blissful for all those reasons that are dull to the reader but never to the traveler: cold drinks, a flush toilet and sink, the shade of a sidewalk umbrella. Cars motored slowly past our table, forced to proceed at a civilized pace because old Loreto's downtown streets are made from paving stones.

After lunch, we bought groceries and fuel. By taxi we transported twenty gallons of drinking water back to the boat. We visited the port authority, but it was padlocked. Still, we expected that some town official might spy us and send an emissary. But everyone's uniforms must have been dirty that day. No officials took the time or trouble to visit us, even though we sat all afternoon at the dock, waiting to be castigated for going ashore without permission.

As the windstorm roared on, sandy grit flew through the air and the palm trees lining Loreto's seawall bent wildly. The waves built into plunging rollers. Every school-age child seemed to be on the dirty beach next to the harbor's breakwater, bodysurfing the swells as they rolled in. Tired of swimming, some of the kids roamed the harbor docks, chasing each other up and down narrow planks and rotting ramps. Aryeh stared at the boys, and then at me. I looked at the derelict piers and algae-covered ramps, imagining broken bones and skull contusions, and finally relented.

"Go ahead," I said. "Just wear your life jacket."

We'd gone to some effort to teach Aryeh Spanish before the trip, for rare social occasions like these. But we needn't have bothered. These boys, ages seven to ten, used only the most cursory Spanish themselves. Mostly they spoke the international tongue of boyhood: *Ptshew! Ptshewwww!* and other mouth-generated shooting sounds, while they pretended to kill each other.

Aryeh aimed his index finger with theatrical precision and was embraced by the local boys immediately. Tziporah loved the excitement too, even when the boys drew close to press their hands lightly against her pale skin. If Tziporah took even a single step away from me, toward the dock's edge, the boys ceased their chase for the moment and slid into position behind us, forming a silent and protective barrier between her and the dangerous drop-off to the green harbor water below.

Armando, Alberto, and Jesús all had thin, brown legs and bare feet and bright, impish smiles. They were fishermen, they said. From the beach and docks they caught triggerfish and bull's-eye puffers, which they sold in town.

In La Paz, Steinbeck and Ricketts also encountered many eager young boys near the docks wanting to sell them tidal specimens. Once the *Western Flyer's* crew started passing out ten-centavo coins, word got out that there were strange men in a boat who would pay good money for worthless things, and the deluge began. "If we had not left the second night," the *Log's* authors wrote, "they would have swamped the boat." Among the specimen-hawking boys was one who had speared a puffer, but this he would not sell. Steinbeck and Ricketts tried to buy it from him, but he refused, saying he'd been commissioned by a local man to get this fish so that its liver could be used to poison a cat.

"Our" boys said they sold their puffers for human consumption, but we questioned the truth of this, since the latter fish are exceptionally poisonous. In Japan, only the most talented chefs are allowed to clean and serve the puffers—*fugu*—in a way that avoids its lethal tissues. We'd never seen the fish for sale in Mexico, though the boys claimed it was the tastiest of all seafoods if prepared well. It is possible they were telling the truth. People everywhere will consume remarkable things. But more likely, the boys were too proud to admit that they were selling fish that was only good for killing flies and cats.

Armando, Alberto, and Jesús proved their ichthyological knowledge in other ways. I brought out armloads of identification guides, and their faces lit up to see photographs of organisms they'd previously seen only in real life, just as our faces frequently lit up to see things in real life that we'd previously seen only in photos. They turned the pages of each guidebook carefully. "*Puerco,*" they said. "Triggerfish," I responded. "*Pargo,*" they said. "Snapper," I responded. They did not tire of this process, and wanted to identify every fish in the book, and hear an identification for every picture that stumped them. Like Adam in the garden, we were creating a whole new world together just by naming it.

Next, Brian gave them small gifts: pocket magnifying glasses that we'd brought by the dozens. Immediately they were restless boys again, chasing after each other and attempting to focus the magnifiers on each other's skin or on their own hands, yelping gaily when they produced a burn. But this game didn't last long. Mischief exhausted, the boys discovered the magnifiers' more orthodox purpose. They crawled around the docks, faces pressed to the little plastic tools, investigating every barnacle and sea star cemented to the piers. One boy pocketed an extra magnifier without permission. It wasn't idle thievery or greed. The boys shyly turned away other gifts and accepted only token handfuls of any food we offered them. Something about this magic looking-glass must have been irresistible, and we took pleasure in imagining this same young thief might grow up to become a tidepool ecologist.

Doug gave the boys a tour of the boat and let them touch his private things: tools and so on. He spoke to them in elementary Spanish, displaying a tenderness that surprised us. He might even have shared his crackers with them, had they known to ask.

Late that afternoon, as the storm died down, we took out the rarely used video camera and captured the boys' faces on it, while they called each other names: Whale, and Monkey Face. When we played the footage back to them, using the camera's built-in screen, Armando, Alberto, and Jesús roared with laughter and begged to see it over and over, until the camera's warning light flashed. Seeing their smiles and hearing their gleeful howls seemed more important than saving our only battery, even if it meant we'd capture no more marine organisms on tape. We liked these young fishermen and did not want to leave them.

"When will we see them again?" Aryeh asked.

"I don't know," I said. "Maybe the next time we're in Loreto. And there will be other kids in other villages, I'm sure."

The boys may not have understood Aryeh's words, but they understood his tone, and the crestfallen expression on his face. One of them untied a woven, Guatemalan-style friendship bracelet from his own ankle and placed it in Aryeh's hand.

The northerly had blown itself out. The sea was almost calm now, and we were eager to leave the shallow harbor and find a proper anchorage by nightfall. The boys helped us stow the last heavy bags of water in the sailboat's hold. We prepared to back away from the dock. Still scrambling to be helpful, one boy threw off the stern line tethering us to the dock—

too soon, it turned out. Our kayak towline was tangled around the motor and no one was at the tiller.

"Fuck!" Doug howled, tripping over himself to get control of the boat before we slammed into a row of pangas. We were accustomed to the skipper's explosions, but the little fishermen on the dock looked shocked.

"That's okay, that's okay," Doug shouted toward their still, thin bodies after we had untangled lines and corrected our drift. "Next time, only after I tell you to throw the line!"

Brian, usually silent about such matters, muttered under his breath, "There he goes again." And then louder, to the startled boys, hoping to revive and reassure them: *"Hasta luego mis amigos!"*

APPARITIONS

Later that day, the last of the post-storm's puffs vanished and we were left only with following seas—low, rolling, southbound waves that preserved the storm's memory for a few more hours.

"This sucks," Doug said at dusk, abruptly vacating the helm just when the light, too, was failing us.

Brian and I conferred briefly, then started the motor. In these conditions, the sails were practically useless, but we could putt all the way to Puerto Escondido with few worries. Just the sound of the engine deepened Doug's funk. He curled up in his bunk, where he'd generally stay from now on, whenever the motor was running. At least we'd staked out our domains—he clung to his sails, we were soothed by the motor.

A week earlier, this unexpected desertion by the captain would have mortified me, but I was in familiar territory now. Not only could Brian and I handle the engine together, but we recognized this coastline, some of which we'd kayaked before. As darkness fell, that knowledge would serve us well.

During daylight hours, Doug navigated mostly by sight, steering vaguely from point to point, and drifting where the wind pushed him. Occasionally, when pressed, he would whip out a handheld global-positioning-system receiver to determine his position. Brian and I were slow learners as far as sail-handling was concerned, but we were comfortable with old-fashioned navigation and had a natural feel for how the coast would unfold. We didn't trust technology alone to tell us where we were. Nor did we trust our own eyes.

Sight alone means little in a land of mirages. Under a bright sun, the Sea of Cortez plays tricks, causing distant points to appear near, near points to appear far, and islands to hover above the water, as if levitating, with a neat blue line of waves rolling underneath them.

As Steinbeck wrote after his Cortez trip in *The Pearl,* a novella set in Baja, "Thus it might be that the people of the Gulf trust things of the spirit and things of the imagination, but they do not trust their eyes to show them distance or clear outline or any optical exactness. . . . There was no certainty in seeing, no proof that what you saw was there or was not there. And the people of the Gulf expected all places were that way, and it was not strange to them."

Simple chart and compass were Brian's and my favored tools, but we knew to treat even these with proper skepticism. In Spanish, the word for compass is *brújula,* from the verb *brujulear,* to uncover, to guess, to suspect. But it also shares the root of the word *bruja,* which means sorcerer or witch.

"How is a witch like a compass?" I once asked a Mexican boat captain, and he laughed, admitting that he'd never considered the link between the two words. "I guess that only a witch can see in all directions, and know what lies beyond," he'd said. "The witch and the compass are both diviners."

We loved this notion of navigation as being equal parts sorcery and technology. It fit well along a coastline that so many authors have described in magical terms. "The very air here is miraculous," Steinbeck and Ricketts wrote, "and outlines of reality change with the moment. The sky sucks up the land and disgorges it. A dream hangs over the whole region, a brooding kind of hallucination."

Darkness, in some ways, was more honest than daylight. There were few hazards along this sheer coast, and a ghostly outline of the mountains was visible just off our starboard side. Isla Danzante and Isla Carmen— long, spiny islands of red rock—were also visible in the moonlight, ahead of us and to the port side. By compass, Brian and I were able to predict where a navigation light stood on the southern end of Carmen, and when the light appeared just where it should be, glimmering like a distant star, it seemed less a confirmation of reality than a supernatural favor. Another light appeared on the northern end of Danzante, and the two little lights blinked at each other, communicating across the narrow black channel that separates them.

Even with our motor humming, we couldn't quite keep pace with the following seas. Each confused wave lifted our boat and set us down in the next trough, where the *Zuiva* shimmied indecisively before being lifted again. On each cresting wave, the motor lifted briefly out of the water, where it made a little gurgling noise in protest. It took a steady hand on the tiller to keep the boat from turning into the waves. But these waves were not too big or choppy, and the mild pitch-and-roll was pleasantly hypnotizing, with just enough thrill every time the cadence shifted, stretching our nerves taut.

The children were asleep below, and for the first time Brian and I manned the cockpit together, admiring the scenery all around us. We sailed close against the Sierra de la Giganta; these striated, mesa-topped peaks look like castle turrets set flush against the sea. Most of this "Range of the Giants" is sedimentary rock, laid down when this whole region was covered by the sea. It's easy to imagine this sheer coast as the rocky lair of mythical immortals.

Giants may no longer live in these peaks, but they certainly swim its adjacent waters. Whale sharks from twenty to fifty feet long have been spotted frequently in the middle and southern Cortez. These immense gray fish—not whales at all—hover close to the sea's surface, sieving plankton with the slow grace of zeppelins. Lucky scuba divers occasionally grab a free ride on a whale shark's back.

We sailed with the constellation of Orion overhead, framed by the rigging's steel cables. Moonlight glinted off the roughly textured waters all around us. Out of one corner of my eye, I spotted what looked like a shark fin slicing through a silver ribbon of water, just feet away from the boat. My heartbeat quickened. This was something smaller and speedier than a peaceful whale shark. I reminded myself to breathe again, just in time to see two more fins lined up in parallel formation, carving the waves before disappearing into the ebony depths.

It took several more double-fin sightings before Brian and I realized these weren't sharks at all, but manta rays. What had appeared to be two sharks swimming side by side were really the two gracefully upturned fins of each single enormous ray. Early naturalists sometimes called the rays devilfish, perhaps because they have two fleshy horns, which the fish use to herd planktonic crustaceans and small fish into their slotlike mouths. Once we recognized them for what they were—peaceful gliders—the great mantas no longer seemed frightening.

Tiny Colletto had seen these same pelagic giants, along this same stretch of shore, and had repeatedly harpooned them, but had never succeeded in landing one. The thickest line, thick enough to tow a fishing boat, simply snapped when the speared ray dove deeply.

The largest rays have wingspans to eighteen and a half feet, and weigh over two thousand pounds. In the family Mobulidae, there are ten to fourteen species (three on the Pacific), "all poorly known," our Peterson Field Guide informed us. This *poorly known* pleased us more than a ream of statistics, because it was thrilling—especially at night, especially on the moonlit gulf—to imagine we were seeing an animal still shrouded in mystery. Every one of the rays we saw was traveling in the same direction, due north, as if heading to some midnight leviathan's convention.

Without incident we arrived late at Puerto Escondido, the Cortez's finest natural harbor. The hourglass-shaped "Hidden Port" is nearly enclosed by a hilly peninsula, except for its entrance, which is a fast-flowing, navigable channel barely sixty-five feet wide. One could easily sail past Puerto Escondido, past its outer navigation light (broken) and the three dozen yachts hiding within its farthest reaches, without any hint of what lies within. The top part of this hourglass is a mile-wide, multilobed cove, reinforced on one side by concrete seawalls. The bottom part of the hourglass is a smaller cove called the Waiting Room, itself a decent anchorage, well-protected and concealed.

Once, there were ambitious plans to develop this perfect hurricane-hole into a world-class harbor with marina facilities, condominiums, and resort amenities. When we'd last visited, in 1992, there were some signs of this happening. A yacht brokerage firm called the Moorings operated from one harborside building, and the port captain's office was open. A grid of straight, broad streets had been laid down and modern street signs were erected. But this time, the old Moorings building was boarded up and the empty port captain's office looked neglected, if not abandoned altogether. The streets were still there, empty and waiting, with their little signs pointing the way to a "there" that wasn't anywhere in particular.

Rumors suggest that the grandest plans for development, hatched in the 1980s, fizzled because of shenanigans involving missing money and fleet-footed international investors. It is a story as old as the conquistadors, illustrating what is both the best and worst about Baja. In this "other Mexico," as mainlanders sometimes call Baja, dreamers aim high. When they succeed at developing the desert, it is an impressive feat. When they fail, usually because of corruption or incompetence, their failures are worth applauding more than any success, because only in failure is the Cortez preserved. Someday, though, this port will be developed in earnest. It can't be avoided. The profits to be made here are too great to be ignored, and for every three or four con men who run off with the funds, there is likely to be at least one who stays to finish pouring the concrete.

We puttered around the Waiting Room, weaving between eight other sailboats, until we found a suitable anchorage. Our nearest neighbor was a hypermodern motor yacht, a USS *Enterprise* on water, or at least a jumbo jet. It could have crushed the *Zuiva* into toothpicks. This monstrosity was brilliantly lit. There wasn't a sharp angle on it. Its white, rounded curves glowed against the black harbor water. Through an airliner-style row of windows we could squint into the yacht's penthouse-like interior, where I saw framed paintings on the walls, white carpeting, and a flash of color—two people waltzing quickly by, with drinks in their hands. From the back deck of the boat, billows of smoke poured forth, enveloping us in a barbecue-scented fog. I both hated the rich people inside and wished they would call us over so that we could become best friends. We heated our quesadilla dinner slowly, ready to put aside the tortillas at a moment's notice, but no invitation came.

Since the port captain's office appeared permanently closed, we had to wait another day, until Monday, for one of us to commandeer an expensive taxi ride back to Loreto, to register our presence with the authorities there. It seemed backward and silly to pay good money to return to a place we'd already been by boat, but Doug volunteered for the job and all went well.

Meanwhile, Brian, Aryeh, Tziporah, and I headed a half-mile inland to a trailer park resort, one of Escondido's few surviving developments. After two nights recouping our energies at the trailer park pool, we returned to the Waiting Room. Using the *Zuiva* as our base, we spent our last day in Puerto Escondido paddling and tidepooling. None of the shore around the steep-sided harbor was good for walking, so we investigated the shallows by kayak, just as Steinbeck and Ricketts had explored most of its margins by skiff.

In 1940, Puerto Escondido was completely undeveloped and one of the best collecting stations along the whole gulf. Its richness was in its diversity. In a small and easily explored area, it combined every kind of environment: sand bottom, stone shore, broken rock, boulders, mud, still and protected waters, and fast-flowing current at the constricted harbor entrance. "A textbook exhibit for ecologists," the *Log*'s authors wrote.

Now partly developed, the port still served as a textbook example of a different kind, demonstrating natural and artificial environments side by side. Most of its eastern shore remained in an unaltered state: mangroves and mud on the eastern side of the Waiting Room, a shoreline of rocky bluffs and broken-rock beaches on the eastern side of the inner harbor, and some sandy shoals to the north. The lower western shore was dedicated to man, boat, and progress: concrete seawalls, a breakwater, several small docks. At the largest pier, a large gray military vessel, the *Totoran,* was docked.

Curious about the *Totoran,* I left my family sitting back on a small dock and walked toward the pier. When the sailors saw me coming they stood, staring, and watched my approach. As I drew near, my hopes for a guided tour or even civil conversation dwindled. The sailors began to whistle and hiss like deflating tires—sounds that were meant, no doubt, to sound seductive. I turned back, walked to the dock where my family was waiting, and got Aryeh. This time I walked to the pier and sat down directly in front of the gate, simultaneously trying to make eye contact and look relaxed, with my five-year-old son at my side. But playing the Madonna was no more successful. This time the sailors appeared to be suddenly busy—studying their shoes, or pacing the *Totoran*'s deck.

Aryeh and I returned to the small dock where we'd left Brian and Tziporah. We all climbed back into our family kayak and paddled past a seawall and under a small arched bridge into a Venetian-style canal, along which several unfinished condominium-style buildings had been partially erected from an adobelike material. Jutting from the buildings were wooden timbers, cracked and warped. Whether this was a sign of shoddy workmanship or proof that this project had been long-abandoned, we couldn't tell. The closer we paddled, the ghostlier the half-finished buildings appeared.

Where Puerto Escondido's natural shoreline had been obliterated, we saw only barnacles and chalky tube worms. But a quarter-mile away, we saw a surprising amount of life. The placid Waiting Room was rimmed by mangrove roots and muck—just the kind of muddy, odoriferous area one usually chooses to avoid, rarely appreciating all the life it contains.

Between the tidally exposed roots, numerous vermicelli-thin tentacles swayed in the sluggish current, anchored to larger tubes embedded in the muddy bottom. One of the species of wispy creatures had nearly translucent tentacles arranged around a darker center, like a black-eyed Susan. The other had darker tentacles. From the kayak, we stared down at these for some time—burrowing anemones? sea cucumbers?—before summoning our nerve to dig one up. As soon as the creature was lifted out of the water, it collapsed into a limp, black pile of slime, demonstrating once again how the most beautiful subtidal creatures become gross when yanked rudely from their proper homes. Anemone, we decided, and left the remaining specimens unmolested.

In deeper water, we found three kinds of sea urchins—relatives of the sea stars—inhabiting the sea bottom. The first was black-spined, a common kind we'd seen before. But the next two were new to us. The largest, a brown urchin, had flame-tipped spines. It weighed at least two pounds. Another species, the flower urchin, had short, pale pink spines. Between the spines were flesh-colored circles spotted with bright red. Each spot looked like a blood-tinged bit of toilet paper covering the face of an imprudent shaver. We scooped up this flower urchin with a paddle blade, examining it from all angles. (Later we would read that the urchin delivers a dangerous toxin through these pretty pink little pedicellaria.)

The urchin is a study in simple hydraulics—proof that neither brains, bones, nor brawn are necessary for locomotion. In place of bony skeleton, the urchin has a pincushion-shaped frame called a test. The test itself, a slightly squashed and mostly hollow ball, is divided into longitudinal rows, like sections of an orange. Each row is covered with spines and nubby pores, through which emerge water-filled, sucker-tipped tube feet that look like rubber-tipped hairbrush bristles. The spines and tube feet are fitted into the test in ball-and-socket fashion, and can move in all directions.

Hundreds of independent movements would seem to require complex orchestration, but the urchin proves this isn't so. It has no brain or complex nervous system. A simple nerve-cell network suffices to direct each protuberance's small movements, and the sum of those small coordinated movements suffices to propel the urchin along at a reasonable pace. In 500 million years, through several worldwide extinction events that snuffed out the dinosaurs, the trilobites, and even many of the urchin's fellow echinoderms, the sea urchin itself hasn't changed much at all. It doesn't need to, evidently. We set the flower urchin on our kayak deck for a while, and listened to the rasp of stiltlike spines against hull as the urchin made its slow but determined escape.

At Puerto Escondido, Steinbeck and Ricketts found "six to eight" species of cucumbers and eleven of sea stars—a number that impressed them. We didn't find nearly as many species. But we did spot, in a short time, less-common representatives from each category. Even near a muddy little panga-landing beach, just next to the harbor's fenced-in garbage cans, pretty tropical fish darted between algae-covered rocks.

Harbor life had left its mark upon the shore, in the form of stray bits of refuse and the limp-necked carcass of one grebe—cause of mortality, unknown—floating in a mat of seaweed. But it was the life here, not the death or decay, that surprised us. Paddling at sunset, we were surprised by slapping sounds on the water behind us. These were loud, awkward spanks, without a hint of piscine grace. We managed to look over our shoulders at the right moment in time to see a small, diamond-shaped UFO levitating two feet above the water. It flashed its pearly white underside at us and wiggled its outstretched fins in a frantic birdlike motion. Then gravity had a talk with the ray, and it belly-flopped and sank.

Turning the kayak around, we watched many more rays repeat the motion. These were not the giant mantas we'd seen gliding past the sailboat a few nights earlier, but smaller cousins, probably mobulas. No one knows why they leap, but their presence here at dusk hinted at a fair source of food—small fishes or crustaceans—even amidst the dozens of fluttering sails and diesel-billowing motor yachts. Later that night, Brian lowered a waterproof flashlight over the rail of the anchored *Zuiva* and saw clouds of plankton filling the water with a milky glow. Whales and whale sharks have been reported even at Puerto Escondido's busy, tide-churned entrance, possibly drawn by this abundance of microscopic life.

One's expectations for a harbor are rooted in one's own experience. Brian and I both grew up on Lake Michigan, near one of the country's worst-polluted harbors. Waukegan, Illinois, claimed to be the "coho capital," but you were foolish to eat any coho you caught there—it was laced with PCBs and other toxins. One of Waukegan's worst industrial polluters was the very same outboard-engine company whose nifty little eight-horsepower model we had purchased in Mulegé and used, quite happily, to motor into Puerto Escondido.

Having grown up along a poison-soaked shore, I considered it remarkable that so many fish, rays, sea stars, cucumbers, and anemones still existed within a well-used, nearly enclosed harbor. But give it time: the condos, once completed, may release their sewage directly into the harbor, and other nautical visitors (people just like us, plus a tax-bracket or two) will leave their mark upon the water and the shore. It takes sophisticated coordination to build a place, something Escondido's investors have managed to do only in fits and starts. But it does not take much coordination to ruin it. The ruining can take place in seemingly random, spontaneous acts—dumped waste here, seeping fuel there, the removal of mangroves to make way for more docks. Like the urchin's reflex-driven locomotion, it does not have to be centrally planned. Little movements suffice to propel change.

Near the end of their collecting time at Puerto Escondido, Steinbeck and Ricketts saw two collie-shaped animals appear at the water's edge— civet cats, they guessed. But the light was dim, and the animals slinked away, blending into the shoreline vegetation.

Paddling back to the *Zuiva,* we too saw a quiet hunter hiding among the mangroves. He was a dark-skinned man dressed in rags, camped out next to a tattered tarp, on the wilder side of the harbor's entrance. He saw us paddling toward him and hunched a little closer to his smoky campfire. Even from a distance, his high cheekbones—Indian cheek-bones—shone a brilliant copper.

The man seemed like an apparition, like the mobulas and the quick-vanishing civet-cats: a hint of wildness in a hidden port that seemed des-tined to become less wild. If this man was a relic, then there was one less reason to be optimistic about the Sea of Cortez's future. If he was an emblem of resilience, then there was cause for hope.

Next to him was heaped a great mound of bivalve shells. But he did not want us to know about his catch.

We wanted to gaze into his lined face and see the future; he wanted to be left alone with his dinner. Between us, the incoming tide pumped—a pulse of cleansing current flowing into the harbor's mouth.

"What do you have there?" I called to him as we passed, paddling hard. "Scallops? Oysters?"

"Nothing," he lied. "I don't have anything."

LIFEBOAT

That night we returned late from our tidepooling. The moon had lit our way home. It was far past dinnertime. We hauled ourselves aboard—wet, cold, and tired from paddling—with a glimmer of hope in our hearts that dinner might be waiting. But Doug hadn't prepared anything, of course. "How's that chicken cacciatore coming?" we might have asked in Carol's honor, if Doug had any sense of humor. Or at least, thinking of Tex: "Ever thinking about doing some of those dishes?" But Doug's knitted eyebrow cautioned against any joshing. We tiptoed around him, washing two-day-crusty bowls and firing up the stove to boil noodles.

Tziporah was too hungry to wait. She fussed and arched her back and finally broke into tears. That was normal enough—a late night, a late dinner, a fussy kid who would quiet down as soon as she had a bowl in her hands. But Doug didn't see it that way. He sat in the cockpit outside the cabin, his back to us, spine ramrod straight. When I stepped through the open doorway to offer him food, I saw that he had his hands clapped hard over his ears, like the hear-no-evil monkey. His eyes were big and round; his jaws were clenched. Even after Tziporah's crying faded, he looked panic-stricken.

Prior to this night, Brian, the kids, and I spent two layover days camped at the nearby trailer park while Doug slept aboard the boat. We had expected this time apart to reenergize him. But the opposite seemed to be true. Solitude seemed to have tipped Doug even farther over the edge—a hint that this was no simple crankiness, but something more organic, fundamental, and cumulative.

"Think he'll still be here in the morning?" Brian whispered.

The next day Doug was still with us, in body if not in spirit. Gray clouds clotted the sky. It was the first overcast morning we'd seen in nineteen days. There was little wind and the waves were not high, but they were choppy. It was a Cortez pattern we were beginning to know all too well: not thrilling, not frightening, just purgatorial. *Zuiva* bobbed and rolled. Aryeh vomited. Tziporah moaned.

"This is how it used to be for the explorers," I said to Aryeh, who was harnessed and shackled into a secure position in a corner of the cockpit. Despite the fresh air, he still looked green around the gills. "Endless days like this. Years like this."

I began to tell him about Columbus and Baranov and Captain Cook and scurvy. As long as he was going to be miserable, I thought, at least he should be getting an education.

"Worms in their biscuits? Is that true?" he asked.

"It's true," came Brian's response from the cabin.

I steered the tiller. Behind me, Doug managed the sails. Aryeh slumped in his cockpit corner, listening with heavy lids as I told him about Georg Steller, the German naturalist who sailed with Russia's Vitus Bering east from the Kamchatka Peninsula, in 1741. They made landfall at Kayak Island for ten hours, the first Europeans to go ashore in Bolshaya Zemlya, the Great Land, what we now call Alaska.

Ten hours. That is the important part of the story, the heartbreaking part. Because Steller, a talented botanist and physician, had waited, traveled, suffered, and sacrificed for ten years, to see his efforts rewarded with a single day ashore. That's all the time he got to explore the new land they had set out to discover, and even that amount of time was awarded him only grudgingly. He used the time well. In about the same time Steinbeck and Ricketts would have spent tidepooling in a single location and pickling their catch, Steller gathered plant samples, drew conclusions about the island's mammal population, identified a new bird as a West Coast jay (now the Steller's jay), and raided an empty Native home for samples of fish, arrows, and other implements. Then he sat on the beach and wrote up his report, completing before day's end the first scientific paper ever written on Alaska natural history. When the water-gathering crew came in a yawl to pick him up, they threatened to leave him if he didn't climb in at once.

"Why didn't the crew like him?" Aryeh asked.

"They thought he was snooty. They didn't care about his studies of the plants and animals. He was a naturalist; they were sailors," I said. And then, noticing that Doug was listening, too: "Just different people, I suppose."

"But the important thing," I continued, "is that Steller had to sail for so long just to get ashore for a little while. That's the way it was. Of course, they should have listened to him. He was right about a lot of things—the plants, where to find freshwater and how to avoid scurvy. A lot of the sailors who didn't like him ended up dying."

Aryeh nodded solemnly at this.

"As for Captain Bering," I added, "he stayed in his cabin most of the time, depressed. I think a lot of the famous explorers were depressed."

For the first time, Doug spoke up. "I can relate to that," he said.

It may have seemed strange to be discussing Russians and their subarctic miseries that took place so far from the czar's realm, but that realm extended into the very waters we were sailing. The Russians had their own Ricketts. I. G. Voznesenskii came to Isla Carmen, the island off Loreto that we were now passing, in 1841. The Russians depended on salt mined at Isla Carmen for the preservation of furs and sent a ship into the gulf once every three years. Voznesenskii's 1841–42 trip was one of these tours of duty. On behalf of the Zoological Museum of the Imperial Academy of Sciences, Saint Petersburg, he managed to collect plant specimens representing 113 species.

A century earlier, the Baja Peninsula was crawling with missionaries who made their own collections and natural history reports. One of the most famous was Miguel del Barco, a Jesuit who served for thirty years as a California missionary. His *Historia Natural y Crónica de la Antigua California* is a gem, full of keen observations as well as whopper mistakes. Barco warned his countrymen about manta rays that smothered pearl divers in their blanketlike wings (a fanciful extension of the ray's name— *manta* means "blanket" in Spanish). Based on the eyewitness report of another missionary, he also reported with painful sincerity the existence of a type of mermaid, or *pez mulier.* "Because we found it dry and flattened like a cod, we could not analyze its anatomy very well. Nonetheless, the face, neck, shoulders, and white breasts looked as if it had worn a corset and had its breasts exposed, although I do not recall if one could distinguish the nipples."

The emphasis on white breasts says it all: the missionaries' fantasies and fears deeply affected what they saw. And what they drew: There are no sketches in all of Barco's report except for one of the fish that didn't exist—the pez mulier.

Knowledge has always been a slippery, subjective thing, whether stalked by men of God, science, or literature. If history proves anything, it is that we're more often wrong than right. Sometimes our blunders reveal us more than our successes.

Near the end of the sailing day, the air continued to be strangely cool, with menacing clouds. I stayed at the tiller through the afternoon as the waves grew taller with each passing hour.

"Pick a point and steer to it," Doug barked behind me as we angled closer toward land. I followed his command, but he continued to shake his head, agitated. "Make up your mind. Where are you aiming? Dark hump or dip?"

It wasn't that easy, of course. The coast ahead was a distant wall of chocolate-covered bluffs. There were dozens of humps and dozens of dips, and all of them looked different according to the perspective of the viewer.

Tiller duty gave me plenty of time—too much time—to muse unhappily. My thought mirrored the darkening clouds and I began to imagine deceitful scenarios, my children endangered by this moody captain who always put himself first.

While I stewed, Doug was busy at the stern, half-turned away from me. *What was he doing back there?* Each time I glanced over my shoulder I could see his hands moving steadily, working at something near the engine, tying and retying, fussing with our kayak towline. *The kayak towline?*

But no, I was being ridiculous. Even if he'd wanted to make us angry or seek revenge for some slight, he wouldn't untie the kayak. It was our dinghy, the only reliable way ashore if something happened to the *Zuiva*. The cheap inflatable rowboat we'd brought was a joke—we hadn't used it since Ecomundo. It lay in a crumpled heap below one bunk. The kayak was our true lifeboat.

I'd already started mumbling to myself. Now this word—"lifeboat"— made me chuckle nervously, remembering the classic survival film of the same name, directed by Alfred Hitchcock. The World War II–era movie was all about cramped spaces and unstable personalities; in a nutshell, everything we had experienced in our days aboard the *Zuiva*.

John Steinbeck wrote the story. He lobbied with partial success to remove his name from the credits after disagreements about the screenplay's editing. I'd watched the movie several times without realizing the Steinbeck connection, but once the connection was made, it was hard not to see this sober tale as a shadow of the *Log*. Castaways of different classes and genders, squeezed together onto one boat, under a blistering sun—it sounded familiar.

Biographers suggest that Steinbeck developed the idea from war events, including U-boat sinkings and the real-life ordeals of survivors rescued from the Pacific in 1942. But who needs that kind of inspiration when you've spent your own time at sea, sharing a seventy-six-foot seiner with five irritable crewmen and an alienated wife? At least it beat sharing a twenty-four-foot sailboat with a testy brother-in-law.

I tried one last time to see what Doug was doing at the stern. Then I laughed: Who was being aberrant now? Who was being paranoid? Not Doug, but me. Me! I concentrated on the horizon again. *Too long aboard this damn boat. I hate sailing.*

Time passed. Twenty minutes? Thirty?

Brian poked his head into the cockpit. He looked at me, smiling, and then looked past me. His face fell. "Where's the kayak?" he shouted.

Doug and I both turned around. We saw the towline dragging in the water, and no sign of the kayak anywhere.

"The rope must have come untied somehow," Doug said.

"When did it happen?" Brian asked. "How far could it be?"

I squinted out to sea. Nothing but gray choppy waves. "I don't know!"

There was no time to tell Brian of my suspicions. Doug looked as astonished as Brian. Either Doug was a fine actor, or the kayak really had slipped away on its own.

"I'd been worrying about that happening," Doug said. "I've been trying to find a way to tie it better. Damn it!"

Was he telling the truth? Is that exactly what he had been doing back there? Was this just bad luck?

Doug jumped into action, with more vigor than he'd displayed in days. "Get your binoculars," he instructed Brian, while he started the motor and swung the sailboat back in the direction we'd come. "Once you spot it, never take your eyes off it."

Meanwhile, Aryeh started calling for me, panic in his voice. I lumbered belowdecks to find him in the forward berth, vomiting.

"Aw crap," I grunted. "Perfect timing. That's okay, honey. Everything's going to be okay."

I grabbed a T-shirt to swab up the sour mess. "I can't stay with you. We lost the kayak. Just hold tight and watch Tziporah. You'll be fine."

"Mommy!" he wailed as I left him there, ashen-faced.

On deck, Brian and Doug were gliding in tight circles around each other. *Sails down. Find the gaff. Got the binocs? Hold on.* They were cooperating better than they had cooperated all trip. Doug was trying harder than I'd ever seen him try to do anything. I had left the kids alone belowdecks and they were holding themselves together, minus a lunch or two. It had taken a major blunder to bring us together as a team, but now we were reacting swiftly and with competence.

"I see it!" Brian shouted.

"Don't lose it. Just keep pointing," Doug instructed.

When the distant kayak was in a trough, hidden between waves, we could not see it. Nor could we see the kayak when the sailboat pitched and rolled between waves. Only when everything lined up just right, kayak and sailboat cresting, could we spy the distant flash of blue-and-black hull, still upright on the waves. It looked so lonely there.

We battled the waves all the way north until we were near the kayak. Then it swept past us. We circled and tried again, fighting chop wherever we turned. This time Doug draped his body low over the lifelines and managed to snag the kayak. He and Brian whooped and grunted as they struggled to swing the kayak into place behind the stern, securing it once more, even as waves slapped the *Zuiva*'s sides.

"We did it!" I said. "Imagine if that had been a person. We made a rescue!"

"Not bad," Doug said, smiling. "Not bad."

All three of us beamed. No one looked more relieved than Doug. Surely he was innocent.

But I was not: I had thought Doug capable of malice and sabotage.

The rescue itself had been a fine moment, but after the euphoria mellowed, I was left with all the feelings that had been festering before the day's drama. This was no way to live, day in and day out—stressed, bullied, driven to paranoia. The *Zuiva* brought out a little of the best in us and a whole lot of the worst.

AGUA VERDE

We anchored off Agua Verde, a fishing and goatherding community, and tidepooled downshore from the village, toward Marcial Reef, along some rocky ledges. (Sulfur sea cucumbers, snails and crustaceans, not much else.) A paunchy Mexican man paced the boulders while we held up unimpressive specimens. We'd never seen a Mexican stroll the beach without a sense of purpose—harvesting something, or selling something. But his hands were empty. At first we thought he was eyeing us suspiciously, which made us tidepool even more slowly and with exaggerated gestures, holding up each creature—*Another snail. Hmmm. Very nice*—to show him we weren't up to any funny business. Only after noting the third wad of brown-stained toilet paper wedged between rocks did we figure out he wasn't watching us, just waiting for us to leave. Leaving the area—a communal outdoor toilet, we realized belatedly—we chose our footsteps far more carefully than we had on the way in.

We walked into Agua Verde, a sand plain between rocky headlands, dotted with wooden shacks and animal corrals assembled from sticks. There were no streets, only dirt ribbons where the valley's scrubby vegetation had been worn away by feet and tires. Pigs and goats rooted under withered shade trees. On the beach, members of a visiting Mexican church group smiled at us from their Easter-week campsite on the beach. A woman gave us directions. A man waved at us from his back porch. Aside from our afternoon visit with the Loreto boys, this was more social interaction than we'd had in weeks.

We were looking for the village's government-subsidized canned-goods store. But we found something better: a baseball game. At a dusty intersection between shacks, four young boys had set up a milk crate and some cracked plastic sandals to mark the bases. Two of the boys were barefoot. The other two—probably from the visiting church group—wore new shoes, stiff white shirts, and name badges.

Brian, Tziporah, Aryeh, and I nodded at the boys, then made ourselves comfortable in a bald patch of ground beneath a palo verde tree. Aryeh squatted on his haunches, face glowing. Just the sight of other boys made him happy.

"Should I ask them?" I said after a while. Aryeh's eyebrows lifted—*I dunno*. But his body told a different story. He hunched forward, like a sprinter at the starting blocks, ready to race into the game if someone only would tell him to go.

"Can he play?" I called out in Spanish.

The boys, all three or four years older than Aryeh, smiled and waved him over. I felt the same gratefulness to them that I'd felt toward Armando, Alberto, and Jesús in Loreto. And I remembered a line from the *Log:* "It would be interesting to see whether a nation governed by the small boys of Mexico would not be a better, happier nation than those ruled by old men. . . ."

Aryeh stood in the catcher's spot, replacing the milk crate. To prove himself, he sprinted after every foul ball until his cheeks were flushed and patchy. At one point, a large woman appeared from the dark shadows of her shack and lambasted the outfielder. The boy dashed off, bare feet raising clouds of dust as he ran, and rounded up some wayward goats. The shepherd had been distracted from his duties by the game. But he was soon back in position, eyes flitting between the batter and his roaming flock.

Finally, we had to go. I called to Aryeh, but he just stared back, eyes round and pleading, jerking his head in the direction of the batter.

"I get it," I said. "Come here and I'll tell you how to say it. But you'll have to ask yourself this time."

Aryeh repeated the phrase to the best of his ability. *"Sí, sí"* the boys responded enthusiastically. One pressed the bat into his hands. Then my son stood at home plate—or rather, home sandal—facing the pitcher. His face was red. His legs trembled.

He missed the first pitch. By a mile. The pitcher, one of the better-dressed, name-tag boys, looked at me. I shrugged. Aryeh missed the second pitch. At home, we'd tossed a ball back and forth but he'd never played a real game of team baseball. The pitcher flashed a nervous grin at Aryeh and then looked at me again, as if some translation would bridge the gap. But no words could help. I smiled. Inside, though, I was squirming. *He'll remember this scene forever,* I pleaded inwardly. *I know it shouldn't matter, but if he could just hit one ball.*

The pitcher tried again, aiming the slowest underhand toss he could manage. Aryeh swung. *Crrr-rack!* The ball flew into the air but Aryeh didn't move. He was in shock. There was a long pause, and then all four boys started laughing and clapping and gesturing wildly toward first base. *"Corre, corre!"* they shouted to Aryeh. And this time, no translation was necessary.

A short walk from the game, still looking for the mini-mart, we came to a one-room, cinder-block church. Little girls in dresses played in front of the building. The outside of the church was painted white, a pure white box with wooden shutters, surrounded by coffee-colored dirt paths. Its doors were open. The inside looked as dark and refreshingly damp as a cave.

I wasn't appropriately attired, but I longed to go inside. It wasn't Jesus or Mary calling me; it was cleanliness and shade. Traveling in temperate places, I'd never understood the allure of missions, but here in the desert, it all made sense. The water of baptism, the dark quiet of morning services, a shining floor swept free of sandy grit: a true refuge. Not from the devil, but from the elements.

One of the girls outside assured me that my clothes were acceptable. After a few minutes in front of the altar, we continued on our way. Leaving the church, we crossed paths with some other Americans, fellow sailboaters, who had also come ashore to visit Agua Verde's grocery store. Clearly this was a popular shore stop; a half-dozen masts were visible out on the bay. The contrast between luxury yachts—all much larger than the *Zuiva*—anchored a stone's throw from one-room shacks and pigpens made me uncomfortable. But it didn't seem to bother the yachties, or the Agua Verde children, who skipped behind us in merry little bands of three and four.

We traded hometowns and destinations with the Americans. They said farewell by stuffing Aryeh's and Tziporah's pockets with suckers, Sweet-tarts, and Smarties. "We always bring candy with us when we anchor here," one of the lady sailors said.

The next small group of children we encountered immediately sized us up. "Candy?" they asked in English. Aryeh peeled one roll of candies from his pocket and began to hand them out. He pried the first pastel-colored Smartie out of the package slowly. Four small dark hands waited under his nose. Then five. Then seven. Aryeh dug in with one fingernail, trying to extract and separate the aspirin-sized candies more quickly. *Where were all these kids coming from?* He emptied one sleeve of cellophane and fished into his pockets for another, while still more children materialized. Preteenagers twice his size showed up, encircling him.

Brian, Tziporah, and I stepped back as the local children stepped forward, forming a gentle but persistent barrier around him. We lost sight of his hands. Then his head. All we could hear was the rustling of wrappers and the persistent request: *Candy? Candy?*

When the crowd finally cleared he was still standing there, looked a little dazed. His pockets were turned inside out. He was brandishing a sucker.

"At least I still have one," he said.

By the time we found the mini-mart and made our way back to the beach, the waves had built into low rollers. The Americans who had stuffed Aryeh's pockets with the candy had come ashore in a motorized dinghy. We watched them wade thigh-deep into the shallows, fighting the pull and crash of the surf, trying to keep their boat facing straight into the waves. A bigger wave rolled in before they could push past the low breakers. It turned their small boat sideways and swamped it.

After lending them a hand bailing and relaunching, we pulled our own kayak to the waterline, ready to jump in, rearrange kids, and paddle hard as soon as a big wave passed. If the surf grew any bigger, we wouldn't be able to paddle back to *Zuiva's* anchorage, and we'd be stuck here in Agua Verde.

Wouldn't be so bad, I thought, remembering the baseball game, the church, the children. But we were already in the kayak, paddling through the curling waves.

THE PEARL

We visited the coastline near Marcial Reef, just around the corner from Agua Verde. After that, we had no more official tidepooling stations to visit until Isla San José, several days south. So though we anchored and beachcombed here and there, our main purpose was simply to make miles. Doug ate most of his meals in the cockpit, his back toward us. Or he stood on one of the cockpit benches with his bowl rested on top of the hatch, so that Brian and I ate our own meals staring, through the cockpit doorway, at the captain's hairy calves.

The farther south we sailed, the more yachts we saw motoring by—three or four a day. They were luxury charter boats, three times as big as the *Zuiva*. Once, we passed a sumptuous yacht within waving distance and I saw women in bikinis lying in deck chairs and men resting their arms on second-story rails, holding beer bottles.

"Do you see that?" I said to Brian. "They're just laying around. Can you imagine? Do you think they have *ice?*"

The sight of this elegant passing boat reminded me of a comment made by Tiny—coincidentally, not far from here—when he saw a sleek, black yacht sail by.

"Nobody but a pansy'd sail on a thing like that," he'd said fiercely, according to the *Log*. And then more gently, "But I've never been sure I ain't queer."

Now that we were getting closer to La Paz, Southern Baja's biggest city, we also saw more fish camps along the shore—little Agua Verdes, with shacks and panga-lined beaches. Here and there, topping spiny tree-less ridgelines, simple crosses overlooked the blue gulf. The crosses seemed an attempt to lay claim to hostile territory, for man and for God. But the crosses looked so small staring down from mountains of red rock—like little cocktail spears. At midday, vultures corkscrewed about them, riding the hot-air thermals. You could see hope in those little black crosses, or you could see desperation.

John Steinbeck had been inspired to write one of his most famous stories, *The Pearl,* after visiting nearby La Paz. He heard the folktale in Baja, briefly summarized it in the *Log,* then spun it into a book-length parable a few years later. The legend of the pearl was just one of many things he took away from the Cortez—one of the stories, settings, and symbols that fed his later work for a decade.

La Paz had changed since Steinbeck's day; now it was a bustling city. But just a few miles away, the past lived on. In the fishing villages north of La Paz, faith still mattered, and young men like Kino, Steinbeck's ill-fated protagonist, still hoped to find treasures in the sea. Not pearls though: After centuries of exploitation, the pearls disappeared quite suddenly just a year or two before the *Western Flyer's* visit, stricken by a mysterious virus or natural blight.

We decided to read *The Pearl* aloud one afternoon as we sailed. The kids listened eagerly. So did Doug. Brian and I had read this story many years before—the story about the great pearl, how it was found and how it was lost, only after it had torn a hole in the lives of a simple Indian family. On first reading, it had seemed overdramatic and outdated. Now, we read it in Baja and it seemed less an overwrought parable than a starkly realistic account.

As always, Steinbeck took great care to describe his natural setting: the Baja he came to know well in 1940. In many ways it was the same Baja we'd been sailing and walking and tidepooling for weeks. "The beach was yellow sand, but at the water's edge a rubble of shell and algae took its place. Fiddler crabs bubbled and sputtered in their holes in the sand." And: "Spotted botete, the poison fish, lay on the bottom in the eel-grass beds, and the bright-colored swimming crabs scampered over them."

Aryeh and Tziporah nodded—*crabs, yes, and botete. Harry Potter,* our other read-aloud, was escapist fantasy. This was life. For young Tziporah especially, whose toddler memories barely held for more than a week or two before blending or fading, the setting seemed like everything she had ever known.

In the story, Kino finds an enormous perfect pearl, "the Pearl of the World." First it attracts friends: the doctor who will treat their ailing son now that the Indian family has credit, and the priest who will finally marry poor Kino to his common-law wife, Juana. But these are only false friends. The pearl arouses envy. It leads to discontent and violence. The town's pearl appraisers, in collusion, refuse to offer Kino a fair price for the treasure. Men arrive in the dark of night to steal it. This gift from the gods, which should have bought Kino happiness and health and leisure, instead robs him of friendship and security. It threatens his family, muting the happy little "Song of the Family" which runs like a current through the story.

"All manner of people grew interested in Kino—people with things to sell and people with favors to ask. . . . The essence of pearl mixed with essence of men and a curious dark residue was precipitated. Every man suddenly became related to Kino's pearl, and Kino's pearl went into the dreams, the speculations, the schemes, the plans, the futures, the wishes, the needs, the lusts, the hungers, of everyone, and only one person stood in the way and that was Kino, so that he became curiously every man's enemy."

Steinbeck romanticized the Indians a little, as he romanticized many things, but at least he did not insult them or despise them, as nearly all other writers of the period did. Steinbeck was the rare Baja gringo who saw the Indians' lives as valuable, who saw their close relationship to the land and the sea as enviable, who did not think they should be "improved" or changed. Steinbeck had learned, in part from Ricketts, that sometimes things and people "just are," and often progress is a sham.

Steinbeck seemed to be saying: *Be careful what you wish for,* and addressing not only Baja natives but himself. "All manner of people grew interested in Kino—people with things to sell and people with favors to ask." Wasn't that like John's own recent experience? And wasn't the best-selling *Grapes of Wrath* a pearl, bringing him wealth and fame, but also notoriety and discontent? Like Kino, he'd felt exposed by this sudden new prosperity. People had begged Steinbeck for money, burned his books, and threatened to kill him. He had been warned, just prior to leaving for Baja, that someone was trying to set him up on rape charges. False friends surrounded him. Some old friends abandoned him. Writerly comrades were the least forgiving—they didn't understand why he should be the one to strike it big, when they had not. They hurried to dump him before he had a chance to dump them.

Steinbeck himself had seen how new wealth and fame could drown out the sweet, simple "Song of Family." Kino had struck Juana when she tried to get rid of the poisonous pearl; John had alienated and cheated on Carol. In Baja, Steinbeck was still mulling over all he had lost and all that he soon would lose, so that when he heard the parable of the pearl it stuck to him like a cactus burr, implanting itself in his imagination.

At the end of Steinbeck's story, Kino reclaims his life by throwing the Pearl of the World back into the ocean. The treasure that was never meant to be sinks under the waves, rejected. Steinbeck tried to do the same thing with his fame. While *Grapes* still dominated the best-seller charts, Steinbeck turned away from fiction and headed south to the Sea of Cortez, to write a very different kind of book.

These parallels fascinated Brian and me. But Aryeh and Tziporah were intrigued by a different aspect of the story—the very beginning. *The Pearl* opens in cinematic style with the "camera" fixed on Kino and his awakening family. As Kino opens his eyes to the dawn light, his eyes become the lens, panning across the simple brush hut to observe his dark-eyed wife, Juana. Kino looks to the hanging box where his baby son, Coyotito, sleeps. The Indian couple proceed silently with their morning routine. The sun warms the brush house, "breaking through its crevices in long streaks." Then one of those streaks falls upon the ropes of Coyotito's hanging basket. A tiny movement there on the ropes draws the attention of Kino and Juana. They freeze.

The scorpion moves down the rope toward the baby box. Under her breath, Juana utters an ancient magic spell and then, just for good measure, a Hail Mary. Kino glides toward the box and reaches for the scorpion. The scorpion, sensing danger, stops, and its tail rises up over its back in little jerks and the curved thorn on the tail's end glistens.

As we read the story aloud in the *Zuiva*'s cabin, Aryeh and Tziporah leaned forward on their bunks, both wanting and not wanting to hear its resolution. "And then what?" Aryeh asked.

"And at that moment," I read quickly, trying to get the worst of it behind us, "the laughing Coyotito shook the rope and the scorpion fell."

The scorpion stung the baby. A collective moan filled the *Zuiva*'s small cabin. A few paragraphs later, the danger was spelled out clearly: "An adult might be very ill from the sting, but a baby could die easily from the poison. First, they knew, would come swelling and fever and tightened throat, and then cramps in the stomach, and then Coyotito might die if enough of the poison had gone in."

I looked up to see Aryeh and Tziporah's expressions. Both of them looked queasy, with parted lips and wrinkled brows. But that was not the end of the story. The baby was treated quickly and did not die—which was lucky for us and our delicate audience. We all could exhale.

Two days south of Agua Verde we followed the fading sunlight into a cove near the village of Nópolo. I stirred a boiling supper while Brian and Doug coordinated a frantic drift around the small bay, swinging the lead line and testing the anchor to see where it would hold. All of us were famished for dinner, eager to eat, but just as eager to get ashore for one glimpse of town before darkness made exploration impossible.

Even before we could finish pulling down sails and lighting the lanterns, two young boys awkwardly poled their way toward us in a flat-bottomed rowboat, using a single oar. They called out joyful greetings as they approached. Aryeh jumped up and down watching them, like a castaway who has sighted rescue. These boys—any boys—were his fellow countrymen, his liberators. We helped Aryeh squeeze into his life jacket and fumbled with the buckles, pinching fingers in our rush. As soon as the rowboat was pulled alongside the *Zuiva* and quick introductions were made, we lowered Aryeh over the rails and into the waiting boat.

"Here," I said to Alfredo and José, as soon as we'd traded rushed introductions. "Take him! Be careful! Go play on the beach! We'll be there soon."

It was amazing, even to us, how much Brian and I had changed. Not only did we permit our children to talk with strangers here in Baja, but we handed them over so that every scarce moment on land, amidst other human beings—especially human beings less than four feet tall—would not be wasted.

When the rest of us walked ashore in Nópolo, we were greeted by several adults and many more children. This village was even smaller than Agua Verde, but more permanent-looking. The houses were built of cinder block, arranged in a few neat lines close to shore, and painted tropical-pastel shades of peach, turquoise, and banana. Dusk obscured the spaces between the houses, but in the fading light, everything looked unusually clean and orderly. The village was only about thirty years old, one of the boys estimated. It had been started by eight families who left the city of La Paz to find a more peaceful place to raise their children, worship God, and fish. They'd ferried all their building supplies by motorized panga, since Nópolo is hemmed in by canyons and no roads lead out in any direction. Now, about seventy villagers lived there.

We were invited into the crowded kitchen of one of the homes, where a family sat around a steel-legged kitchen table, eating a late-night dinner of breakfast cereal. Nearby, a table held canisters of other instant, modern foods—Nestlé coffee, hot chocolate drink mix, more cereal. These were not Indian villagers huddled around a fire patting tortillas. These were modern Mexicans, on the move, looking for peace and prosperity. In Baja, a third of all residents were born elsewhere. Baja Sur was, for Mexicans, a western frontier state—a place, like our California or Alaska, to start fresh.

The family that owned this particular house did not rise from their chairs, but more villagers crowded into the kitchen and stood close to us, introducing themselves and asking us questions. They expressed polite interest in our mention of tidal invertebrates. I explained that we were curious about the health of the Sea of Cortez.

"How is the fishing?" I asked.

"It's good," a woman answered.

"More than before? Less than before?"

"It always goes up and down. More of this, less of that. But it's good."

This was the same answer I'd heard in Agua Verde. Both times, I was surprised, since in my travels among fishing villages in Atlantic Canada and Alaska, I was accustomed to fishermen's grievances—*everything is worse now; it's nothing like it was; when I was boy.* In Baja, too, ten years earlier, I'd heard little from small-scale fishermen but worry and complaint.

I tried not to read too much into people's comments in either case. But I did notice that many pangas were pulled ashore in both villages, and all the motors—sixty-five horsepower and above—looked powerful and shiny and well-cared for. Seeing this, one might have assumed the fisheries were doing very well indeed. But assumptions are a funny thing. Powerful outboards could just as easily suggest that fishermen must motor fast and far to catch fish that once thrived close to shore.

Two young women with short, stylish haircuts introduced themselves as visiting missionaries, on leave from college in La Paz. One of them studied journalism; the other, international law. These women were nothing like Steinbeck's silent, doe-eyed Juana, who superstitiously kept a cloth over her face to prevent breathing the evil night air. But they were like Juana and Kino in their love for this small village and its closely knit community. "It's beautiful here," one of the women said about why the families had chosen this isolated cove to settle. "Much better than La Paz."

Brian had brought more plastic magnifying glasses to give the children, and these were accepted in a flurry of small brown hands. By the time we left the house, it was so dark we barely could see the waterline where we'd left our kayak. Children still swooped and darted all around us like bats, the little magnifying glasses clutched in their fingers. Back on board the *Zuiva*, where we finally ate the cold dinner I'd made under sail, we still could hear the voices of parents sitting on their porches, laughing softly and murmuring. Occasionally a flashlight would click on and we'd see a father swing the beam out toward the beach, to track the motions of playing children.

Brian wrote in his journal, "I was surprised at how strong a feeling came over me—a feeling like I wanted to throw myself into this family. To be one of them—sitting outside, easily chatting in the dark. . . . It is amazing to think that we have yearned and planned and paid for the opportunity to uproot ourselves at great cost, turning ourselves into refugees, so that we may stare hungrily into other people's well-lit homes and listen desperately to their contented conversations."

That night I made loops of duct tape and helped Aryeh decorate the fiberglass ceiling of the forward berth with crayon drawings he and I had made, with nausea-plagued effort, while under sail. Planets and space-ships, mostly. The drawings made the sailboat look more child-friendly. He needed these comforting touches of domesticity; we all did. Why had I taken so long to help my son claim this space?

While Brian and I had strived to become short-order experts on habitat, neither of us seemed to understand the simple concept of home.

EXTINGUISHED

The next day Alberto and José poled themselves from shore and came aboard to see the *Zuiva*. It was a breezeless morning, blazing hot.

"When will the wind come?" Doug asked the boys, using a mixture of English, Spanish, and pantomime.

"Mmm, maybe ten o'clock," one of them answered.

But ten came and went, and the sun only beat down harder on the deck, glinting off the metal hardware and turning every surface and seat cushion into a hot-plate.

I tried to describe a common kind of snail to them, to discover its Spanish name, and they had puzzled over my description and guessed, "Is it a fish?"

"No," I said. "It's in a shell. It's only this big," holding up my fingers a half-inch apart.

"Oh!" one of them piped up. "Is it a *foca?*"

"A seal? No!" I laughed. "It has a shell. It's only this big! It's a kind of *caracol.*"

The boys nodded their heads, still perplexed.

Steinbeck and Ricketts had noticed, too: If something is commonly eaten, everyone knows about it—fishermen, and their children, too. But if something is not harvested regularly, it may blanket the shore but go unnoticed day after day.

Alberto and José helped Doug thread a new rope through some sailing hardware, to replace one that had frayed. This small act of cooperation, despite the language barrier, seemed to cheer Doug. Whether due to Doug's good mood, or the good example shown by the Nópolo boys, Aryeh also presented himself for nautical duty. For the first time all trip, Doug found something helpful for Aryeh to do, rather than banishing him to the cabin.

While Aryeh swabbed the deck with seawater, Brian and I took turns diving off the boat, snorkeling for specimens. The cove was rich and deep, with cold, jade-colored water. Underwater caves and crevices created inviting shadows along the cove's bluffy headlands. So far this trip, we hadn't snorkeled for more than a few minutes anywhere except at Ecomundo and Punta Púlpito. The farther south we sailed, the closer we ventured toward the subtropics, which officially start just south of La Paz. The cove at Nópolo showed us how much we had been missing. King angelfish and parrotfish cruised between underwater boulders. Large, intricate sea fans extended their lacy fingers into the water. Several species of sea urchins and many slender sea stars, with gently dimpled gray- and blue-banded arms, glittered on the sea bottom. We brought the sea stars to the surface, one by one, to show them to Tziporah and Aryeh, then returned them to their homes on the sun-dappled seafloor.

On the cove floor, the water was numbingly cold. On the sun-warmed surface, twenty to thirty feet above, it was still chilly. But between coral-encrusted boulders, there were tendrils of warm current. When I swam into these sudden pockets of heat, it felt like a person's hand was dropping suddenly onto my shoulder or thigh. Then I'd flipper forward, again into the cold mainstream current, and the hand would be gone. Even if I backed around in a circle, I couldn't find the same warm spots again once I'd passed through them. They were like flashes of insight that slipped away as soon as one tried to wrestle them into submission, or like the elusive fragments of fast-fading dreams.

Those warm, invisible pulses startled me. I'd always been a reluctant snorkeler, afraid to be alone in the water. To keep from wheeling around and splashing frantically back to the sailboat, I had to ignore my own jumpiness and the hollow rasping echo of my breath in my ears. When I did manage to stay calm, I was rewarded. Fluorescent-colored fish lured me just a few feet farther, a few feet deeper.

All this was wonderful and invigorating. It made me wonder how Steinbeck and Ricketts had tidepooled every day in knee-high water, for over a month, without mentioning the even more astounding colors and communities in slightly deeper water. A few times in the *Log,* they mentioned a crew member diving, quickly and purposefully, to retrieve something from deeper than a hand could reach—"expecting at any moment to be attacked by one of those monsters we do not believe in." But I had a feeling this was Tiny or Carol (both avid swimmers), not Ricketts or Steinbeck, because there were few details of the subsurface view.

Steinbeck knew how to swim. As for Ricketts, I wasn't sure. I did know that he avoided wetting his hair and expressed far less interest in deep-sea creatures than in littoral ones. It was almost as if they'd made a pact: In Baja, they were searching for answers in the shallow tidepools, in that life-filled margin between habitats. To dwell on richness elsewhere was to miss a point that was both scientific and philosophical: that edges are where the answers lie. Cannery Row itself had been such an edge—a human version of a tidepool, as Steinbeck himself described it—a place where people of different classes and backgrounds and beliefs fetched up against the barrier of the Pacific Ocean and mixed, sometimes with comic results.

There was a less philosophical explanation for Steinbeck's and Ricketts's apathy toward the abyss. Modern diving hadn't been invented yet in 1940. Cousteau's Aqualung, the predecessor to modern scuba, was a World War II innovation. Man had plunged into the depths since ancient times, and in Baja, centuries of native pearlers dove until their ears bled. But modern visitors—tourists, even scientists—rarely followed their example. Simple snorkeling, as sport or hobby, was foiled by a lack of proper equipment.

The lightweight, quick-sealing masks and pliable, mass-produced flippers that we'd bought in a San Diego sporting goods store would have been treasures for the *Western Flyer*'s crew. If it had been written ten years later, the *Log* might have been a substantially different book.

Brian and I took turns snorkeling for several hours, switching every twenty minutes to warm up and visit with the children on the sailboat's white-hot deck. Our wet shoulders flared angry pink from the sun exposure, but the warmth felt good. Everything felt good. Nópolo filled us with the tantalizing sense of secrets-to-be-revealed, either in the water or later, among the friendly houses on shore, and we did not want to leave. But Doug was getting antsy.

"Those kids said the wind was going to pick up, and look at this," he said, gesturing to the flat blue sea east of our anchorage.

All morning, Tziporah had waited patiently while Brian and I snorkeled. Aryeh had scrubbed the deck. Both of them had petitioned frequently to go ashore. Now it was noon and they were hungry as well as bored. I scrounged for a quick lunch and promised to let them play on the beach as soon as we'd all eaten.

A few puffs of wind sketched light spirals on the otherwise glassy cove. Doug perked up and started unwrapping the sails. At the same time, he noticed that I'd opened a jar of salmon to feed the children.

"Don't give them that. They'll just eat it up and it will be gone."

Yes, I wanted to say. *That's how food generally works.*

Instead I said, "We could make some rice to go with it, but that will take a few minutes. And I notice you're getting the boat ready."

"Don't forget," Brian added, "we promised to take the kids ashore. We should let them stretch their legs, at least."

"Are we gonna just sit here when there's wind?" Doug shot back. "I don't want to sit here when there's wind." And then, to Aryeh, in a haughty voice, "And how long do you plan to be on the beach?"

"About a third of an hour," Aryeh answered with as much maturity as he could muster. Never mind that he didn't know how to tell time or what a "third" really represented.

Doug stomped and clomped around, fussing with lines and tossing projectiles—hardware, a spoon, sunglasses—from the cockpit through the cabin door to his bunk.

"I think we should just go," I whispered to Brian.

"But we told the kids," he whispered back. "Aryeh *really* wants to get off the boat."

My whisper became a low growl. "And how happy do you think he's going to be when we have a hell-sail with Doug mad at us again? Let's just get out of here and keep Doug happy."

We broke the news to the children while Doug lifted anchor and started the motor. Aryeh protested. I tried to cajole him. "We're going to an island next—Isla San José. A mysterious island."

"It'll take forever," he moaned. I was having the same thoughts.

"No, no, just a few hours, I'm sure. Then we'll spend lots of time on the beach there."

Aryeh quieted, Tziporah was neither crying nor vomiting, the rice was almost ready, everything seemed as good as it ever was on board the *Zuiva*. Brian offered to lend Doug a hand at the tiller, but the captain declined. "I've got it under control," he said.

He had recently confessed that sailing alone was often easier than sailing with help, and that being an instructor was the aspect of the trip he hated most. Still, Brian sat in the cockpit doorway, half inside the cabin and half out, to demonstrate his willingness to assist at a moment's notice.

"Kill the motor," Doug called a few minutes later from the front deck of the boat, where he was raising the foresail. Brian scurried to the stern, where he stopped the engine and began lifting it out of the water.

Suddenly a gust of wind caught the foresail and the boat swung around. "What the hell are you doing?" Doug howled.

"Pulling up the motor," Brian said.

"You've got to pay attention! Take the tiller! Steer!"

"But you told me the tiller didn't need attending," Brian called back wearily.

"It does when the sails are up."

"Sorry. Beginner's mistake."

This admission was followed by a tirade by the captain. It seemed to go on forever, and for once, I felt some wifely resentment on my husband's behalf as I watched him shrug off the insults.

"Listen Doug," Brian said, "I apologized already. You said you didn't need help at the tiller so I didn't take the tiller."

Doug's rant started up again. Brian hung his head and slumped into the cabin, where I handed him a bowl of rice and salmon. "That's okay," I said quietly. "Just give him some space."

To show the captain there were no hard feelings, I brought him a bowl of lunch and offered to take the tiller myself, but he repeated his desire to be alone. I didn't notice whether he ate the lunch or just shoved it aside. Back in the cabin, Brian and I opened the *Log* to read about our next two tidepooling stations—Amortajada Bay, on Isla San José; and a little offshore islet called Cayo. The *Log*'s authors had called Cayo "black and mysterious." We read Steinbeck's and Ricketts's descriptions aloud, playing up the dreaminess of San José's hot yellow beaches, and the intrigue of Cayo's dark rocks. Aryeh began to sit up straighter, to ask questions, and we could feel him slowly letting go of Nópolo—the friendly boys, the ride in the rowboat, the promised beach afternoon that was cut short.

Steinbeck and Ricketts described seeing iron rings set high in the rocky bluffs on Cayo. Surely they wouldn't be there still. But Aryeh's interest was piqued, and we wanted to urge him toward curiosity and enthusiasm, to forestall any tantrums or whine sessions that might trigger similar tantrums in the captain. It was hard enough keeping a child emotionally stabilized; harder yet balancing a child's moods with those of an unstable adult.

"Maybe the rings are still there. Maybe there's treasure," Aryeh said hopefully.

"Probably not," I said. "But you never know."

By this time, the light breezes that had lured Doug prematurely into the gulf had disappeared. The single gust that had spun the boat around had been like an opera singer testing his voice—a hearty blast, followed by silence. We bobbed in place, a little closer to the bluffy shore than was prudent. The water was oily smooth. The long, low island of San José shimmered in the far distance. It was going to be a scorcher. We should have stayed at Nópolo.

Doug ducked his head into the cabin, saw us eating and smiling and reading the *Log* to Aryeh and Tziporah. On other days, he'd peered in to see me cradling a sick child, wiping vomit from a chin, scrubbing the floor on hands and knees, or scattering papers in a desperate search for some book or chart. That never bothered him, but seeing us all happy and peaceful made him seethe.

"This sucks," he yelled. "I want to go back. I'm sick of being your tour guide while you all sit in there having a party. You do it! I quit!"

Doug disappeared out of view. We heard heavy steps on the foredeck. "Go back?" I whispered to Brian. "Back to Nópolo, back to California— what?"

The captain had abandoned his post before, north of Puerto Escondido, but never so explosively, and never so early in the day or so close to a sheer wall of bluffs. How deep was the water? Were there any offshore boulders to beware? Had Doug been checking the charts over the last few minutes or just stewing?

There was a good reason mutiny was a serious offense in the nautical world, punishable by death. You couldn't just walk off a boat, or throw aside the tiller, or let go of the anchor any old place. You couldn't keep spazzing out at sea, or someday the sea would spaz back and bite you in the butt. That cliff, for instance. We were bobbing, inch by inch, closer to a sheer wall of rock.

"That's it," I barked, and turned to Aryeh. "This is an emergency situation. We're on our own and we need your help. We're all alone. Doug isn't helping us."

Brian tried to mollify me, saying that Doug would snap out of it soon and we still had a chance to make it to Isla San José. But I felt like a mother lion whose cubs had been threatened by a mangy hyena. No more.

"We're taking charge now," I said. "We're going to go slow and we're going to have fun, and everybody is going to help."

Aryeh and Tziporah pulled on their life jackets. For the first time, we harnessed Tziporah in the cockpit, so she could be part of the action without requiring an adult's constant steadying hand. All four of us had never been in the cockpit together, while under sail. For the first time, I looked into the faces of my entire family and saw not a single nausea-creased brow. The fresh air, the sun—this was it! With the captain out of view, we almost could pretend he didn't exist.

Brian and Aryeh tacked slowly away from the bluff—incredibly slowly, since there was no wind. But this was adequately thrilling for Aryeh, who shouted, "I'm doing it! I know how to sail!"

After some time had passed, we heard footsteps and the clank of metal. We squinted toward the pulpit and there was Doug, changing the sail. He hadn't communicated his intentions to us. Brian looked relieved, but I protested. A lighter sail would be trickier to handle, and this wasn't the time for tricky sailing.

"No. He can't do that. If we're the ones sailing, we make the decisions."

"Doug," Brian called out. "If you put up that sail, I'll need your help to sail it."

I turned to Brian. "No, we don't *want* his help. No more back-and-forth. This isn't safe anymore. I don't trust him. We have to make our own decisions and stick to them."

Doug ignored us both and hoisted the drifter. Even that light sail fluttered aimlessly.

Isla San José was still a good day's sail away, but the village of San Evaristo, straight south along the coast, was only two hours by motorsail. Brian wanted to push for the island. But I didn't want to get stuck farther out to sea with a tyrant. I told Brian that we should stay close to shore until we had more gas.

"Put on the motor, Brian."

Brian looked to me, to Doug, to the kids, to the bluffs, to the gas level in our single auxiliary tank. We had just enough to make San Evaristo.

I repeated the command. "We're in charge now. Brian, put on the motor."

There were a few more exchanges over the next two hours, but they were mere epilogues to the day's drama. There were suggestions and threats back and forth—"You really should put the sails up," Doug called out once from his position on the forward deck. And, "it would save *your* gas!" I reassured both Brian and Doug that I would be responsible for finding more gas at San Evaristo, no matter what it took—begging from fishermen, hitchhiking inland, something.

Now, en route to San Evaristo, we motored peacefully. Every droning minute sucked more energy out of Doug. He hated windlessness and he hated motoring; we knew he did. It made us enjoy the comforting thrum of the engine even more.

"Some light had gone out of him," Steinbeck said facetiously about Tex, after the *Western Flyer*'s crew had bullied the engineer into doing the dishes.

Doug's bulb had been dimming all the way since Bahía Concepción—perhaps since Tijuana. But en route to San Evaristo, his flickering enthusiasm was snuffed out for good.

It didn't help that he was stretched out on the foredeck, roasting in the midday sun. It was maybe one hundred degrees up there, even hotter with the glassy green water glinting all around him. The former captain sprawled on the deck in front of the mast, morose and martyred, unshaven, his cheeks patched with sunburn, his dark hair streaming over his bare shoulders.

At some point Doug stopped talking. We would not hear him utter more than a few words over the next six hours, and not a single word during the twenty-four hours following that.

"Some light had gone out of him," Steinbeck wrote.

But my world felt a little brighter.

At San Evaristo, I tried to explain to some Mexican men what had happened. The men were here on Easter vacation with their families, camping on the beach under thatched huts, alongside another half-dozen families.

"We need to buy gasoline," I said. "And our captain is very sick."

I wasn't sure why I was telling them this. Was I looking for sympathy, or simply trying to establish our grave need? The beefiest man said something to his wife, who nodded grimly at me. Then he motioned me to climb into his open-sided Jeep, parked next to their hut. He said he would give me a ride to the outskirts of town, where a local man sold gasoline from barrels behind his house.

Before we pulled away from the beach, two more men jumped into the Jeep's backseat and the story passed from the driver to his comrades: "Her captain—the husband of her sister—he's sick."

It's true enough, I told myself. Maybe Doug wasn't physically ill—aside from dehydration and sunburn. But mental illness seemed like a real possibility.

"Where's his wife?" the Jeep's driver asked. Mexicans rarely failed to assume that every man had a wife, and every woman a husband. To be alone or unmarried was suspect.

"In La Paz," I said.

"Well, that's why he doesn't feel well," the driver said.

The backseat men assented to this with nods and friendly grunts. I liked these men for thinking a wife's absence was enough to cripple a skipper.

"I know," I rambled nervously. "I keep telling him—hurry up, let's get to La Paz and see her, you'll feel better. But he won't move. He feels like he wants to die. But we do not want to die. That's why we need the gasoline."

The Jeep whined and shook and spun its wheels on the steep, sandy road leading away from the beach and into the cactus-covered hills. We veered sharply to avoid wandering goats and cows. When we arrived at the house, a man came out, scratching his belly, and shook hands with the men who had accompanied me. He siphoned gas from a barrel into my five-gallon container, charged me a fair price, and disappeared back into his cool, dark kitchen.

Back in the Jeep, we all veered and vibrated back down the twisting road to the beach, where I loaded the container into my kayak and paddled back to the boat. Easy. The kindness of strangers. As opposed to the fickleness of in-laws.

On board the *Zuiva,* Captain Doug was curled up in the crumpled foresail.

Now, with gas, we had more options. Brian and I could motor-sail onward to La Paz, where Eliza awaited us, passing one of our tidepooling stations, at Isla San José, along the way.

Or we could stay put and someone could go, by land, into La Paz and bring Eliza back to our present anchorage, in San Evaristo, where she might be able to rouse Doug from his vegetative state.

Neither of these choices answered the long-term question: After Eliza came, then what? We'd nearly completed one important leg of our trip, from Mulegé to La Paz. After that we'd planned to take a one-week break from the sailboat anyway, since the southern cape region—including the reef at Cabo Pulmo, where anchoring is prohibited—was best reached by road. But that left four more sailing legs at least: back north from La Paz to Mulegé, even farther north to Bahía de los Angeles, somehow over to the mainland side of the gulf, and back again to Ecomundo, where we'd started. Having Eliza on board might offset Doug's tyrannical influence, but surely, all six of us didn't plan to complete the rest of this circular voyage.

Brian, optimistic to the extreme, hadn't discounted the captain completely, even though Doug was presently motionless, half-wrapped in the sail and half-exposed to the broiling sun. "He's just pouting," Brian said.

"Pouting, are you kidding?" I said. "I think he's flipped his lid. Did you take a look at him?"

"He's curled up in the fetal position."

"The fetal position?" I whispered. "It's a nervous breakdown!"

If the captain refused to sail, and we made him walk the plank, who was mutinying, him or us? Him, we decided. Even if he hadn't physically abandoned the *Zuiva,* he had mentally skipped town long ago. We had learned a lot in the last three weeks—*almost* enough to sail the *Zuiva.* Almost. Especially if we stayed loaded with gas. Brian and I spent part of a day speculating whether we could make Doug leave, while we continued the trip ourselves. The whole time we talked, Doug stayed on the foredeck, silent and out of view.

Meanwhile, the children seemed unaware that anything was more amiss than usual. They reveled in the broad, shallow cove where we'd anchored. The beach formed a gently curving comma, enclosing sparkling blue-green waters. The entire cove bottom was white. Braids of light and shadow reflected off the underwater sand, the way light shimmers at the bottom of a swimming pool. For the first time, Brian and I managed to talk Aryeh and Tziporah into swimming directly from the boat. In their life jackets, they doggy-paddled around the *Zuiva,* alternately clinging to us or daring to tread solo, and occasionally hauling themselves onto the deck of the kayak, which floated alongside the sailboat. When Aryeh or Tziporah spotted a pufferfish swimming by, its spine-covered, balloon-shaped body propelled by small, whirring fins, they shrieked and whooped and kicked into the safety of our arms. This was the part of sailing we loved—the part when we weren't sailing at all. By dusk, the children were happily exhausted.

That night we made spaghetti and ate it on the back deck, under a bright dome of stars. We called out to Doug, offering him some, but he ignored us. We steeled ourselves to enjoy the night despite the fallen captain's creepy, inert presence on the foredeck.

Looking toward shore, we saw lights kindled in the largest hut. A beam of lamplight spilled down the beach, toward the water's edge, like a path inviting us to the hut. Our boat cast its own hazy glow upon the water, and beyond this dull glow our anchor chain reached toward shore, brilliant with green phosphorescence. But the shore beam and the glowing chain did not meet. Then singing voices rose up and floated across the water to us, bridging the darkness.

"Should we go? Wouldn't it be fun?" I asked Brian. But Tziporah had fallen asleep in my arms, and Aryeh's lids were heavy.

Squinting, we could just barely make out the fuzzy silhouettes of people gathering in one of the largest huts, lined up on several parallel benches and facing a cluster of instrumentalists. Despite the distance, the voices and the twang of guitar strings were loud and clear, somehow amplified by the sweeping curve of the bay. The singers—men mostly— delighted the crowd by harmonizing, their braided voices undulating together in melodic coyotelike whines and vocal slides. Sometimes, the audience clapped. Other times, they burst into laughter, and it was clear that these were not simply songs but stories. Most of the lyrics escaped us, but the words "love" and "waiting" were frequently repeated, as well as the word "dawn" wailed forlornly, again and again. *La madrugada:*

when the rooster crows, when lovers part, when the fisherman sets out, hoping. The time of truth. The hour of reckoning.

"I want to fall asleep to the music," Aryeh murmured, and he did just that—nodding off in the cockpit, his head on my lap, while I stroked his hair.

As we listened to the music, Brian and I quietly talked, as we had all day in bits and pieces, about what we should do next. No, we didn't feel comfortable sailing the boat alone. Yes, we wanted to continue traveling in the footsteps of Steinbeck and Ricketts. On the one hand, traveling by any means other than the *Zuiva* felt like failure, since this is how we had envisioned the trip from the beginning. On the other hand, Steinbeck and Ricketts were themselves pragmatists. They'd abandoned their own plans to travel the Cortez coast by truck once they realized a boat would be easier.

Our own boating experience had been such a boondoggle that any other means—car, thumb, kayak, or all three—seemed preferable to the *Zuiva*. I thought I knew what Ricketts would have counseled: adaptation. The world has no patience, he would have told us, for the animal that will not adapt. And then he would have recited one of his favorite Zen maxims: "When you are caught by the tide, don't fight it, drift with it and see where it takes you."

Brian and I let these thoughts settle, amidst a dozen other justifications, into the benthic murk of our minds. And meanwhile, we kept listening to the soothing night music: *la madrugada, la madrugada*—dawn, when all accounts shall be settled.

We leaned toward the music, toward the beam of light that almost but didn't quite make it to our anchorage, and we wished we were on shore, instead of aboard a gringo boat. It was okay, I thought, if the sailing part of our trip ended here. And maybe it was more than okay. It was a relief. A blessing. We had felt something missing all trip, and perhaps it was caused by this distance from shore, by the fact we had traveled thousands of miles from our home to Baja only to find ourselves, every day and every night, a few thousand feet farther away from the tidepools and the villages and the towns than we would have liked. How nice it would be to travel by land.

When we fell asleep, the water was lapping gently against the hull. But a few hours later a fierce wind kicked up and spun the boat around and around in circles, like a weathervane. The wind wailed and bayed all night, rising and falling. The shifting wind direction seemed like a parody of our indecision, and the boat's dance around the compass points echoed the tug-of-war that had existed these last few weeks between Doug, and Brian and me. All night I worried that we were dragging anchor, and it seemed that Doug was having the same worries, because I heard him thumping around the boat's outer deck every few hours, an inconsolable phantom rattling chains.

By morning we were still anchored securely. And a bigger surprise: Doug had returned to his bunk inside the cabin. The spell had broken. His monastic immersion in the foresail's folds was over.

By afternoon we had persuaded him to start talking again. He was surly, but surprisingly honest. "I guess I just don't get along with other people," he said. "That's one of the things I wanted to learn to do on this trip, but I guess I failed."

He seemed too depressed to stay on the *Zuiva,* and too depressed to face the daunting prospect of heading inland and hitchhiking all the way to La Paz. I tried to remind him how nice it would be to see my sister—his wife—and how nice it would be to sit at a restaurant and sleep in a motel bed. But he just shrugged. "I don't care about that."

Go, we told him. *Go to La Paz. You need to get away for a few days anyway. Get Eliza and come back. This boat's not going anywhere. We're not going anywhere.*

Brian paddled Doug ashore and left him there, clutching a lightly packed overnight bag and sighing. From the *Zuiva* we watched him hike slowly up a dusty desert hill, toward the outskirts of San Evaristo.

CAYO'S RIDDLE

The next day, we were just completing an afternoon paddle and snorkel around the bay. We had gathered a few scallops for dinner, and Brian was preparing to drag a fishing line behind us to supplement the meal. Suddenly I felt the need to be back at the *Zuiva*.

"You don't think your sister is waiting for us, do you?" Brian asked.

It didn't make any sense, since we'd told Doug to take his time in La Paz. But we paddled faster, around a rocky point, and there on the San Evaristo beach stood Eliza, pale and Rubenesquely lovely, in her black bathing suit. When she spotted the kayak, she jumped up and down—that's when we knew it really was her—and instead of waiting for us to paddle the final quarter-mile to shore she dropped her bag, jumped in the water, and started swimming.

After a few minutes we pulled up alongside her and she grabbed onto the side of the kayak, panting and grinning. Even while treading water, she chatted at a ferocious pace—about how she'd rented an expensive car to drive here as soon as she met Doug, and how perilous the road had been from La Paz, and how it was just crazy the stories she'd heard from Doug about our trip and all its tensions. Compared to Doug's silence, her garrulousness came as a pleasant shock. Since their marriage a year earlier, he hadn't managed to squelch her verbose, sunny demeanor. Maybe, I hoped, that was their secret: She was the yin to his yang.

"Let's get to the *Zuiva*," I said. "We'll talk more there." And we reunited a second time at the boat's stern.

As soon as Brian had collected her baggage from the beach (and Doug, too, waiting quietly), Eliza plunked down on Doug's bunk. She was still wet from the swim, and still smiling, her eyes scrunched up into happy moon-slits, and her glossy black hair streaming over her round shoulders. Sometimes people ask if she's part Mexican, or American Indian, or Asian—she's none of these, though she can fit in just about anywhere.

Eliza began spilling out the contents of one of her bags. First, a camera she'd bought for me, to replace the one that had broken early in the trip. Then, snack foods and other surprises. "Be careful there," I started to say. "Doug doesn't like . . . the sheets are getting messed up . . . here, let's put the food away . . ." Until I finally stopped, realizing she didn't care at all.

Out of her bag came fine cheeses and crackers, tins of smoked eel, and crinkly black sheets of nori, the dried seaweed that surrounds sushi rolls. She handed the nori to Aryeh and Tziporah—a strange gift for children, I thought. But they ate it like candy, with such eagerness that I wondered if it contained some vitamin they'd been lacking. They giggled and clapped, enamored of this magic Auntie who extracted exotic gifts from dark folds.

Unlike Doug, who had kept count of his cracker boxes, Eliza was not a saver. She opened practically everything at once. And then she looked around at our things to see what else invited immediate consumption. She spotted the bottle of Kahlúa we'd been keeping in a cupboard since Loreto.

"We don't have milk or anything to go with it," I apologized. But she shrugged, upended the bottle, and drank it straight.

"Oh," I said. "Good idea. Why didn't we think of that?" And Brian and I drank some. She'd only been on board the *Zuiva* for ten minutes, and we were feeling better already.

Eliza understood the nature of our trip and had read the *Log,* something Doug had never done. "You can still make it to La Paz for Easter," she said, remembering that Steinbeck and Ricketts had spent the holiday there. We were just miles away from finally making our trips link up, just a few driving hours from becoming chronologically in sync. Maybe we could find a mass to attend, as the *Western Flyer*'s crew had. "The rental car is on the beach. It's a bad road, but you can make it."

As the sun set, we briefly considered packing quickly and racing ashore. But it was hard to turn away from my sister's beaming face. Also, we still had the scallops and hachas that we'd gathered earlier in the day—a perfect meal to share, with more Kahlúa straight from the bottle to wash it down. We had a choice to make: hurry to catch up with Steinbeck and Ricketts, or sit back and enjoy our own place and moment in time. So, we decided: forget Easter.

Later, we would realize that we hadn't really missed anything. The holiday of Easter already had shaped our impressions of this shore, from Loreto to San Evaristo: the friendly campers on the shore of Agua Verde, the festive atmosphere at Nópolo and San Evaristo, the vacationing men who had helped me find gas, the evening singers with their soulful songs about *la madrugada*. Even Doug's luck with hitchhiking so quickly and effortlessly into La Paz could be attributed to Easter: The driver who picked him up was feeling especially charitable.

With Eliza around, Doug acted like a chastened and repentant son. She massaged his shoulders, or simply laid one small, strong hand against his arm, and he collapsed into relaxation, his head bowed. His single furry eyebrow no longer contracted into a menacing ridge. We noticed, instead, the boyish face we hadn't seen in weeks: long dark eyelashes and a flashing white smile. That night aboard the *Zuiva,* Eliza cajoled us into talking about all that had happened. This prompted another round of noisy outbursts from Doug, but these were the weary, benign exhalations of a deflating balloon. We listened to him whine and flap and knew, now, that everything would be okay.

The *Zuiva's* long-term future was decided: All six of us would not fit for more than a day or two. So, Eliza and Doug alone would continue sailing south just to La Paz, where they needed to reload the boat with groceries and supplies. We'd meet them in La Paz and share a week of overland travel. Then Brian, the kids, and I would continue our circular route overland, while Eliza and Doug sailed the boat back to its home anchorage in Bahía Concepción. I felt a little nervous leaving the boat's return trip in Doug's hands. Brian and I were willing to hire someone to skipper the boat back rather than risk Doug's wrath or mental instability. But Doug assured me: Sailing alone with Eliza was not the same. It was something they wanted to do. We all breathed a sigh of relief.

With those details settled, we decided to risk one more day on the boat together—all of us—so that Eliza and I could share at least one day at sea. From San Evaristo, we could see Isla San José, a seventeen-mile-long spine of crumpled rock just across the narrow Canal de San José, which we'd missed visiting because of Doug's final outburst. Two of our official tidepooling stations were there. The next day at dawn—*la madrugada,* mirror-calm—we revved up and motored across the channel.

"Should I put up the sails?" Doug asked meekly.

"No," Eliza answered, smiling but firm. "We said we would motor. Remember?"

And that was that.

En route to the desert island, we read aloud from the *Log* again, recalling for Eliza all the mysterious details of the island and its little islet, Cayo. She listened with raised eyebrows and round eyes, grinning at the mention of chains and black rocks. She asked questions. She looked at the map. Unlike Doug ("Look at all that shit . . . oh right, for studying bugs . . ."), Eliza seemed to understand our mission here in Baja. With Eliza present, we felt a renewed sense of hope and purpose.

Brian and I turned to the first sentence of the *Log*'s fourteenth chapter. "The beach was hot and yellow," we intoned with the solemnity of séance participants, trying to rouse the ghosts of Steinbeck and Ricketts. "Hot and yellow," Eliza repeated, nodding respectfully. Aided by this spirit of collective concentration, we could imagine once again Steinbeck's lumbering frame, pant legs rolled to the knee, postholing up a broad and sandy beach.

We motored into the waters of Bahía Amortajada and anchored on the north side of this bay, about a half-mile from Isla San José. The dawn's soft loveliness had burned away, and now the sun blazed so powerfully it hurt our eyes. The distant beach, just a tawny streak at this distance, smoldered in the heat. The green water all around us sparkled with the fierceness of cut glass. We could feel the effects of last night's grievance-airing session; we'd all stayed up too late, our throats were dry and our eyes, bloodshot.

Another sailboat pulled up near us, preparing to anchor, and as they passed, a bikini-clad woman called out, "How's the beach?"

"Hot and yellow," Eliza deadpanned back. Then she and Doug collapsed into siesta mode on the bunks.

Brian, Aryeh, Tziporah, and I lowered our tidepooling gear into the kayak and paddled to the island. It was, as the *Western Flyer*'s crew had recalled, a silent place—"spooky," as Sparky had said in his memoir. We heard no birdsong, not even the gentle *shush* of waves on the beach.

The beach was a series of terraced berms: a steep slope of cobbles, then a few level feet, then another steep slope of rocks, so that climbing inland felt like scaling a small pyramid. Beyond the cobbles were berms of ancient-looking shells, washed up in broad stripes parallel to the water. I squatted down to study some of the shells, and the chipped ones had the heft and gritty texture of pottery fragments. The shells were many times larger than the shells we normally found. Many were larger than my hand, and a few were as long as my forearm. They were thick, and bleached a dusty gray-white, like ancient Roman urns. There was a Pompeiian solemnity to this quiet beach, with its graveyard of heavy, ash-colored shells. We could not sit—not easily, anyway—because the shells were so hot. As we walked, the shells shifted under our feet, filling our ears with a hollow glassy clatter.

Far behind the beach, a thin stripe of green shimmered seductively: the mangroves. Steinbeck and Ricketts had mentioned them. They surround a small, hidden lagoon. We postholed through more hot shells and rocks and gravel—slow going—until the sweet, grassy smell of the mangroves reached us. But the smell was only briefly seductive. Stepping nearer, it enveloped us in an overpoweringly sweet cloud—rich, fetid, a floral stink that hinted at death. Our feet sank into muddy ooze, and burrowing crabs waved their pincers at us before retreating into their burrows. We tried to press farther into the mangroves, to see more of the lagoon beyond, and sharp branches snagged our arms and painted them with a rust-colored sap. By the time we returned to the ocean's edge, we were sunburnt, smelly, and covered with welts.

The white-hot cobble-and-shell beach appeared lifeless, discounting a few buglike isopods and a lonely elbow crab. The tide was up, and the bay's bottom was mostly sand, so there weren't any discrete tidal pools to explore. We gave up on wading and pulled on flippers, hoping for a good swim if nothing else.

Slipping into the green water of Bahía Amortajada, everything changed. Brian and I took turns snorkeling in just a few feet of water, and lifting our stunned faces out of the water to call out breathlessly, *Feather-duster worms!*

There's a miniature seaweed forest out there, too. And some white coral.

Sponges! Triggerfish and rainbow wrasses!

Brian swam even farther out, to a rock reef. In water just deeper than his head, sandy-floored canyons ran between boulders. He flippered between large schools of yellowtail. He came face-to-face with a large green moray eel, its close-set eyes fixed on him like two small chips of glittering obsidian.

If we'd only walked the beach—"hot and yellow"—we never would have known. Above and behind the waterline, Isla San José was a mausoleum; below the waterline, a pulsing, fluorescent-colored discotheque. It reminded me of a famous scene from the *Star Wars* movies, where the hero steps from searing, blowing sand dunes into an interstellar bar, where he is suddenly bombarded with noise and color and strangeness and all those unfamiliar alien faces. Except these aliens were real: anemones and feather-duster worms and other exotics that darted in front of our masks, or slipped lightning-fast back into their shells, tubes, or crevices before we could identify them.

It was the contrast—scorching, seemingly lifeless desert next to cool, frenetic sea—that we loved most about the Sea of Cortez. It startled our senses into high gear. It made us feel small and plain, and also immensely lucky.

There are places in the world where one travels miles, days, deeper and deeper into the heart of some jungle or across a vast arctic plain to find life, color, natural worlds of drama and splendor. Here, hidden universes lay not miles away, but inches away—just a bit farther, just a few inches deeper. In Baja, we felt less like intrepid explorers than like children at a peephole. It was all there and we only had to look.

"Cayo lay about a mile and a half from our anchorage and seemed to blacken the air around it," Steinbeck and Ricketts wrote about the small, strange islet off Isla San José.

We paddled there against a stiff, building wind. The men's intriguing description of iron rings set in the rocks kept us going, even though it was hard kayaking with two children—one asleep, one eager to be ashore—against the afternoon waves.

This was the islet Steinbeck and Ricketts had described as mysterious and "burned," with black rocks and a "sparse, unhappy fauna." When we'd sailed west past the islet, en route to our anchorage in Bahía Amortajada, Cayo had indeed looked dark. But as we paddled toward it now, heading east, it looked surprisingly light-colored. Only the boulders at waterline were dark red. The rest of the islet—boulders just above waterline, sloping steeply to crumbling, flat-topped bluffs—all looked tan or chalky white. We squinted as we paddled into the waves, trying to imagine what trick of sunlight or shadows could account for the difference.

There are no anchorages near Cayo, and no beaches or smooth niches to allow even the smallest boat to land easily. The whole islet is surrounded by large, wave-splashed boulders, some smooth and rounded, and others blocky and fissured, like immense molars. To land, we had to stand up in the kayak (ours was an exceptionally wide and stable model) in knee-deep water. Then we had to jump onto a boulder, hand over kids and nets and water bottles, and tie our bobbing boat's towline around a rock, while the wind whistled around us. After we'd secured the kayak, reflected waves continued to grab it and bang it against the boulders. We knew our stay here, like that of Steinbeck and Ricketts, would be brief.

We boulder-hopped twenty feet inland, crouching here and there to look for invertebrates wedged between the rocks. We saw sea cucumbers and anemones, but they were small, pale specimens—this fact, at least, confirmed the *Western Flyer* crew's observations. The only brightly colored species we saw was the Sally Lightfoot crab, queen of this islet sixty years ago and queen of it still.

The Sally Lightfoot, *Grapsus grapsus,* foiled the *Western Flyer* crew on many occasions. These common crabs have a kiln-fired look, with glaze-bright shells—red and purple and brownish orange—all overlaid with a caramel-colored gloss. They are as big as dinner plates, with thick pincers. The Sally Lightfoots creep over the rocks, tap-tap-tapping with their scythe-shaped legs. Hundreds will gather where the habitat is right. They love caves, sandstone shelves, or any slag of rock surrounded by water.

When watched from afar, each crab seems to mind its own business—skittering forward into a crevice, or backing away from a splashing wave, or baking motionless under the Baja sun. But when a human approaches they all become alert, and move as a herd.

If Sally Lightfoots always dashed away at top speed, they wouldn't be so maddening—as the *Log*'s authors noted before us. Instead, the crabs square off with any pursuer, waving their black-tipped stalk eyes defiantly. If you shadow them slowly, they creep away slowly, giving you false hope in your own cunning. If they sense you're going to speed up—the merest tightening of muscles, the beginning of a crouch—then they, too, speed up. If you corner them near a drop-off, they leap, demonstrating an acrobatic agility that verges on the nightmarish. If you run at them full tilt, Steinbeck and Ricketts warned, "they seem to disappear in little puffs of blue smoke."

The *Western Flyer*'s Tiny slipped and hurt his arm chasing Sally Lightfoots. He never forgave them, and added them to his hit list of marine animals, like the manta ray, that he wished to maim or kill. Steinbeck and Ricketts managed to catch a few, with difficulty. The average human who is intent on catching a Sally Lightfoot, they said, will be forced to "scream curses . . . hurl himself at them, and . . . come up foaming with rage and bruised all over his chest."

At Cayo, we were surprised to watch our five-year-old son catch one Sally Lightfoot after another with no difficulty, using a simple short-handled net. Perhaps the crabs' evasive intelligence is based on a perception of something other than the pursuer's posture or movements. Perhaps the Sally Lightfoots, tap-tap-tapping hauntingly at the rocks, perceive instead the darkness of the pursuer's heart. That might explain why bloodthirsty Tiny chased them to distraction, without success; why Steinbeck and Ricketts (and Brian and I, for that matter) caught some but not many; and why a child could simply bend over and scoop up any crab he liked.

We set the crabs free and stepped cautiously inland. The islet was shaped like an exclamation point. We had landed, conveniently, at a saddle of boulders that nearly cleaved the islet in two—the space between the vertical exclamation dash and its dot. To our left and to our right, bluffs rose to narrow, grassy plateaus. Steinbeck and Ricketts had followed a trail across the left plateau. We felt a responsibility to explore and report in their footsteps, but something stopped us.

We looked around again: white, not dark. Distinctly white. The rocks, described as black in 1940, were stained now with milky splats of guano, as was the flattened grass atop the bluffs. The air smelled like fertilizer. Gobs of oily excrement floated in soupy niches between the wave-battered boulders. Dull-witted, slow-moving flies bobbed and weaved in the gusting wind.

I had brought the *Log* with me and I opened it now, mumbling under my breath, *What bird was it that they saw?* I found the page that described their sighting of a single animal: one black crow (probably a raven, actually), which squawked its disapproval at them. Frankly, it seemed like poetic license—a deathly quiet islet, mysterious chains, and a raven's warning. Crows and ravens weren't even all that common in these parts. Who did Steinbeck think he was kidding?

But just as I read the passage I heard a ratchety caw and looked up, squinting toward the sun, to see a familiar black shape overhead. No birds in sight, and then that well-timed corvoid squawk. It was like some cosmic joke.

The raven sighting didn't explain the acres of bird poop, though. All this modern-day guano suggested a sizable bird population, one that might be disturbed if we ventured farther. Many seabirds will desert their nests when approached by hikers, allowing gulls and ravens to attack the seabirds' eggs or drive away its chicks. Even if I couldn't see the nests, I knew they might be on the islet's far shore, or tucked into the nearby bluffs.

While Brian went back to the waterline, to make sure our kayak was still firmly tethered, I walked ten more feet inland, paused, stepped forward again, paused, and finally turned around emphatically. Every minute ashore here felt like an invasion.

"Come on, we're done," I called to everyone on my way back, including Aryeh, who was stalking crabs again, and Tziporah, who was just warming to the idea of an island hike. "No more crabs. Let's go." The fact that they didn't argue suggested an unspoken agreement about this islet's haunted—or at least odoriferous—qualities.

We quickly settled into the kayak and back-paddled into the waves. Whatever we would see at Cayo, we would see by water, from a respectful distance. Staying just offshore, we headed north to trace the island's perimeter. At the saddle, we'd seen little life, but paddling along the islet's steeper northern reaches, many birds came into view: two species of gulls, then pelicans and cormorants, all balancing on barely exposed boulders in the tidal zone. The cormorants stretched and refolded their wings, air-drying them in the stiff breeze. The pelicans had that grumpy, greasy-feathered look they get when hunkered down too close to splashing waves, their necks drawn back between their ruffled shoulders and their long slim beaks tucked low against their chests.

The brown pelicans we saw had juveniles among them—hefty juveniles, as big as their parents, but with the darker, mottled coloring of youth. We watched for any signs of anxiety, but all the birds stayed perched where they were, hunched into the same wind we were fighting with our paddles.

Above and behind the pelicans, in the dun-colored bluffs, were fuzzy gull chicks, wedged into well-camouflaged holes. Passing a vertical crevice, we spied a dark bird on a hidden nest—possibly a booby, though at this distance we couldn't be sure. A flurry of tiny yellow-orange beaks flashed in the light. Then a wave lifted our kayak and we lost sight of the hungry brood.

The more birds we saw, the farther offshore Brian and I tried to steer the kayak. In this month of April, a nesting time for many birds, we did not want to trespass. At the same time, we were thrilled by this unexpected abundance. Make no mistake, this was not a major nesting area—there were dozens of birds, not the thousands that might be found at major Cortez island rookeries. But the dozens of birds (representing seven species, including the frigates and ravens now circling overhead) were a contrast to the near-lifelessness reported by Steinbeck and Ricketts.

Paddling hard, with heads bent low, we had time to think and to wonder. My mind kept dwelling on preconceptions. With great difficulty, Western society has begun to abandon its faith in the notion of linear progress—the idea that our world will inevitably improve, year after year, thanks to mankind's ceaseless tinkerings. But in that notion's place, I had found myself clinging to an opposite and equally questionable assumption: that everything in the world, from social problems to the environment's health, becomes inevitably worse.

Our doomsday-trained minds had prepared us to see fewer life-forms than the *Western Flyer's* crew had seen, not more. At previous tidepooling stops, we'd explained perceptive differences various ways: the tides were in or out, we were having a good day where Steinbeck and Ricketts had hangovers, our eyes were fresh where theirs were tired, or vice-versa. But here, the evidence was clear. In fact, it was literally black and white. They had seen one crow, and black rocks. We saw dozens of birds, an ecosystem seemingly restored (or newly established), and white rocks. We didn't know what it meant. But this surprise alone made the paddle to Cayo worthwhile.

Then, near the island's northern reaches, we saw the iron rings.

"There!" I shouted to Aryeh, while trying to steady the kayak against reflected waves. "Do you see them? Set into the bluffs. Look higher."

We saw rings of two sizes, about ten feet above sea level, and old frayed ropes trailing down the bluff face. On the rubbly beach below the face was an old length of chain and many large shell middens. Steinbeck and Ricketts had questioned the rings' purpose, assuming that a boat couldn't lie safely against this exposed islet—or at least not for long. Perhaps they were stymied by their own familiarity with larger motorboats and fancy sailboats. Arriving by kayak, we had no trouble imagining a native wooden boat—a *cayuco*—or a modern, indestructible panga tying up to this islet.

If there was something worth gathering from the island, people would find a way to secure any kind of vessel, big or small. Steinbeck and Ricketts had managed to come ashore in their rowboat. And we'd done the same thing, landing at the island's saddle, where we'd tied up to a boulder. The amazing thing was not that people landed here, but that the chains and rings they used to secure their boats had lasted so many years in this corrosive environment.

But *why* tie up here? Steinbeck and Ricketts had seen the rings and chains. Walking on shore, they had also seen clamshells and turtle shells and even a fresh pile of turtle meat next to a recently abandoned firepit. As they noted, "There is no wood whatever on the island with which to build fires; it would have to be brought here. There is no water whatever. And once arrived, there is no anchorage. Why people would bring clams and turtles and wood and water to an islet where there was no protection we do not know. A mile and a half away [on Isla San José] they could have beached easily and have found both wood and water. It is a riddle we cannot answer. . . ."

The answer to their sixty-year-old riddle, we thought, might be related to our own: Why was the island white now, where it had been black? Perhaps, Brian and I thought, people had come here to mine the guano. Perhaps they came to dive for turtles—thus the shells and meat—and, secondarily, scared away many of the birds. Or maybe—and this was our best guess—they came to collect bird eggs.

The author Ray Cannon once wrote a column describing egg harvesting on Isla La Raza, an island in the Midriffs of the Sea of Cortez that is the sole nesting place for white elegant terns. Early Indian harvesters gathered tern eggs selectively, by walking among them and feeling for fresh ones—the recently laid eggs felt slick. But modern commercial harvesters took another approach. They smashed all the tern eggs and waited a day or two for the birds to lay new ones, so they wouldn't have to distinguish between older eggs and new ones. The elegant tern's survival was threatened until 1964, when Isla La Raza was declared a wildfowl sanctuary. The protection of Isla la Raza was an early and bold stab at Baja island conservation, unparalleled until recently.

Perhaps here, too, at Cayo, commercial harvesters had been shortsighted in their harvesting techniques. When Steinbeck and Ricketts arrived in 1940, it is possible they were seeing the islet at its nadir—the scorch marks of harvesters' campfires still fresh, but the birds practically wiped out.

Later, in La Paz and Loreto, we talked with conservation officials, tourism operators, scuba enthusiasts, and a biologist, trying to find someone who could tell us about Cayo's history or bird population. We never found anyone who knew much about this heap of guano-covered rock. Like Steinbeck and Ricketts, we were left with a feeling that this whole area— Isla San José, with its ancient shells and scorched feel, and Cayo, with its iron rings—had a mysterious quality. Our riddle, at least, was a hopeful riddle. Possibly we'd stumbled upon a happy bit of unexpected news: that compared to sixty years earlier, Cayo's bird population had begun to rebound.

As Steinbeck and Ricketts wrote, "There is so much that is strange about this islet that we will set much of it down. It is nearly all questions, but perhaps someone reading this may know the answers and tell us."

Cayo left us feeling curious and purposeful, determined to continue our journey even though our means of travel would change. Back at San Evaristo, we packed all our bags and left the *Zuiva*—left our home of three weeks, with Doug and Eliza waving as we turned inland—and felt no regret. *Sometimes you must leave one shore to find another,* the saying goes. Sometimes you have to leave one shore just to get a good night's sleep. I couldn't wait to be in a Mexican city again—ice and showers and a mattress, all within two hours.

On the beach, where Eliza had parked it, a rental car awaited us.

"The road's really bad. I mean, *really* bad," Eliza reminded me again as I kissed her goodbye, promising to meet her again at the marina in La Paz. "Be careful," she said.

"Bad road," I chuckled to Brian. We wedged our backpacks under the kids' feet. The setting sun painted the desert tangerine. Aryeh and Tziporah, exhausted by our day at San José and Cayo, were crimson-cheeked and slack-jawed, ready to fall asleep as soon as the motor hummed. After the difficulties of sailing, the ease of traveling by car seemed almost wrong—an affront to the gods who had guided us through this trip's challenges so far.

"I've driven all over Baja," I rambled to Brian, feeling giddy. "I've hitchhiked all over Mexico. With her, no less! She thinks I don't know about bad roads?"

We drove south toward La Paz. It was a bad road. Even by Baja standards. It headed briefly inland through flatlands of cactus and brush, then followed the coast, narrow and twisting and steep. The road was blanketed with soccer ball–sized rocks and wounded with tire-grabbing dips. There was no shoulder. Even with four-wheel drive, we barely conquered the twisting climbs. The car would shudder and begin to slip backward, sending out rooster-tail plumes of dust and gravel. To defeat each scarred summit, we had to step on the gas and barrel upward aggressively. On a straightaway, this would be frightening enough. But while speeding forward in a cloud of dust, we also had to steer sharply around hairpin curves. Just beyond the curves lay the gulf, sparkling, several hundred feet below.

"All that sailing and kayaking, and this is how the kids are going to die," I lamented. Aryeh and Tziporah slept peacefully, oblivious to the danger and the waxy, nauseous look on their parents' faces.

"My stomach hurts," Brian said, gripping the wheel.

In place of guardrails, the terrifying curves were marked with little white houses, memorializing the precise spot where some less fortunate traveler had met his or her maker. Inside the white houses, votive candles flickered. This ghostly dance of candlelight, framed by a darkening indigo sky, was a more emphatic warning than any highway "caution" sign.

Our drive could have been worse. We could have had traffic to contend with, always a dread when the road narrows to one lane. Instead we were alone—just us and the cardón cactus, gesturing silently to the fresh night air with thick-ridged arms. Then we realized, three hours into our "two-hour" nighttime drive, that our fuel tank was close to empty. Eliza had spelled out that peril, too—no gas stations, no places to get food or water.

Veering around another drop-off, we could see the gulf's silvered surface far below. From this height, the sea looked so much smoother than any boulder-choked road.

"This is why Steinbeck and Ricketts gave up on traveling by truck," Brian said. "Remember?"

"Yeah."

"And this is how we're going to see the rest of the Cortez?"

"Not all of it," I said. "Kayak, buses, pangas, ferries. I don't know. Let's take it one day at a time."

Soon after our gas needle hit empty, the rural side road from San Evaristo met a paved highway that wove through an industrial area and finally headed into the outskirts of La Paz. We drove another quarter-hour on residue and fumes until the broad boulevards of this coastal city, Baja Sur's capital, surrounded us. We stopped at the first roadside grill: picnic tables and an open-air dining hall next to the road, billows of meat-scented smoke, and a portable TV blaring late-night soap operas. A motherly waitress soothed us with steaming cups of cinnamon- and nut-flavored hot chocolate. Then she surrounded us with platters of grilled steak and warm tortillas and pickled jalapenos. By the final midnight taco, we couldn't remember much of anything—*what road? anemones? John and Ed who?*—and wanted only to slip between the cool sheets of a motel bed.

PART TWO

Fall

from

Grace

LA PAZ

Appetites are cultivated over weeks, but satiated in mere days. The *Western Flyer's* crew spent a long weekend in La Paz attending a Catholic mass (described lovingly in the *Log*) and patronizing prostitutes (almost entirely omitted). Steinbeck and Ricketts made one short, veiled reference to these latter activities. In his own memoir, Sparky Enea was more frank.

"We were never ashamed of what we did in different ports," Sparky wrote many years later. "When Steinbeck would question us we would tell him, 'We are only human and we are doing what we have to do. After all we are single and in the prime of life.' Every time we said it, Steinbeck would roar with laughter."

This confirmed what Steinbeck already believed about his fellow men: that they weren't so different from the tidepool creatures, whose simple but spirited lives revolved around consumption and reproduction. The thought didn't ignite his moral sensibilities. It simply made him laugh. A few years later, when he was stuck in the trenches of European warfare as a correspondent, and was desperate again for that joyful laughter, he would remember back to men like Sparky and Tiny, and reflect on the days spent splashing through tidepools. Those nostalgic memories and oceanic metaphors, intertwined, would inspire his first postwar book, *Cannery Row*.

In La Paz, our appetites were tame compared to Sparky's. We wanted to eat and be clean and promenade every night along the *malecón,* a seawall that attracts families and lovers and tourists and giggling teens, strolling arm in arm. We wanted to feel the *coromuel* breeze, a local wind that stirs most evenings and blows toward land, soothing a hot city.

Brian and I hadn't visited La Paz since before the children were born. I had told Aryeh about the city's sidewalk seafood stands, offering various kinds of marine delicacies, stewed in lime juice and served in big plastic cups. Driving into downtown La Paz our first full day, Aryeh spotted a man working behind a brightly painted stand—an island in the morning stream of sidewalk pedestrians.

"There, there! Clam cocktails!" Aryeh pointed. But looking closer, we saw the man was not selling clams or oysters, but cell phones. Down the road, where bars and taco joints once stood, several cybercafes now advertised their services: Internet access, with cappuccino on the side. All this was new: the communications network, the easy-access espresso, the laconic college students perched on cafe stools, tapping away at computer keyboards.

Near the waterfront, a large video billboard mounted in an exterior wall flashed moving images of "Scubaja" excursions, featuring manta rays and whales and neon-suited scuba divers. Everywhere downtown, dozens of sandwich boards and window displays advertised sea-kayak rentals, guided snorkeling trips, whale-watching excursions. You couldn't walk two blocks without seeing posters of Kool-Aid-colored kayaks and fuzzy photos of whale tails piled up on brochure tables. A decade earlier, the La Paz outdoor scene had been dominated by a few kayak and scuba companies. Now there were more than thirty ecotourist outfitters promising encounters with marine wildlife.

We had arrived during spring break. Well-heeled ladies with Mexico City accents congregated in the fine hotel lobbies, their arms weighed down with chunky golden bangles. A new cruise ship dock, festooned with white Christmas lights, jutted at a right angle from the *malecón*. Young men in jerseys played soccer and volleyball on the fine sand beach in front of the seawall, next to swing sets and sherbet-colored tires, sunk into the sand as playthings. The festive atmosphere seemed more than a tourist construction. The local children, too, seemed well dressed and well fed; as they played along the waterfront, a great many of them dribbled ice cream onto their sharply creased jumpers and Disney-character T-shirts. But away from downtown, away from the ocean's cooling breezes, the city seemed to lose itself, sprawling into endless grids of sun-blasted suburbs: wilting landscape shrubbery and cinder-block houses tattooed with graffiti.

In 1940 the *Log*'s authors had noted the erection of a fancy hotel along the shore and had predicted that with the addition of many more hotels, this "beautiful poor bedraggled old town will bloom with a Floridian ugliness." Steinbeck and Ricketts were right: the modern explosion of pastel-colored high-rises along the *malecón* did bring Florida to mind, and the daily traffic snarls at every intersection made this city of 164,000 feel like a metropolis of one million or more. But La Paz had its own energy—a sophisticated, international energy that seemed both modern and *antigua*, faithful to its centuries-long history as a stopping place for conquerors, traders, and profiteers. Motorboats and sailboats had replaced the native canoes once paddled by the local Nayarit Indians, and the waterfront of simple, iron-shuttered colonial houses had filled in with restaurants and shops and marinas. But the romantic seawall was still there, and a "cloud of delight," in the words of the *Log*, still hung over the city "from the time when it was the great pearl center of the world."

As a city, La Paz was vibrant and cultured. But it was still a city, with a heavily trampled shore. Steinbeck and Ricketts tidepooled in several La Paz area locations. In town, they relied on children (the ubiquitous local boys) to find organisms for them. Brian and I did the same, reclining lazily in the muggy afternoon heat under a palapa—a thatched shade hut—while Aryeh and Tziporah sifted through the apparently sterile urban sand.

"You won't find much," I said, hot and bored, and feeling the first pinched, gassy pains of what would develop, soon, into full-blown intestinal distress. "Too many people here. And the water's turbid."

"Oh yeah, what's this?" Aryeh said, discovering a buglike creature scavenging just above the surf line.

"Good. An isopod." But still, it hardly seemed worth abandoning the palapa's shade. Nearby, several Mexican children chased each other around playground equipment and a baby waddled about, bare-bottomed.

Ignoring the allure of the nearby swing set, Aryeh went to the water's edge again, where the tide had washed a thin collar of algae onto the beach, like a bathtub ring. He returned with damp, salty tendrils—green and brown. We sorted the seaweed fragments, five different kinds, into piles. "You call this no life?" he admonished us.

The next day, when the tide fell even lower, exposing a band of rocks, Brian and I roused ourselves from apathy. In front of a large hotel, where we expected to find little, we chased armies of hermit crabs, scooped up sulfur sea cucumbers, and uncovered writhing masses of stinging polychaete worms. Not bad, we thought, but still colorless compared to what we had seen in less-populated areas. To see more, we'd need to get farther away from the city.

When Eliza and Doug sailed into La Paz, three days after our own arrival, we met them at the harborfront. Over dinner, they sketched a few scenes from their voyage together, omitting much, and filling the restaurant with both laughter and awkward pauses. We heard enough to sense that Eliza's trip with the captain had been as bumpy as our own, which was reassuring and worrisome, in equal measure. In less than a year they would be separated. Like John and Carol's own post-Cortez fracture, there are some travel postscripts best told plainly and briefly, or not at all.

We unhitched the kayak from *Zuiva*'s stern so that we could explore more of the La Paz area shoreline. An hour before dusk, Brian, the children, and I paddled across the La Paz channel, past a hundred masts, to El Mogote, a mostly undeveloped, mangrove-lined peninsula opposite the city, and one of the *Log*'s collecting stations. Elsewhere dusk is a tranquil time, but not in La Paz, the home of *coromuel* winds. As the sun dipped low, the channel grew increasingly choppy. Every paddle stroke lifted blowing spray into our faces, but the muscular paddling felt good after several soft days in town.

El Mogote is surrounded by treacherous shoals that discourage casual visitation. To sail too close without local knowledge of the area is to risk shipwreck, a fact demonstrated to us by the half-sunken ship skeletons we paddled around as we neared the Mogote's sandy shore. In one case, we paddled directly over a wreck, with broken bow on our left and a few feet of stern protruding crookedly, like a snapped femur, on our right. It felt good to be in a small, practically draftless boat that could navigate these obstacles with ease, even with the wind blowing hard. I wondered if this is how the native Indians in their *canoas* must have felt, dodging around the shipwrecks of arrogant conquistadors and missionaries. Often, it is better to be small, and to travel light.

Stepping ashore at El Mogote, wet and chilled by the evening wind, we did not feel predisposed to liking the place. The mangroves enclosing the shore looked dark and sinister, their wet, barnacle-encrusted roots exposed by the falling tide. Those slimy, black roots never fail to arouse my dental anxieties—in the dark, moist gaps I imagine the plant equivalent of gum disease. When the surf bubbles up between the roots, it makes a sound like breathing, and in that same breath a foul smell blooms outward, like a dying gasp.

Steinbeck and Ricketts had bad things to say about the mangroves, too. "We suppose it is the combination of foul odor and the impenetrable quality of the mangrove roots which gives one a feeling of dislike for these saltwater-eating bushes. We sat quietly and watched the moving life in the forests of the roots, and it seemed to us that there was stealthy murder everywhere. On the surf-swept rocks it was a fierce and hungry and joyous killing, committed with energy and ferocity. But here it was like stalking, quiet murder. The roots gave off clicking sounds, and the odor was disgusting. We felt that we were watching something horrible."

Having capitalized playfully on the sinister aspects of a dark and stinky shore, Steinbeck and Ricketts surely knew, as we knew, that mangroves are not really villainous. In fact, the saltwater-tolerant bushes are essential. The mangrove's network of stiltlike, air-breathing roots helps bind the shore, protecting it from erosion. The mangroves provide a habitat for crustaceans, mollusks, echinoderms, and more. The silty, detritus-rich environment around the mangrove roots is a nursery for baby fish and many other marine organisms.

When mangroves are removed, ripples pulse through the food chain. Cut away the mangroves to clear beaches and build tourist resorts, and soon you will not have the delicious shrimp to serve your hotel guests. The shrimp, like the fish, are born and bred in the mangroves. Once the wild shrimp are gone, countries may turn to aquaculture—shrimp farming—which requires even more mangrove removal. These bushes, which once covered three-fourths of the world's tropical/subtropical coast, now fringe less than half. This deforestation tragedy mirrors the destruction of the tropical rain forests. But since mangroves are dark and smelly and a little sinister, the world hardly weeps.

Steinbeck and Ricketts proved the fecundity of these mangrove forests by finding many species here: dentaliums, a mollusk in a long, tooth-shaped shell; sponges and tunicates; heart-urchins, brittlestars, anemones, sea cucumbers, and flatworms of several kinds.

Our tide was not low enough to reveal much foreshore, so we had to dig around the foul mangrove roots to find intertidal creatures. The waves were slapping against the roots and stirring up sediment, so we could not see beneath the water's surface. Brian persevered in the search, grabbing blindly at slimy handfuls—sea cucumbers and anemones. I gave up and walked farther inland, to prowl the dry shore.

In the place of live animals or even shells, I found what looked, from a distance, like ivory knitting needles. Closer, I realized they were the long, thin bones of a dead pelican. And I found garbage. At first I picked up plastic wrapper shreds, shoving them into my pocket for later disposal, until I started noticing the futility of such an effort. There was garbage everywhere on this beach—more than we had ever seen in Baja, which by world standards remains a surprisingly clean place overall.

I made a survey: plastic Pepsi and 7 UP bottles, Modelo beer cans, drinkable-yogurt containers. Soon I had forgotten about marine organisms entirely. Brian was yards down the beach, up to his elbows in mangrove muck, but I was more interested in this beach detritus: emptied pints of motor oil, candy wrappers, one-gallon water jugs, butter tubs. Nearly all of the litter was plastic, resilient to the wearing effects of the sand and the sea.

In the *Western Flyer*'s time, at least some forms of litter weren't so casually discarded. Steinbeck and Ricketts wrote about the La Paz men who, even if a "trifle intoxicated" after socializing with the crew, would not forget to bring home their armloads of empty tomato cans. "They value tin cans very highly."

But now most Bajacalifornios, like their neighbors to the north, are more wasteful. We had only to think about our own garbage aboard the *Zuiva*—all the wrappers and cans and diapers that had filled the boat's cramped cabin, awaiting proper disposal in town. Finally, now, we could dispose of them. But who knows how well La Paz monitors its dump? Some of our litter might someday wash up here, in the mangroves.

The same feeling I'd had while kayaking around shipwrecks en route to El Mogote—*better to be small, and travel light*—I had again. This time traveling light meant something different. It meant: better to use less, to waste less.

Later, I would stumble across *The Octopus's Garden,* a book by Cindy Lee Van Dover, the first woman to pilot the submersible *Alvin,* which has allowed Woods Hole scientists to explore deep-sea hydrothermal vents. To my surprise and dismay, I read Dover's words:

"I would like to write that the floor beneath the open sea is beautifully pristine, a place where one is for once removed from the impact of humanity on nature, a place clean of the litter and debris of modern life. But even in the deep sea we leave our spoor. The worst I have encountered was in a small hollow at just over nineteen hundred meters depth in Guaymas Basin, halfway up the Gulf of California (on the mainland side)—Steinbeck's memorable Sea of Cortez. White plastic bags of trash had settled into the leeside of a stand of slender, branched black coral nippled with minute fleshy polyps. The bags were frayed and their contents spilled onto the mud. I remember feeling shame at the desecration of something so beautiful. I suppose the bags were dropped over the side of some ship passing by."

After surveying the garbage at El Mogote, I returned to the stinky mangroves. They did not seem so foul or murderous now.

All the way to San Evaristo, I had managed to avoid intestinal maladies. But in La Paz, a city of street food and excess, Montezuma's revenge struck hard. The city had caused my distress, and now that I was dependent on fast access to plumbing, I didn't want to leave the city. It was a vicious cycle.

Several times each day, Brian, the kids, and I returned to our fourteen-dollar-a-night family-style hotel room, one of a dozen pale blue rooms bordering a courtyard filled with birdcages and kitchen appliances. We napped or rested or visited the toilet, which was located inside the narrow room's shower stall, within spray range of the shower itself. This architectural arrangement was new to me. Feasibly, one could bathe and eliminate at the same time, and all without missing the day's soap operas, which blared on the central hotel TV, positioned just outside our door.

Our fellow hotel guests were mostly mainland Mexicans, here in Baja for work or a cheap vacation. Often, the man of the family would disappear into the city all day, while the mother and her young children stayed in the courtyard. They cooked their meals on a central stove, hung sink-washed shirts and socks over hotel chairs to dry, and watched the courtyard TV. At afternoon's sultry peak, we watched the soaps alongside our fellow guests. But understanding only bits and pieces, we usually fell asleep—an entire family, sweaty and snoozing, on red Naugahyde love seats. Evening sounds awoke us: the muffled bass of a stereo, blaring from inside one of the rooms, or the sound of a baby wailing, long and loud, for dinner.

On another day, we walked six blocks from our budget digs to one of La Paz's ritziest hotels. Pretending to be guests, we spent an afternoon swimming in a deluxe pool. Again, our fellow guests were Mexicans, though of a different class from those families staying at the fourteen-dollar-a-night *hostería*. Here, there were young men, but no blaring stereos. Here there were babies, but when they cried, the wails were indignant and brief. A warm towel or cold drink was never far away.

Being American allowed us to wander between worlds. The poor families staying in the budget hostería couldn't have crashed the luxury hotel to use the pool; something in the way they dressed, moved, or spoke would have given them away. And the wealthy developer wouldn't have bothered visiting the hostería. No less than the tidepool animals, each social class had its own niche and habitat. But we did not, and this intrigued our fellow guests, who wanted to sort and categorize us every bit as much as we had sorted and categorized every living thing we had seen on our own trip.

Guests from both hotels quizzed us on our backgrounds: Jobs? Family? Where were we from? Why were we here?

The biggest clue by which they judged each other—accent—was missing. Our Spanish was a hodgepodge of all the places we had been, and anyway, it was not our first language. Our otherness disguised us. It allowed us to move from place to place, from zone to zone, in search of a larger picture.

Not all of the sidewalk stands had converted from selling seafood to selling cell phones. Every day we found a new place to sample cocktails made from *pulpo* (octopus), *camarones* (shrimp), and *almejas* (clams). We ate standing, or crammed on a city bench next to lunching white-collar workers. Each cocktail came with tortilla chips and splashes of hot sauce. These street-corner edibles felt like old friends to us, and roaming from stand to stand felt like a kind of urban tidepooling. Instead of lifting rocks, we turned a corner and found some new bivalve or crustacean to sample.

We wanted to taste even more of the critters we'd spent so much time appreciating in the wild. Tiring of Mexican cuisine, but never tiring of seafood, we were thrilled one day to notice a new restaurant sign, "Sushi Express." It took several visits on different days—appetites sharpening all the while—before we found the restaurant open. Inside, the walls were painted persimmon. Halogen lamps cast cones of light on a black-trimmed bar. The air-conditioner hissed reassuringly. Our waiter brought little ceramic bowls, chopsticks, and two kinds of soy sauce. Any skepticism about the authenticity of our imminent dining experience vanished. We all rubbed our hands together, while the waiter stood by our table, glum and distracted, head turned away from us and eyes riveted on the TV blaring over the bar. The bartender and a fastidiously dressed hostess, in suit and heels, were staring at the same program.

"National specialties?" I said, reading from the sushi menu. "We'll have a plate of those."

"No," he said.

"Excuse me?"

"We don't have them."

We smiled, consulted with the children, studied the menu, gave up on finding anything exotic, like sea cucumber or sea urchin, and finally settled on the old raw-fish standby.

"Tuna rolls," I said. "Please."

"No," he said, without offering any suggestions.

"Then what kind of fish do you have?"

"No fish." Finally, he interrupted his TV-focused stare and briefly met my own gaze. "Listen, we don't have anything."

"Nothing?"

"And," he added quickly, "no wasabi either."

"No wasabi? In a Japanese restaurant?" How could you have sushi without this green horseradish?

He fixed me with a testy look.

"What's over there?" I asked the waiter, gesturing to the bar, where a fishy-looking slab sat under glass.

"Crab."

See? I smiled, proud of my own persistence. "Crab! That would be great." And I slapped the menu shut.

So that's what we got. Or almost. It wasn't real crab, the feisty, hard-shelled creatures we'd encountered on every rocky shore from here to Mulegé. Instead it was surimi, the precooked fish flakes made of pollock, a bottom fish harvested thousands of miles north of Baja.

"Why not real crab?" I quizzed our waiter when he brought the bill. "And why don't you have any fish? Are they hard to obtain? The ocean is so close—a few blocks away . . ."

"Listen. I'm from Guadalajara," he said. "I don't know anything about seafood."

"There's a fish market just blocks from here . . ." I started to say again.

"Go there, then," he said, and sashayed away with our credit card.

Following the waiter's advice, we woke early the next morning, ahead of the day's heat, and headed to the market: a city block under one roof, divided into a labyrinth of stalls and corridors. The sights and smells were overwhelming—overripe bananas and papayas, sour meat, buzzing juice blenders, a guitar being tuned, cash registers ringing as people purchased sandals and straw hats and radios and breakfast cereal. We held tightly to Aryeh's hand and lifted Tziporah onto our shoulders, trying not to lose track of them and each other in the crowds.

At the fish stalls, merchants were packing away their crates of seafood. Most of the day's ice had already melted. Flies settled upon the remaining fish, red and yellow panfish with bulbous, unseeing eyes. We recognized some of the common fish names, and learned a few new ones: *cabrilla, chivato,* and *lisa*—some from the Sea of Cortez, and others hauled by road from the Pacific.

I explained to several vendors that we were interested in the health of the Cortez. Three men paused from stacking their crates.

"How are the fish doing?" I asked. "Do you have less of them now? More of them?"

"Oh, less of them," one of the men said.

I perked up and took out my journalist's notebook.

"Less than five years ago? Less than ten years ago?"

The man didn't blink. "Less than before Easter," he said, shaking his head. "Easter comes and everybody buys up all the seafood."

ELEGY FOR A SEA CUCUMBER

In Loreto I had seen a flier, posted near the harbor, cautioning local fishermen against harvesting endangered species. I puzzled through the dense Spanish and Latin text, expecting to see familiar names: vaquita, the rare porpoise; totoaba, the gulf fish; any of the sea turtles. What I read shocked me. The endangered animal—*en peligro*—was *Isostichopus fuscus*. A humble sea cucumber.

It is easy to love some animals passionately—the gray whale, for example. The year leading up to our Baja trip, whale-lovers clamored to protect a Pacific lagoon from development by a jointly owned Mexican-Japanese salt-mining company called Exportada de Sal. Baja's Pacific lagoons are critical habitats, used by the migrating whales for calving their young.

Concerned contributors mailed $5 million to the Natural Resources Defense Council in response to mailings about the threatened lagoon, and three weeks before our trip, Mexican president Ernesto Zedillo canceled the San Ignacio Lagoon salt project. Gray whales—once slaughtered, now slowly recovering—make good mascots, easily embraced and marketed.

Not so the equally imperiled sea cucumber.

A holothurian, as members of this class of animals are called, will not sidle on up for a back-scratching, or look you in the eye. It has no eyes. Basically the cucumber is a faceless rubbery or leathery gut—a mud-eating tube. Some species breathe through their skin; others through their anuses. Eight to thirty tentacles form a ring around the sea cucumber's mouth. These wispy or flattened tentacles—sometimes they look like the leafy end of a celery stalk—collect diatoms and other edible, microscopic particles from the sand, mud, or water. Then they systematically deliver the food into the cucumber's mouth. Whatever is not digested passes through the gut and out the cucumber's rear end.

Cucumbers burrow or wriggle along the ocean floor, moving along on small tube feet that are usually no larger than warts. I say usually, because sea cucumbers come in five hundred flavors. A few have spikes, though most do not. Some of the most common ones are dark and oblong, like the pickle-shaped sulfur cucumbers we saw frequently all over Baja. Others are slimier, thinner-skinned, less robust: think of used condoms left in a muddy ditch. There are medium-sized ones that looked like long-necked beer bottles or overstuffed sausages. The largest ones look like half-deflated footballs.

Isostichopus fuscus—a large, dark-brown cucumber with orange warts, or teats—falls into this last, more elite, category. Its value to the culinary world—yes, sea cucumbers are eaten, thus their imperiled status—is in its texture and heft. With a soft, knobby dermis, *I. fuscus* is a prized food in Asia. The Baja commercial fishery for this exotic export started in 1988. Unregulated and inadequately documented, the fishery peaked in 1991. It dwindled thereafter, probably due to overharvesting. Or at least the Mexican authorities assume so. Lacking reliable catch records or a careful assessment of the cucumber's health, the federal government closed the fishery in 1994—an election year, when more conservation-oriented politicos took the nation's helm. *I. fuscus* was labeled "endangered," pending further studies.

The cucumber plows the ocean floor as it travels and eats, alone or in mysterious herds a thousand-strong. *Isostichopus fuscus* lives in shallow waters, from the tidal zone to two hundred feet deep. But other sea cucumbers are deep-sea dwellers; in fact, the deeper one goes, the more these mud-eaters predominate. Scientists speculate that without these voracious "vacuum cleaners of the sea" (in author Robert Hendrickson's words), the buildup of detritus on the ocean floor might suffocate more-fragile organisms.

That's the sea cucumber's serious side. But it can be playful. The cucumber is not only the seafloor's vacuum, but its whoopie cushion as well. When you lift a cucumber out of a tidepool, it responds to the change in pressure by flattening and drooping. Sometimes it spurts a hearty stream of water from one end, which only strengthens the resemblance between the cucumber and its male-anatomy look-alike (big laughs from tidepoolers who have spent too long in the tropical sun).

Provoking a flaccid sea cucumber into wetting itself isn't animal cruelty. Honest. We know the sea cucumber is not bothered by this, because when the cucumber *is* at all bothered, it does something different. It eviscerates. Some cucumbers rupture their own guts and extrude sticky hollow threads called Cuvierian tubules. In some species, the tubules discharge a short-lived toxin. Other cucumbers go all out and explosively discharge other organs as well. The ability to turn itself practically inside-out—to spew its insides and survive—is the sea cucumber's greatest survival trick. It does this to distract predators, which become entangled in and repelled by the sticky explosion. In one experiment, 96 percent of predators continued to steer clear of a sea cucumber days after it had eviscerated at them. Clearly, even small-brained crabs have a hard time forgetting the traumatic experience of being whipped with sticky intestines.

Sometimes the sea cucumber will eviscerate to seek revenge against a particular parasitic fish that insists on living on the cucumber's anus and nibbling its insides. The sea cucumber regenerates its internal organs in about two weeks. During this time, its digestive life comes to a halt. It feeds sparingly or not at all in a state of quiescence or semihibernation.

"Life has one final end, to be alive; and all the tricks and mechanisms, all the successes and all the failures, are aimed at that end," Steinbeck and Ricketts wrote. The sea cucumber's tricks have sustained it for longer than most species: 470 million years, according to the oldest known sea cucumber fossil.

A target for humor in Steinbeck's time and our own, the cucumber is strange, fascinating, and no doubt ecologically essential. But how many tourists, besides Brian, the kids, and me, would want to pet one?

"I want to see one," said Eliza when we were in La Paz. In a week, she and Doug would be sailing the *Zuiva* back north, to Ecomundo. For now, she had time to help me visit a few more La Paz–area tidepools, following the *Western Flyer*'s wake toward one specific creature's habitat.

West across the peninsula, in Baja's Pacific lagoons, spring whale-watching season was petering out. Here on Baja's Cortez coast, my sister and I booked ourselves on a different kind of commercial tour: a cucumber-watching expedition to nearby Isla Espíritu Santo, in search of endangered *I. fuscus*. Sort of.

To be honest, the trip we signed up for was—officially—a group snorkel-with-the-sea-lions outing. A visit to the sea lions of Los Islotes, protected islets at the north end of Isla Espíritu Santo (about an hour's panga ride from La Paz), is one of that city's most popular day trips. I talked to the tour company beforehand, explaining my personal mission: to look for sea cucumbers and other local invertebrates. Furthermore I explained the framework of our larger, *Log*-inspired trip. Steinbeck and Ricketts had tidepooled at two places on Espíritu Santo: a sandy stretch at the island's south tip, and a coral-head environment at Bahía San Gabriel. If we could talk the tour guides into making a few detours along the way, we could have it all: a chance to look for holothurians, a few more marks for our S&R checklist, and—as long as we'd paid for the encounter—a few minutes of fun with the sea lions, too.

Years earlier, Brian and I had circumnavigated Espíritu Santo's thirty-five-mile coastline by kayak—a dreamy four-day trip marked by shimmering white-sand beaches, deeply indented jade-green coves, and caves with walls that wore a moving armor of scarlet Sally Lightfoot crabs. This time, Brian volunteered to stay at the hotel with Aryeh and Tziporah so that Eliza and I could focus all our energies on the holothurian hunt.

We joined five other tourists in a roomy panga early in the morning, before the sun had gathered its strength, and were shuttled across the four-mile-wide channel that separates La Paz's Playa Tecolote from Isla Espíritu Santo. The night's *coromuel* winds hadn't yet given way to morning calm. It was a good day to be in a panga, instead of a kayak or sailboat. The wind blew hard against us and we slammed over choppy waters, outboard engine roaring and tailbones smarting with every wave.

After nearly a month of independent travel it felt strange to be part of a tour group. On the positive side, it was a relief to leave the navigation to a professional. And not since my childhood has someone packed me potato chips and bologna-and-mustard sandwiches. But as part of a group, I could not pretend that I was exploring unknown places. I was on the tourist trail now, and I would see—as I had rarely seen—what happens when desert islands and commercial tour groups collide.

Seated closest to Eliza and me was a young American woman, with long brown braids and an earnest smile, who was studying Spanish at a language school in La Paz. Eliza and I chatted with her, and with a petite man from northern California who said he was a real estate agent, vacationing in Mexico alone. He wore a banana-colored jogging suit and had a small, lightbulb-shaped head. He talked vaguely but at length, in a high, girlish voice, about faraway places where he'd worked—oil countries, mostly. "CIA," Eliza whispered to me. "I'm sure of it."

A wealthy Mexican family occupied the far side of the panga: quiet father, increasingly seasick mother, and their seven-year-old daughter. The parents were fully dressed in synthetic resort-wear, with no intention to swim, though that was the advertised highlight of this island excursion.

When we arrived at Los Islotes, a cluster of low rocks covered by more than three hundred sea lions, the tour guide stopped the panga just offshore and gave us directions. We were allowed to swim near the sea lions, but not approach, bother, or corner them. We were supposed to maintain a distance of at least twenty feet from the sea lions' rocky haul-outs. And we were supposed to avoid resting our flippers against the coral heads—knobs of coral dotting the reef next to the islet—which made this shallow snorkeling area so vibrant and full of life.

Within fifteen minutes I watched the banana man violate all three rules. He hadn't been able to find a place to change into his swimsuit (the rest of us had worn our suits under our clothes) and so had been forced to swim fully clad in heavy yellow cotton. Then, when he'd tried to swim toward a sea lion (violating rule one), a mischievous young male had turned the tables and aggressively cornered him.

Eliza and I watched as the man came up gasping for air and stood, with flippers firmly planted, on a coral head. This might have been a brief violation of rule three, but he extended his stay above water by sitting back on an exposed boulder (too close to the haul-outs, violating rule two as well) to take a break from swimming.

Meanwhile three other tour boats had approached Los Islotes and discharged their own snorkeling and scuba diving clients. Every boat except ours had anchored closer than twenty feet. Compounding the problem, surely every boat had at least one rule-shirking banana man aboard. Over the course of a year, thousands of boat trips are made to this small colony. Doesn't any of this activity disturb the sea lions, never mind the islet's other sea life—pelicans, coral, fish?

"They're friendly. The sea lions like to play," our tour guide assured me. "It does not bother them."

For the most part, I believed him. Peering underwater with my mask, I watched streamlined sea lions torpedo under and around me, jetting through their own collars of bubbles. The sea lions were surprisingly long

and lean, their necks outstretched and their fins angled back as they exe-
cuted high-speed glides. Often in pairs, the sea lions made bombing runs
past various swimming humans, and seemed especially attracted to the
scuba divers prowling the seafloor forty feet down. The juvenile sea lions
liked to hover above the scuba divers and nose the bubbles rising in silver
chains above the divers' heads. When a sea lion rose through the blue water
and darted close to me, I could see its wet, dog-brown eyes, and the rim of
white around each brown retina. The sea lion looked startled but also curious and puppy-playful. If I'd had a stick in hand, I might have thrown it.

All this was a treat, of course—every bit as fun as petting a whale, and
almost fun enough to make me forget about the lowly sea cucumber
altogether. But part of me suspected I was reveling in something I might
later denounce. I could see how a sea lion's anxious circling might be
misinterpreted as playfulness. And I wondered, more specifically, about
the wisdom of swimming near sea lions during breeding season, a testos-
terone-heightened time when males become more territorial. In La Paz,
I had read one tourism brochure that described the breeding season as
June to September. "It's too hot to go to Los Islotes during the summer
anyway," my tour guide said.

"So you won't take tourists there in the summer?" I asked.

"Well, if they sign up . . ."

Later, I read another tourism brochure that said breeding occurred in
April and May. I had the sneaking suspicion that "breeding season" managed
to move around the calendar, according to the needs of tour operators.

The rules for sea lion–snorkeler interaction seemed equally flexible.
One of the same tour companies that advocated giving sea lions their
space also decorated their full-color brochures with a photograph of a
sea lion nibbling on a snorkeler's camera. Another photo showed a sea
lion sitting fully atop a paddler's kayak, inches away from the grinning
paddler herself. Maybe it was a good thing the sea cucumber was ugly—
at least it was spared all this attention. Not for the first time, I questioned
the "eco" in ecotourism.

Harassing sea lions is forbidden by Mexican law, but tourist dollars
seemed to speak louder than regulations. If Espíritu Santo was a test case
for island tourism, the verdict was mixed: On the one hand, I hadn't
heard anyone say with certainty that tourism had harmed any species on
the island. Furthermore, tourist exuberance might impact the sea lions

less than outright slaughter. In parts of Baja where travelers are few, sea lions are used as shark bait, or shot simply because fishermen view them as competition for fish. On the other hand, with so many scuba divers and snorkelers and kayakers visiting the island, I couldn't imagine Isla Espíritu Santo remaining pristine.

For now, though, there was much to see—not only the frolicking sea lions, but a circus of brightly colored fish and invertebrates in the aquamarine waters surrounding Los Islotes. The young American woman disappeared into the deeps with a scuba partner. Banana man leaned back on his haul-out rock, the seven-year-old girl bobbed around in a life preserver while her parents stayed aboard the panga, and Eliza and I swam as far as we dared away from them all.

This subtropical reef was the most active one I'd seen so far. Schools of gray surgeonfish with lemon-yellow tails cruised beneath us. Bright green parrotfish nibbled the coral. On underwater boulders, we spotted sea stars we hadn't seen before: bright blue and purple, with slim arms. Lacy sea fans protruded, like graceful Spanish mantillas, from submerged rock.

As our Baja trip took us south, the colors grew brighter and the waters warmer. Not quite warm enough, however. Too soon, I was shivering and we were forced to retreat back to the tour boat, to warm up on deck. Our fellow tourists were grateful to see us. We had just started exploring, but they were ready to go, especially the green-gilled Mexican mom, who kept asking when we'd go ashore for a lunch break.

"How was it?" the tour guide asked with evident pride as he stowed our snorkeling equipment and prepared to motor to another location for lunch. "Good?"

"It was beautiful! Great!"

"You found what you're looking for?"

"Some, but not the cucumber. I'm hoping to see it at San Gabriel. We're stopping at that bay, yes?"

The seasick mom overheard our Spanish conversation. "Cucumber? What's this?"

The guide tried to explain, but she only looked blank, until I stepped in: "A marine animal."

"Oh," she said and turned away, disinterested as soon as she realized we weren't discussing lunch.

We ate our sandwiches and chips and drank our American soda on a perfect white-sand beach backed by cactus-studded bluffs. The turquoise shallows were warm and dazzling. This was the kind of Espíritu Santo beach I'd shared with Brian—and Brian alone—seven years earlier. We didn't have any proprietary right to solitude then, and I didn't have any right to solitude now. But still, I felt myself rolling my eyes as more pangas arrived, disgorging their swimsuit-clad day-trippers on the sand. When I dropped a few potato-chip crumbs on the sand, a bold chipmunk darted close and stole the salty bits. At a conservative estimate of twenty per day during all but the hottest months, perhaps six thousand picnickers visit this small beach each year. Lots of crumbs. I tried to shoo the little rodent away, but he was no dummy. He knew we gringos are suckers for cute, dewy-eyed wildlife.

The *ejido* (communal land-holding organization) that owns the island has been itching to develop it, I was told. But for now, the only permanent structures on all of Espíritu Santo were a few old wells and the crumbling foundations of some buildings used during the pearl trade, vestiges of a long-gone era. Considering the proximity of La Paz, Espíritu Santo's present wildness was phenomenal.

Eliza and I were in no rush to leave. But some of our fellow tourists seemed antsy, ready to reboard the boat even before the engine started. There were murmurs about piña coladas and other delights waiting in La Paz. Keeping his promise, however, our tour guide explained that we'd be making one more stop, at Bahía San Gabriel. The Mexican mom sighed deeply; her daughter leaned against her and promptly fell asleep. Several people checked their watches. Banana man, who had been so gregarious en route to Los Islotes, barely looked at Eliza and me now. "Searching for little marine animals," the guide explained brusquely. I sensed I had lost an ally.

We motored to the bay's mouth and stopped in water that was about twenty feet deep. There was some disagreement between the guide and his assistant about where to anchor; I didn't understand their murmuring but I knew I'd better hurry. I pulled on mask and snorkel and plunged overboard. Eliza joined me and we swam a few times under the boat, but we didn't see much life in the first minute or two. None of our fellow day-trippers joined us in the water. They were tired. They were sunburnt. They were hot, but they had satisfied their swimming urges. They had no interest in "little marine animals."

"Good?" the guide asked when I came up for air.

"Not too good," I said, trying to sound more knowledgeable and efficient than I felt. I'd never been pressured to find marine life on demand.

Even I wasn't sure what I was looking for—the endangered *I. fuscus* certainly; that would be a coup. But I also wanted a general, albeit briefly taken, snapshot of the whole bay. Steinbeck and Ricketts had found scads of life here: "literally millions" of *Holothuria lubrica,* the smaller, more common sulfur sea cucumber; as well as squirming knots of brittlestars, three species of urchins, ten kinds of crabs, four of shrimps, various anemones and worms, clams and sponges, snails and bryozoa. Most of those species had been found near rocks, and we were anchored offshore over sand that was dotted with knobs of coral. Clearly, we needed to get closer to the beach—*on* the beach, really. But before that, I wanted to get one more look at these knobs of coral.

"Let me go again," I said, and dove under the boat. The gulf's only true coral reef—an extensive, living system—is at Cabo Pulmo. The coral I found myself studying now were isolated coral heads, about as big around as a bicycle wheel. The coral was greenish brown and stony. Several knobs had light tan patches—areas that looked dead, though I wasn't anywhere close to being sure.

When Eliza swam past I motioned to the seafloor, and also to our sagging anchor chain, which grazed one of the coral patches.

"Good?" the guide asked when I surfaced.

"Coral," I said, panting. "with *manchas*—maybe dead spots."

Up until now, the guide had humored us. Now he shook his head and sputtered. "But you don't know that. You're not an expert. You're not a coral biologist."

If a tan spot did indicate death, it could have been caused by one of many factors, including the fatal bleaching that occurs when sea temperatures warm, killing a symbiotic algae that lives inside the coral.

"You're right. I don't know coral," I said. If I'd had more breath and less diplomacy, I might have added: *But I know not to anchor on coral heads.*

The guide helped Eliza and me aboard, and we motored toward the head of the bay, anchoring this time in water less than ten feet deep. Our last chance. The guide tapped his watch as I pulled on my flippers.

As soon as Eliza and I plunged overboard we began to see invertebrates scattered on the white-sand seafloor: clumps of sedentary snails, a large sea urchin, two species of slim-rayed sea stars, some green fluorescent blobs I couldn't identify. No cucumbers yet, but this looked like the place. A box-shaped pufferfish swam past us, its tiny fins a windup-toy blur. This was a rich bay—a place to savor. I knew it would be even richer on the edge where the sand flats merged with boulder foreshore.

"This is silly," I told Eliza. "We don't have much time. We should really swim to shore. That's where Steinbeck and Ricketts were." But the beach was far away—a shimmering stripe of tan above the turquoise water. We flippered over sand flats for five minutes, and stood up to get our bearings. The water was no deeper than our waists, but still, land looked far away. We put our masked faces down in the water and swam hard again. After a few more minutes, the water was so shallow it was hard to swim at all. With masks down, we were practically scraping our noses on the sand. But we weren't at the rocky zone yet. We tried standing and walking, but wading was no easier than snorkeling. Our flippers made us clumsy and we had to choose every footstep carefully, for fear of stepping on sea urchins or stingrays.

Still, Eliza was game. She looked toward the anchored panga—just a small bobbing dot—and she looked toward the beach. "What now?"

"I don't think we'll get to tidepool on shore. They're not going to wait for us that long. Let's look here."

We snorkeled in place briefly, lifting various specimens out of the water for closer examination and returning them to their proper places on the sand.

"What's this?" said Eliza the next time she raised her head. In her hand—and sagging well beyond it—lay a large, rust-colored blob with orange teats. A deflated football. Not gushy or slimy at all, but pliable. Hideous. And gorgeous.

"You found it!" I whooped, pressing a finger against the fleshy animal. "A sea cucumber!"

Not only a sea cucumber, but *the* sea cucumber: *Isostichopus fuscus*. Its size conformed with a scientific study I'd read, which suggested that many of today's remaining *I. fuscus* cucumbers are the survivors of the 1988–1994 overharvesting debacle. Based on its size, I guessed that this squashed football would have been a baby pickle in 1994.

We admired the cucumber for a short while. It seemed anticlimactic to put it back after so eager a search, but we were more like birders than collectors: Spotting *I. fuscus* was our only goal.

If two frantic and scientifically unpedigreed snorkelers searching randomly could locate a specimen, then perhaps this imperiled species had a chance. The people on the boat will be pleased, I thought, to know their patience had made this moment possible. But that warmhearted sentiment was drowned out by the roar of the panga's outboard motor, revving in the distance. Just warming up, I thought. Except that the anchor had been pulled up, and it looked like the boat was moving— only slowly, but still . . .

"They wouldn't leave without us, would they?" I asked Eliza. "They can't leave us here." We were paying customers. And this was a desert island. No water except for those old wells, several coves away. No food except lizard meat and tourists' breadcrumbs.

"Wait!" we called out, pumping our flippered legs as fast as they'd go.

Months after our return from Baja, I stumbled upon the proceedings of the 10th International Echinoderm Conference and discovered a strange universe of holothurian researchers. The conference featured papers and posters on sea-cuke circadian rhythms, intestinal regeneration, migration, reproduction, and gene-sequencing. An Auckland researcher reviewed the commercial uses of temperate sea cucumbers: An extract of boiled skin is drunk as a tonic in Malaysia, guts and gonads are consumed salted or dried, and the muscle bands of some species are used as clam substitutes. Scientists from South Africa have suggested the cucumber as a possible bioindicator of heavy metals (the cucumber accumulates aluminum from polluted waters). Many holothurian researchers today focus on aquaculture—the raising and breeding of sea cucumbers, a necessity in a world where wild cukes of the edible kind are becoming increasingly scarce.

All this information is eagerly sought because sea cucumbers are big money, with demand outpacing supply. About eighty thousand tons of cucumber (wet weight) are harvested worldwide each year. Eighty thousand tons equals 160 million pounds. If sea cucumbers were divided into quarter-pounder slices, served on a slab between sesame-seed-covered buns, the world could eat 640 million of them each year.

Every country that eats this variously slippery-leathery delicacy has its own name for the sea cucumber. Indonesians call it trepang. The Thai call it pling khao. The Japanese call it namako. The Portuguese call it bicho de mer—something close to "seaworm." The French, with their talent for making the slimy sound palatable, adapted the Portuguese term into the gallicized "beche-de-mer."

We had to taste one. We never found the chance in Mexico, but later, in a Chinese restaurant in Alaska, Brian, Aryeh, Tziporah, and I sat down to a specially ordered, advance-reservation-required meal of stir-fried, nobby-nippled sea cucumber. It wasn't cheap. The restaurant ordered the dried sea cucumbers from Japan at $17.95 per pound—the price of lobster—and spent three days repeatedly boiling and cooling the reconstituted strips. ("We can't make money from them," the waitress said. "Cost too much and too much work.")

What ended up in our chafing dish looked like strips of a blown tire found roadside. More charitably, it looked a little like black beef, except the beef had little bumps and pores, like the surface of a scrotum. Touching the thin sea cucumber slices, we found them more gelatinous than rubbery. They didn't taste like seafood at all, which was a credit to the cook, who had bathed them in a thick garlic sauce. So this was the meal that graces so many wedding banquets and New Year celebration tables throughout Asia.

"You like it?" the waitress asked.

"It's far better than I thought it would be," I said, searching for honest words.

The cook had tossed in a few green onions and bamboo slices, but mostly it was just the sea cucumber, generously portioned. "And," I added, "that sure is a *lot* of sea cucumber."

She watched us eat a few bites.

"So why exactly do Chinese people like this so much?" I asked.

"Good texture. Good for health." Here she lifted her chin past the staring eyes of Aryeh and Tziporah, and nodded toward Brian, telegraphing a secret message with her eyebrows. "Special for men. Strong."

No one on the boat would have cared. They did not ask us what we saw on the beach near San Gabriel. Chalk it up to queasiness or antsiness or subtler interpersonal dynamics. The other tourists had grown tired of Isla Espíritu Santo and all talk of sea cucumbers, and that was that.

"How long will it take?" the Mexican mother asked the guide, eager to be back in La Paz.

"Not long," the guide answered.

"So much for mañana-land," I whispered to Eliza.

Halfway across the channel that divides Isla Espíritu Santo from the mainland shore of Baja, a furious slapping and splashing erupted behind us. Even over the roar of the outboard motor, we could hear it, and all the tourists and even the guide himself turned and started pointing with excitement. It was a whale's tail, thrashing the water. The guide looked over his shoulder, and toward La Paz, and over his shoulder again. No other part of the whale's body emerged, but the great gray tail, speckled with white, stayed well in view, beating the water like a washerwoman beating her laundry against a rock.

"What is it doing?" someone asked.

"Is it caught or something?"

"Is it a gray or a humpback?"

"Is it hurt?"

"There it goes again!"

Finally, the guide killed the motor and swung the boat around in a careful arc.

"Figures," I growled to Eliza. "They won't wait for a sea cucumber. But they'll wait for a marine mammal."

For better or worse, though, they wouldn't wait long. Even for a whale. After less than a minute watching the water foam, we were on our way back to La Paz again, with the whale's tail still slapping away, tapping out some Morse-code message that none of us could decipher.

NOWHERE AT LAND'S END

Now we headed to a place we feared: Cabo San Lucas, the tourism capital of Baja. If the Los Islotes tourists had seemed uncommitted to a lengthy exploration of Isla Espíritu Santo, they were nonetheless an entirely different breed from the bake-and-slake crowd that fills Cabo's expensive resorts. But we had a mission to fulfill.

We broke down our collapsible kayak into its two thirty-five-pound bags, gathered up the rest of our overweight luggage, and climbed aboard a bus bound for Baja's southern tip. Hours later, when the bus expelled us and our mountains of gear at the appropriate station, we stood for a moment blinking into the bright, hazy sky. "Is this it? Cabo San Lucas?" We saw no beaches or even any hotels, only sprawling city outskirts.

At the bus station, we inquired about buses heading to downtown Cabo San Lucas. There weren't any. Then we asked about buses heading onward to Cabo Pulmo, so that we'd have our escape route from San Lucas fully planned. We hoped to spend only a few hours here and then flee northeast to Pulmo reef by dusk.

"You mean Cabo San Lucas?" the ticket agent asked. No, I told her. I mean Pulmo.

"You mean San José del Cabo?" No. Cabo Pulmo—the reef, Baja's only coral reef, on the Cortez. We have a reservation there tonight.

There is no such place, she informed me. "You are confused. There are two Cabos. Not three."

"Perhaps you are confused," I said. But with pressed lips she wagged her finger at me, and I knew I had gone too far.

Outside the station, a kind man spotted us sitting, dejectedly, on our piles of gear. Tziporah was sunburnt. Aryeh clung to a guitar we'd bought him in La Paz. We all looked a little lost. The man disappeared back into the bus station and came out with a busking guitarist I'd noticed inside the station. The kind stranger mediated in Spanish, gesturing to Aryeh, and making pantomimed introductions. The guitarist smiled, tuned Aryeh's

guitar, and showed him how to strum a chord. After a while, the guitarist's own bus arrived and he departed, bowing.

Just as the first man turned to walk away, we asked him about Pulmo
and described its location, well off the main road leading back to La Paz.
"Do you know how to get there?"

In ten minutes he had rounded up two friends and their beater, a low-
slung sedan with a small trunk and dirty windows. "A taxi," the stranger
announced with a flourish. We negotiated a price—one hundred dollars
for the trip into San Lucas, and then onward to Pulmo. All of us jammed
our bags wherever they would fit: trunk, backseat, front seat. There was
no place left for people. Twine emerged from pockets, and various adults
climbed over the car, attempting to tie and squash and make do. In the
midst of this activity, I pulled Brian aside.

"How do we know we won't get dumped along the road somewhere?
I was thinking more of a real taxi. An official one."

We had judged the stranger trustworthy for one reason only: He had
brought the guitarist to us, mediating the briefest of cultural exchanges,
without asking for anything in return.

Still, we felt wary. The fact that our oversized bags refused to fit into the
sedan offered us an out. The stranger and his two friends finally shrugged
apologetically, admitting defeat, though the thought of that easy c-note
still glittered in their eyes. One of them disappeared, and he came back
with a real taxi driver. The bona fide driver stepped out of his official,
more spacious vehicle and eyed our heap of bags. He eyed the derelict
sedan, snickering. *Amateurs,* his expression seemed to say.

Then the original stranger and his two friends departed, with smiles,
waves, and hearty wishes of good luck. Our new driver was less friendly
but more competent. We explained the stops we needed to make and our
reason for going there—to explore the kind of beach that a visiting biologist would have seen many decades ago.

"A beach? There are many," he said, and started to name them—Playa
Del Amor, Playa Solmar.

"Not a tourist beach. Not pretty, not all sand and hotels," I said. "A
beach with small marine animals—some rocks, some sand. Like the old
Cabo San Lucas." At the mention of "old" he nodded efficiently, and
pulled into traffic.

We were parched from the long bus ride, so along the way, I asked the driver to stop at a downtown pharmacy. Inside, a vacationing American cop was casually cautioning a young male tourist, "Don't steal anything. I mean it. I saw what the jails look like here." Large white letters covered the pharmacy's windows: "Lomotil. Prozac. Zantac." Diarrhea and depression; that about covered the perils here. The smallest plastic flask of water cost two dollars—an insane markup possible in few other Baja towns but this one, where annual visitors outnumber residents more than ten to one. I knew we needed a full gallon of water for the road but I couldn't stomach the price.

As we drove toward the beach we passed strip malls and Graeco-Roman mansions and fake adobe condominiums and signs we hadn't seen since California: "Kentucky Fried Chicken," "Burger King," "McDonalds." Real estate fliers advertised open houses for "discerning buyers only"— meaning buyers who could afford to pay $499,000 to $2 million. Everything was in English. Bars and cafes competed to have the most flip, ironic name: The Nowhere Bar, or What's Up?

Steinbeck and Ricketts wrote about a much simpler San Lucas: "To a man straight off a yacht, it is a miserable little flea-bitten place, poor and smelly. But to one who puts in hungry, in a storm-beaten boat, it must be a place of great comfort and warmth."

Translating that generous sentiment to modern times, we might have said: "To a man who has traveled the rest of Baja first, it is a decadent, tacky, spiritless place. But to one who wants to lay on a white beach and get snockered while fending off earring vendors, it might be okay for a weekend."

In the taxi, I asked Brian, "What's the shortest amount of time we can stay here and still say we came? Does half an hour count?"

The *Western Flyer*'s crew, landing at Cabo San Lucas late at night on March 17, arrived with fewer preconceptions. They had traveled south along the Pacific until rounding this southernmost headland ("cabo" means simply "cape") and welcomed the first sight of land and town that morning would bring. Even so, the town was not impressive even then, for altogether different reasons.

The original Cabo was small and dirty—"very primitive," Sparky recalled. It had been recently wrecked by a winter storm that flooded the town's streets. "Then there were no roofs over the heads of the people," the port captain told the *Western Flyer*'s crew. "Then the babies cried and there was no food. Then the people suffered."

The next winter, a hurricane would deliver even more punishing blows. World War II, when Japanese submarines prowled the waters off Land's End, would practically shut down the village altogether.

Even in 1940 the beaches were strewn with garbage. The sound of gunshots echoed from the cliffs, where men were shooting at cormorants—hated birds with the audacity to eat bait fish that the San Lucas fishermen wanted all for themselves. And in the town's mournful, buggy cantina, where the crew expected to find a little fun at least, they found instead only gloomy young men who could not afford to drink.

Steinbeck and Ricketts recalled: "When we lifted a split of beer to our lips the eyes of the young men rose with our hands, and even the cockroaches lifted their heads. We couldn't stand it. We ordered beer all around, but it was too late. The young men were too far gone in sorrow. They drank their warm beer sadly. Then we bought straw hats, for the sun is deadly here. There should be a kind of ridiculous joy in buying a floppy hat, but those young men, so near to tears, drained even that joy."

The taxi pulled up to Playa Escondida or "Hidden Beach," a small pocket at the neck of a boat harbor. Brian and Tziporah stayed in the car while Aryeh and I picked our way over the boulders. The beach had mustard-colored sand, dotted with rounded rocks. Mexican families picnicked just above the foamy surf line, scrutinizing us as we passed. A baby in a soggy diaper stopped digging to look up at me, her mouth flecked with gravel. My camera thumped against my chest. I took it into my hands with exaggerated motions and focused the macro lens on some gray worm-casings plastered to a boulder. It was a miserable picture, but I took it at several exposures, as if to communicate my wholesome intentions.

Steinbeck and Ricketts described the Cabo beach they visited as "ferocious with life." They collected crabs and snails and sea stars and sea urchins and sponges and tunicates and more. We saw none of those things, and passed the minutes picking idly through the garbage trapped behind the rocks. The tide was only halfway out. If we had searched harder and longer, we would have seen more—but perhaps not much more. A steady parade of feet and shovels and hooks had changed this beach over the years.

A gaggle of skinny men, cigarettes dangling from their lips, eyed us suspiciously. We *looked* suspicious. Why would American tourists visit this cruddy cove, when Cabo had miles of softer, paler, cleaner sand? Twenty minutes away from town, we might have snorkeled among sea fans or chartered a scuba guide to take us to impressive submarine canyons. But we had come to this simpler and grittier beach to tidepool and compare.

A gap-toothed wharf extended from one side of the beach, and Aryeh and I jumped between the rotten planks, weaving around the boys who idled there. Some of them were trying to fish, whipping the water with monofilament handlines. *"Con permiso,"* I said again and again, clutching Aryeh's hand. The wharf anglers made only the most token efforts to let us pass.

"The cannery," I announced, as the realization sank in. Steinbeck and Ricketts had mentioned this very same building. They had collected near here, perhaps turning over these very same rocks. Next to the wharf was an old tuna cannery emblazoned with large, faded letters. All of this—the cannery, the beach alongside it, the whole neighborhood in fact—was slated for new condo development, according to a tourism publication.

The taxi driver had done his job well. We had stepped in Steinbeck's and Ricketts's footsteps. And now we could go.

PULMO REEF

We felt no ambivalence about leaving Cabo San Lucas, though we chided ourselves for wasting money by visiting so briefly. Maybe the whole side trip was a bust. Later, we realized it had prepared us. We had seen, however superficially, a vision of what our next destination could easily become.

Long past sunset, we arrived at the other-other Cabo—not Cabo San Lucas, or San José del Cabo, but Cabo Pulmo, a small village on the east cape that was both trying and not-trying to become like its big brothers to the south and west. We were glad to find that this place did exist, as was our dubious taxi driver, who—one hundred dollars notwithstanding—was ready to turn around and return to his wife's loving embrace rather than drive us even a mile farther along unpaved rural roads.

The tourist complex at Cabo Pulmo consisted of a compound of elegant, solar-powered cabanas tucked a discreet distance away from the beach, a few restaurants, and Pepe's Dive Center, a roadside thatched hut offering scuba services. Gates blocked a handful of side roads, suggesting the presence of a few select mansions or condominiums, or a real estate developer's ambitions to build more of the same. But this village still functioned and look like a real village. Children skipped along the street and cows wandered roadside, corralled in places by barbed-wire fences. Mexican pangas lined the beach.

In the morning I set out in search of information about the reef. I found Pepe, the dive shop owner, next to his open-air palapa, putting the finishing touches on a no-camping sign for the beach.

"How does it look?" he asked playfully. "I'm not an expert painter."

A faded Mexican flag flapped behind him. Laminated fish-identification cards decorated the hut's interior walls. Plastic dinosaurs belonging to Pepe's two young children littered the dirt floor.

I told him I wanted to ask him about the reef and arrange a guided snorkel tour. And also—if he would be so kind—he might help me find

Señor José Luis Murrieta, majordomo of Cabo Pulmo National Marine Park. Pepe said he could help me on both counts. This cheerful, chubby-cheeked Pepe *was* José "Pepe" Murrieta—head of the dive center, and also head of the marine park. One-stop shopping. I could tell this was going to be a good day.

Pepe's first job, he told me, helps subsidize his second. Murrieta, a national park employee who has guarded the Sea of Cortez's only coral reef since 1992, receives no salary. It's the same for many fishery or conservation agents in Mexico. They receive nothing, or next to nothing—barely enough to cover the fuel cost of their patrols. If not for the profits from his tourism operation, Pepe might have little choice but to accept bribes from large-scale commercial fishermen, who find the park's no-fishing prohibitions tedious. "Oh sure, they offered me money," he told me. But still, he made light of the pressures.

Later, his mother-in-law would be more frank. She described seven or eight incidents where large fishing boats from the mainland state of Sinaloa bullied their way into the park's shrimp- and fish-rich boundaries. Only the arrival of a naval gunboat, hailed by Pepe from a distant port, ended that spate of illegal fishing. Illegal fishermen continue to test Pepe's resolve, though he has little authority or muscle to do anything but observe and report infractions. Still, he frequently stops turtle-egg poachers, illegal spear-gunners, and gillnetters on his own, accepting the risk of unarmed patrols.

Pepe's background did not prepare him to be a reef sheriff. He lived in the large mainland cities of Veracruz and Mexico City before moving to Baja in 1985. In Cabo San Lucas, he worked as a bartender. Then, he went for a swim and discovered another universe. Snorkeling led to scuba diving, which led to a new profession. In 1992 Pepe and his U.S.-born wife, Libby, moved to Pulmo and started their dive business. Here, at the eastern Pacific's northernmost coral reef, they found a paradise, not yet lost, but on its way. Visitors were spearfishing, taking coral, and collecting tropical fish. Mexicans were netting fish and shrimp on the reef itself. For twenty years, people from the university in La Paz had talked about making Pulmo a park, but nothing came of it. Finally, the village took matters in its own hands, with Pepe in the lead.

As he told me this story, a local woman in a truck pulled up to the thatched hut. With a wave and a smile, she called out to Pepe. "We found a net. On the beach." Abandoned nets—"ghost nets"—trap and kill untold numbers of turtles, rays, and fish.

"Okay," he called back, promising to take care of it.

Later, a boy ran barefoot down the dirt road and stopped by the hut to deliver Pepe another message. Villagers like this one were his unpaid rangers, Pepe explained. "This whole park is practically run by the community."

Still, there are problems: Tourists who stand on or kick their flippers against the coral. Guides who arrive from distant resorts without enough skill or reef know-how to keep their clients from doing unintentional damage. Boats that anchor on the reef, despite rules forbidding it. Poachers who steal tropical fish for the aquarium trade. And the park has no official management plan. Everything is ad hoc here, from the signs Pepe paints himself, to the Pulmo reef informational brochures that are sponsored by a real estate company that is developing the same area that most conservationists agree should be preserved. (A conflict of interest? "We couldn't afford to print them without help.")

Already, Pepe said, villagers have seen the fruits of their labors. "The sardines are back, more than we've seen for so many years. The sardines attract more fish—jacks, groupers. There are more birds: pelicans, cormorants, ospreys. Manta rays—there are lots now. . . . We have survived a few El Niños."

The park officially opened, with meager federal support, in June 1995. In 1997, sport and commercial fishing were prohibited and about fifty small-scale fishermen, representing three local families, lost their primary livelihoods. They did so willingly, Murrieta said. Every one of them saw the greater tourism opportunities offered by a healthy reef: fish restaurants, guided snorkel tours, cabana and kayak rentals.

We'd been talking for well over an hour now, interrupted only briefly by a few scuba clients who stopped by the hut to book a personal dive lesson. Throughout our interview, Pepe flashed a humble smile, and gestured frequently to the fish pictures hanging on the hut's wall. He jumped up frequently to point out maps that illustrated the many-fingered reef he was describing. Pepe was no biologist; he had to pause and squint to search out the names of certain endemic or key species. But I'd never talked to any Baja tourism operator who was so eager and optimistic—a true and noble amateur, in the Latin sense of the word: *amatus*, a "lover." Pepe loved this reef, and he knew it intimately, from a diver's perspective, if not a scientist's. Whether answering my interminable questions or dealing with clients, he expressed none of the cynicism or simple exhaustion that I had seen in so many guides and expatriates.

A hot afternoon breeze stirred, rattling the palapa's thatched roof. The wind carried the salty scent of the reef toward us, and I longed to be out there, tidepooling and snorkeling. How wonderful it must have been, I thought, for the three families who, until three years ago, harvested this reef, feeding their children directly from its tropical bounty.

"Surely they didn't all want to stop fishing," I said to Pepe. "I've lived in Alaska and in Canada when there was a crisis in the cod fishery. It's the same everywhere. Always, there are some fishermen who don't want to stop."

"No," he said. "Here they understand."

I wanted to believe him.

Among the two dozen Cortez tidepooling stations they visited, Pulmo Reef was one of Steinbeck's and Ricketts's top five favorites. They anchored a mile away and then rowed to the reef, which is really a series of eight hard coral fingers scattered throughout the sparkling, sand-bottomed bay. As the tide went down, parts of the reef's flat, pockmarked surface were gradually exposed, allowing them to walk on its encrusted surface, filling their collecting buckets and tubes and jars. From afar, either one of the men must have looked like Jesus walking on the water.

They wrote, "Clinging to the coral, growing on it, burrowing into it, was a teeming fauna. Every piece of the soft material broken off skittered and pulsed with life—little crabs and worms and snails. One small piece of coral might conceal thirty or forty species, and the colors on the reef were electric."

They broke off pieces of coral and submerged them in pans of seawater. As the water grew stale, "thousands of little roomers which live in the tubes and caves and interstices of the coral [would] come out of hiding and scramble for a new home."

Brian and I had not considered in detail how we would re-create this particular tidepool stop. Now that we were at Pulmo, staring across the waves to the breaker zone where the water beat against the reef, we reread the *Log*'s Pulmo passages and were horrified. Today, walking atop a coral reef is unthinkable. Stampeding all over it, breaking apart pieces of coral like a construction worker jackhammering an old sidewalk, is anathema. We did not waste time lambasting Steinbeck and Ricketts—pulling apart bits of reef was on a par with collecting methods of their time—but we knew that we could not re-create this aspect of their Cortez experience. Our Pulmo would not be their Pulmo.

In fact, in many ways, our Pulmo experience would be better, thanks to technology that missed them by just a few years: the postwar refinement of the common mask and snorkel. They had lamented, "On several occasions we wished for diving equipment, but never more than here at Pulmo, for the under-cut shoreward side of the reef concealed hazy wonders we could not get at. It is not satisfactory to hold one's breath and to look with unglassed eyes through the dim waters."

We hired a guide, chartered a panga, "glassed" our eyes, and headed off to see what they could not.

On a map, Pulmo reef appears well within the Sea of Cortez. But actually, oceanic influences—deep swells and currents—wrap around the entire cape region and bring a taste of the open Pacific to the reef's back door. This was not the bathtub-calm gulf we'd experienced farther north. These were heaving, whirling waters; an ecosystem on the dividing line. As always, that edge produced an unparalleled richness.

Throughout our three-day visit, gusting afternoon winds textured the sea's surface. Even when the breezes died at dusk, waves continued to break against the reef. With so much chop and without the benefit of scuba-diving equipment or skills, we experienced our best snorkeling from protected reef-facing beaches.

One of Pepe's guides transported us by roaring panga to our first of several snorkeling spots. Tziporah had fallen asleep in the motorboat, her face hidden under a hat. While Brian and Aryeh climbed over the gunwales into knee-high water, I settled onto a seat near Tziporah, expecting to miss my first turn at snorkeling. The guide smiled. "Go ahead," he said, gesturing to the water, and then to the napping toddler, curled up on the boat floor. "I'll watch her."

I slid into the water, promising myself I'd snorkel for just a minute or two, not more than a few feet from the boat. But that was like saying one could slip into New York's wildest dance club and emerge before even the first song was over. Beneath the warm and wind-stirred water, a psychedelic party was under way, complete with disco-ball glitter. Colors flashed. Fins whirred. Surf broke against submerged rock, releasing clouds of bubbles. Needles of light flashed just under the surface. I steadied myself in time to realize that a passing quicksilver sheet, so close to the water's mirrored ceiling that it looked like the ceiling itself, was actually a small school of inch-long juvenile swordfish, perfect miniatures of their predatory parents.

But the biggest surprise in this flashy place was the soundtrack. Often, the underwater world is described as silent. It's not. As currents pushed and tugged, waves of sound washed over me: the roiling pulse of moving water, a steady white-noise static of shifting sand and coral debris, and a higher-toned click and pop that I guessed to be shrimp. I added my own noises, inhaling noisily and nervously through my snorkel, and making involuntary grunts of surprise every time a fish careened within inches of my mask, swept by an underwater current.

Above all this, I could hear the persistent scraping sound of a dog worrying its bone. I followed the brittle gnawing to its source. It turned out to be no dog, of course, but a parrotfish grinding its fused, beaklike teeth against the coral. In this way, it scrapes edible algae from the rock. Sometimes it eats the living coral as well. A single large parrotfish can pulverize a ton of coral reef into sand in a year's time.

Nearby, other tropical species probed and tore and circled the coral—idols and surgeonfish, triggerfish with sloping foreheads and horselike incisors, and blue damselfish, small but fiercely territorial. A snorkeler from Cuba or Jamaica might recognize a third or more of these species, which are twins, or analogs, to Caribbean species. Until two to five million years ago, the Sea of Cortez was distantly connected to the Caribbean by a natural rift through Central America—the Panama seaway. In the ages since the seaway closed, species on both sides have continued to evolve, making them distinct species. The idea of a Cortez-Caribbean link was widely recognized only in the 1960s and 1970s; it would have delighted Ricketts, who struggled to understand why, to a West Coast biologist, the Cortez seems both familiar and exotic.

The diversity at Pulmo Reef astounded me. Until now in the Cortez, I had snorkeled mostly among large schools of fish—many fish of one species, one school at a time, roving like hungry gangs above the sea bottom. Here, the fish intermingled in more complex patterns, drawn into closer proximity by the coral. Aside from a lobster, purple gorgonians, brown urchins, and the coral itself, I didn't see many of the smaller invertebrates, but I expected that they, too, were here, probably burrowed under sand and rock to avoid the maelstrom of current. The larger reef vertebrates so dazzled me that I could not focus on any one thing for long.

Tropical fish colors—turquoise, emerald, lemon yellow, stoplight red—drew me ever deeper, and made me forget, however briefly, about my own need to breathe. Some of the fish were flat and round like dinner plates, others were sleek and bullet-shaped. All wore the round-eyed, purse-lipped expressions of the perpetually surprised.

Watching the fish, I could rarely hold my position for more than five seconds before a rush of current sent me tumbling. There was no point in kicking; the trick was to stay level and in place, to avoid being washed sideways into rock or coral. Instead of actively swimming, I simply sprawled, doing my best Peter-Pan-attached-to-guy-wires imitation, using my hands and arms as hyperactive rudders. The fish, I was surprised to see, did the same. Most of each fish's whirring energies seemed spent not on forward motion, but on simple reorientation, a concept that might have had philosophical implications, had I been quiet-minded enough to grasp them. As it was, I was plenty busy just trying to float. Every strong surge prompted a blurry burst of gyrations and flutterings; platter-thin fish that had tipped completely on their sides would rush to upright themselves, while barely avoiding collisions. I'd imagined a tropical reef as a graceful and slow-moving place, an underwater ballet composed of a hundred smaller, purposeful motions. Instead I saw artful chaos—Mobius Dance Company meets rush-hour traffic. And still, out of all this confusion, a community thrived.

This was only the macro view. Closer in, I knew, there were even more intricate dances, more intricate universes, to behold. A hawkfish darted between the olive-colored folds of a branching stony coral, and I strained to hold my breath and focus my vision, to follow the fish's red-spotted body through the metaphorical doorway into places I had never seen. But my lungs would have no part of it. If a mouthful of plastic weren't clogging my mouth, I would have sworn a blue streak then and there, cursing human anatomy. Instead I simply surfaced and spit out my salty plug, gasping.

At Pulmo, Steinbeck and Ricketts were frustrated that they lacked a simple good mask. I owned a good mask and snorkel, and was frustrated that I hadn't yet learned to scuba dive. Daytime scuba divers know that the real secrets await in the dark; that's when coral polyps extend a ring of tentacles beyond their limestone skeletons and feed on passing zooplankton; and that's also when the night-shifters emerge—moray eels and grunts and big-eyed squirrelfish who sleep during the day. Round-the-clock scuba divers go down into the greater depths, into the dark, and curse the weight of their tanks and the fact that even they must ultimately surface. All of us expect a grand vision just around the corner. Every taste of wonder only sharpens our appetite for more.

These were my thoughts as I fought the currents and labored to hold my breath for longer and deeper dives. Then I remembered Tziporah, and hurried back to the panga. After she woke up, I took her to the soft white beach, where she stood in about three inches of deliciously warm water. It was barely enough water to cover my feet, but enough to submerge her lower calves and convince her she was practically swimming.

Aryeh had gone off snorkeling with Brian—the first time all trip that Aryeh was willing to put his face into the water. Tziporah was too young even to try. But at Pulmo, there were tropical fish even in these sandy shallows. She stood, happily pointing out the small rainbow wrasses— red- and yellow- and blue-striped—that darted past her ankles.

"There," she said with a Buddha's contentment. "And there. And there..."

Coral was once mistakenly classified as a plant, and the first man to suggest differently (Jean André Peyssonel, in 1723) was so ridiculed that he quit science altogether. Now we recognize coral as a colony of tiny primitive animals. This colony, in turn, feeds and shelters a larger community: all the fish and invertebrates who live within or beside the reef. It has been called the marine equivalent of the rain forest and the ocean's most diverse ecosystem.

The reef structure is composed of layers upon layers of calcium car-
bonate material, deposited by the living cnidarians (relatives of sea
anemones) who live only inside the structure's tissue-thin outer layer. The
metaphorical possibilities are infinite. Some writers refer to the reef as a
skeleton, but it is more than that—it is a colonial bone heap. These living
cnidarian polyps are like army generals who rely on the accumulation of
their own dead to gain more ground into surrounding territory. Or seen
another way: The polyps are like scientists who stand on the venerable
shoulders of their own forebears to see farther into the unknown. From
Pliny's shoulders a Linnaeus stood, and from Linnaeus's shoulders, a
Darwin—incidentally, the first scientist to explain reef formation, based
on his observations of South Pacific coral atolls.

Cnidarian polyps continually build the reef, replacing the limestone
framework that is gnawed by other animals or ground down, slowly, by
the pulse of the waves. In this way, the coral is engaged in a never-ending
battle with the elements, through which it reshapes the underwater
world. No army of engineers has created so much out of so little. The
Chinese built the Great Wall, but coral polyps built Australia's Great
Barrier Reef, a living structure more than a thousand miles long.

Coral is both strong and sensitive. It survives only within a narrow
range of environmental conditions. First, reef-building corals need warm
water—usually, from sixty-eight to seventy-seven degrees—and bright
light. That limits them to the tropical shallows, between about thirty
degrees north and south of the equator. Second, the water must be clean
and clear. Haphazard shoreline development is probably the greatest hazard to all corals since it washes sediment plumes into the sea, which clog
the delicate pores of the reef, killing it. Beachfront condominiums, for
example, are not reef-friendly. Thus the contradiction of the snorkeling
tourist who buys a seaside retreat that will ultimately destroy the very
reef he has come to explore.

The coral relies on other things, too. The most important of these is a
microscopic algae called zooxanthellae, which gives the coral its greenish
or brownish cast. The coral gives the algae a home and a steady supply of
nutrients in the form of waste material. The zooxanthellae absorb excess
carbon dioxide, process waste, and somehow speed the coral's reef-building abilities. Without the zooxanthellae, coral grow only a tenth as fast.

With their predilection for writing about communities, ecology, and group-man, it is surprising that Steinbeck and Ricketts didn't spend more time musing about Pulmo reef in the *Log*. But even before they came to Baja, Steinbeck and Ricketts brooded frequently on the idea of collective behavior, as represented by simple animals and also by a more complicated one, called man. Sometimes Steinbeck called the collective organism a phalanx, borrowing the word used to describe ancient Greek infantry, marching closely with their shields and lances raised, so that they resembled a single massive, armored animal. The Okies moving West to California, in *The Grapes of Wrath,* were a phalanx—more than, and different from, the sum of their parts.

Men can bond together for ethically neutral ends—simply to survive, no more and no less. But often, collectivism has a more sinister quality, and in spring 1940, the evil side of group-man was on Steinbeck's and Ricketts's minds. The threat of war weighed heavily upon them. As Steinbeck wrote to a friend before his departure for Baja, to explain why he was going: "The world is sick now. There are things in the tide pools easier to understand than Stalinist, Hitlerite, Democrat, capitalist confusion, and voodoo."

Not all phalanxes are sinister, however, or even ethically and reflexively neutral. For brief, shining moments, humans, working as cooperatively and efficiently and intentionally as a single animal with a single mind, have been able to do great good. Steinbeck hoped as much when he wrote *The Moon is Down,* an optimistic war novel that emphasized the power of occupied nations to resist. American critics hated the book and criticized him for advocating resistance; they thought it would lead to even greater German atrocities. (The critics were wrong.)

In occupied Denmark, readers had a different view of the book and its message. They printed the illicit manuscript on hand presses in cellars and even copied it by hand onto scrap paper, held together with twine. The Germans declared possession of *The Moon is Down* a capital crime, but that didn't stop Danes from reading it. The Danish citizenry reacted to Steinbeck's novel like coral to zooxanthellae; without it, they might have fought toward the light and won, but with it they fought ten times as fast and hard.

But what does all this say about Pulmo reef? Only that we strange and varied earth organisms are interconnected in ways beyond our imaginings, that those connections build, destroy, and resist destruction. And all this, even the noble, shining moments, takes place in a world that is not free from affliction.

Perhaps this as it should be. As Steinbeck and Ricketts wrote in the *Log,* we would not be the same species—or the same society—without disease and suffering. "For it is through struggle and sorrow that people are able to participate in one another. . . ."

In the strange way that thoughts often come full circle, their thoughts apply even more directly to coral reefs than to humans, though Steinbeck and Ricketts didn't realize it at the time. Coral reef ecosystems, sensitive and imperiled as they are, do not benefit from environmental constancy. The same disturbances that threaten them—sediments, storms, climatic change, and invading predators—may also, in small quantities, nurture them. One theory suggests that the coral reef's diversity is a result of these disturbances. In a less variable environment, a small number of successful competitors would win out and exclude other species. Instead, disturbances rattle the competition, allowing a more diverse species assemblage to prosper. Of course, if changes happen too quickly, the whole system slides into the abyss. It's happened before: Coral reefs disappeared or almost disappeared three times in earth's geological history.

Two days in a row, we snorkeled from shore and made short forays elsewhere in the bay. One exceptionally windy afternoon, when the central bay was churning and a great school of manta rays was spotted leaping and splashing, we motored to the spot with a guide and waited as Brian, masked and flippered, slipped into the foaming gray-brown water. From the panga, I could make out the pearly flash of mantas' undersides as they rolled and flipped and swam beneath the boat. From the water, Brian could see the giants glide past and then disappear, all too quickly, into the murk. Waves slapped him in the face and turbid water flooded his mask. He lasted only a few minutes, sputtering and choking in the cold waves, while dozens of rays erupted and splashed down around us, more clearly seen above the water than beneath it.

From the missionary Miguel del Barco's time up through Steinbeck's, mantas were feared, and Brian's blind groping in ray-infested waters would have been seen as suicidal folly. But we knew that they are nothing more than gentle giants. Still, the episode demonstrates how far we marinophiles will go to try to make contact with unfamiliar species, to understand.

After each day's snorkeling we poked around the Cabo Pulmo resort compound, admiring the attractive cabanas that are, for the most part, set back a reasonable distance from the beach itself. We puzzled over incongruous details here and there—small squares of green grass, for example, in a place where fertilizer and runoff might have disastrous impacts on the reef.

One day I watched some Mexican fishing guides and their foreign sportfishing clients lower their nets into the water just offshore. They motored away when they saw me photographing them. "Probably catching bait fish," Pepe Murrieta explained to me later. While commercial and sportfishing are prohibited within the park's boundaries, netting bait fish is not, he said. I didn't completely understand this allowance, just as I didn't understand how a real estate company would be an appropriate sponsor for a national park.

By dinnertime I understood a little better. Turns out that Nancy, the American woman who served us dinner at the elegant restaurant bearing her name, is also Pepe's mother-in-law. She's also a real estate agent.

Most of the village is composed of three families, so it shouldn't have come as a shock that Pepe, the reef guardian, is related to one of the people seeking to develop and profit from expanded Cabo Pulmo tourism. The journalist in me smelled a good story, but the budding ecologist in me sniffed something different: not conflict of interest, necessarily, but rather complexity. Ecology doesn't stop at the reef, after all. It continues onto the shore, embracing the people who make a living from the reef's bounty.

Which brought me back to one of my earlier questions: Does everyone at Pulmo really get along as well as Pepe claimed? Did the fishermen really agree to stop fishing without protest? Or did an even more tangled web of relationships and compromises support the national park, in both its failures and its successes? Despite the tenor of those questions, I still felt more optimistic than skeptical. A visit to a coral reef, with all its messy vitality, will do that to you.

In any case, if I had learned anything from Steinbeck and Ricketts so far, it was to avoid premature conclusions. Three days at a reef wasn't adequate for judging the complex ecology of this village. We all left Pulmo with the strange, disorienting feeling that we'd seen a tremendous amount, and nothing at all.

HUNTING

Just south of Loreto, Steinbeck and Ricketts departed on a curious side trip. They joined three local men—a schoolteacher, a customs agent, a ranch owner—plus Indian trackers, on a bighorn sheep-hunting expedition into the Sierra de la Giganta. They lunched at a cascade-fed freshwater pool, which Steinbeck would utilize later as a setting in *The Pearl*. The men shared Spanish stories and jokes around the campfire. The racy punch lines eluded the Americans' understanding, but the camaraderie of the moment needed no translation. "Good friends," one of the Mexicans said to Ricketts, and these two simple words affected him deeply.

In the end, this overnight hunt into the steep cactus-lands produced no *borrego*. The trackers brought back a pocketful of droppings, which they handed to the Americans. Steinbeck and Ricketts accepted this gift with pleasure, amusement, and a little relief: "We intend to do all our future hunting in exactly this way. The ranch owner said a little sadly, 'If they had killed one we could have had our pictures taken with it,' but except for that loss, there was no loss, for none of us likes to have the horns of dead animals around."

In fact, the next time they went hunting, Steinbeck and Ricketts planned to make one slight improvement to their method. ". . . We shall not take a gun, thereby obviating the last remote possibility of having the hunt cluttered up with game." They added, "For ourselves, we have had mounted in a small hardwood plaque one perfect *borrego* dropping. And where another man can say, 'There was an animal, but because I am greater than he, he is dead and I am alive, and there is his head to prove it,' we can say, 'There was an animal, and for all we know there still is and here is the proof of it. He was very healthy when we last heard of him.'"

From Cabo Pulmo, we found our way north by thumb and bus. Brian, the children, and I set our sights on the Midriffs, the gulf's island-studded belt far north of Mulegé, where we would continue the second half of our Cortez tidepool circuit—a route that would take us away from the tourist track of Baja Sur and deeper into the unknown.

First, though, we planned to stop at Loreto. We'd taken shelter there once already but I worried that we'd given this national marine park gateway short shrift. Steinbeck and Ricketts had lingered in this region hunting sheep. I was hunting reliable information. A borrego might have been easier to find.

I spent four days tracking Benito Bermudez, a marine park director I wished to interview. In the spirit of Steinbeck and Ricketts, I tried to enjoy this goose chase: the stifling walks back and forth to Bermudez's office at the Bahía de Loreto National Marine Park headquarters, the fruitless discussions with other park employees who couldn't tell me what I wanted to know. A fisherman tried to help by driving me around town in his pickup truck, but he couldn't locate Benito that day either—it was Cinco de Mayo, a national holiday. Some other fishermen—Americans on vacation—tried to help by buying me margaritas. I accepted. Then it was the weekend. Then it was Monday—merely an extension of an already long weekend, because Mother's Day, a revered holiday in Mexico, was just around the corner. I showered repeatedly between my sorties, just to cool off, and headed out into Loreto's white-hot streets again, my hair dry in minutes, my eyes stinging from the midday glare.

It was so hot that two barefoot, elderly American sportfishermen, crossing the beach between their motorboat and the hotel where they were staying, flayed the soles of their feet. Once they realized how hot the sand was, it was too late. They hopped the rest of the way, a thirty-second dash over coals. Skin hung in pale shreds off both men's feet. The men themselves hardly spoke; they were racked with pain and also embarrassed. I knew this because I acted briefly as their emergency interpreter—a short break from my search for the park director.

All the while my family tossed and turned in a cheap, airless motel room, waiting for me to finish my interview so that we could press on. I tried to feel ready to accept a sheep turd instead of a trophy head, but my heart wasn't in it.

Finally, on a broiling afternoon, I found Benito. The day's relentless heat had wilted me. When we finally shook hands I had to restrain myself from collapsing gratefully into his arms. The park director was fresh, well dressed and professional—elegant in a white, long-sleeved, sharply creased shirt, no sign of sweat, with a fine watch glittering on his wrist. Pepe Murrieta could have passed as a rancher or fisherman. Benito, his Loreto counterpart, looked like a CEO. At a thatched-roofed restaurant overlooking the sea, we ordered cold drinks and got down to business.

The son of a farmer, Benito Bermudez studied biology, received his master's degree in La Paz, and logged time working in Mexico City before accepting his present post when the park opened, in 1996. Pressure came from angry Loreto residents, who watched each day as shrimp trawlers from the distant states of Sonora and Sinaloa scoured the coast between Isla Coronados and Isla Danzante. "There were sometimes twenty anchoring during the day, and more at night," he said—all operating, like lighted offshore villages, within view of Loreto's waterfront. The fish on which local small-scale fishermen depended were quickly disappearing.

Trawlers scrape the seafloor clean, dumping up to ten pounds of non-target species overboard for every one pound of seafood they retain. Steinbeck and Ricketts, ahead of their time in so many ways, were among the first writers to describe this phenomenon and predict its consequences. The trawlers they saw then were foreign; only later did Mexico learn how to destroy its own resources.

The *Log*'s authors described a Japanese trawler fleet near Guaymas on the mainland shore, "dredging with overlapping scoops, bringing up tons of shrimps, rapidly destroying the species so that it may never come back, and with the species destroying the ecological balance of the whole region."

They got permission to board one of the fleet's twelve ships and to pick out samples of every species littering the boat's decks. The Japanese were interested only in the shrimp, not in the countless other fish and animals they tore from the seafloor. All those tons of wasted by-catch were usually thrown back into the ocean.

"We liked the people on this boat very much," the *Log*'s authors wrote. "They were good men, but they were caught in a large destructive machine, good men doing a bad thing. With their many and large boats, with their industry and efficiency, but most of all with their intense energy, these Japanese will obviously soon clean out the shrimps of the region."

It took more than fifty years for Mexico to catch on to Steinbeck's and Ricketts's message. And another ten to *begin* to stop Mexico's trawlers from doing the same damage done earlier by foreign fleets.

In scholarly articles aimed at a modern nature-loving audience, Steinbeck is often lauded for his activist stance against shrimp trawlers. (Never mind that all the comments about the Japanese trawler were really from Ricketts, taken nearly verbatim from his journal.) But in addition to describing waste and prescribing limits in the *Log,* the two men said a disturbing thing. Having decried waste, they added (fourteen pages later) that really, at the macrocosmic level, there is no waste. All the dead by-catch thrown overboard is eaten by something: if not birds or fish then worms or sea cucumbers, and if not cucumbers then bacteria. "The great organism, Life, takes it all and uses it all." And in his private journal, Ricketts went on to poke gentle fun at Tiny's horror about the rampant devastation of sea life they had observed.

I found this prime example of Ricketts's non-teleology—"what is, is"—philosophically soothing but pragmatically irritating. I wondered if Ricketts, visiting the gulf now, would indulge in such laissez-faire musing. Perhaps our time simply doesn't allow for it.

I, for one, didn't take comfort in knowing that wasteful trawling would help feed the seafloor's worms while wiping out its larger invertebrates, fish, turtles, and marine mammals. I didn't want a macrocosmic view so "macro" that it precluded the value of preserving one of the world's most pristine seas. I was more interested in knowing, sixty years later, if the trawlers had been stopped. Even so, I knew that such a question led away from both objectivity and enlightenment, toward heartache.

At Loreto, the creation of a national park has slowed the pillage locally, though big boats still haunt its margins. Benito told me that in February, an out-of-state shrimp trawler was stopped near Agua Verde, ten miles outside the park's southern boundary. The people of Agua Verde couldn't evict the trawler without good cause. But the mere presence of the nearby park has emboldened local, small-scale fishermen for miles around, and authorities were summoned to board the trawler in search of minor infractions. They found an inoperable turtle-excluding device (a device legally required on shrimp trawlers), enough cause to send the trawler packing.

The hardest part of stopping boats is catching them—never easy along an extensive and thinly populated desert coast. But some progress has been made. This year, *Totoran,* the military vessel we saw at Puerto Escondido, added environmental patrolling to its military and antidrug patrol duties. Unlike the park at Cabo Pulmo, Loreto park also has a budget, with added support from the Nature Conservancy, an American nonprofit. Unlike Murrieta, Benito Bermudez receives a salary.

At the Loreto national park, local fishermen—with a fleet of 250 pangas—still work the waters, catching about ten thousand tons of fish each year. That's triple the amount caught by local fishermen five years earlier—although those early numbers are hopelessly suspect. "Before, no one was informed about what they were doing," Bermudez said. "Now, they are registered for the first time. We know the catch of every panga."

The local *pescadores* say the fishing has improved. Bermudez thinks recovery will take longer—another five to ten years. Locals may be making a decent living now, but increasingly, they are landing second-class fish. Other changes complicate the ecological big-picture. Like climate change. "Have you seen all the sargasso seaweed by the waterfront?" he asked me. "We didn't have that before."

And booming ecotourism. The red-rock desert islands that looked so threatening and untrammeled from our beachfront restaurant table are actually fragile and overrun. The park authorities now require paddlers and campers to register for specific campsites and confirm that they are following leave-no-trace camping rules, a level of bureaucratic watchfulness that would have been unheard of just five years ago. Three thousand kayakers visited a single small beach on Isla Carmen in 1999. The park has closed two island beaches altogether, to promote habitat restoration. Nine years earlier, Brian and I had circumnavigated Carmen and Danzante, the islands that Benito was discussing. The same nameless coves and tiny cliff niches we had visited now had names. Worse than names, they had codes—CN5, CT35, DZ7. Those letter-number sets, stripped of all poetry, stripped of even the pretense of wildness, utterly depressed me. And yet, this kind of management, and the death of illusion, were necessary, I knew.

Toward the end of my conversation with Benito Bermudez, Loreto's mayor swept past our table. Like Benito, he was elegantly dressed and unruffled by the heat. Benito hailed him. We talked water quality. Benito lectured adroitly. I tried to keep up, stumbling along in Spanish. The mayor hardly said a word, but only listened politely. The mainland side of the Sea of Cortez, Benito explained, has far more problems than Baja: heavy metals, organic pollution, agricultural chemicals washed into the gulf by farms in the coastal states of Sonora and Sinaloa. Most cities have no sewage treatment plants. Everything washes into the gulf, to be churned by racing currents.

Amazingly, Benito said, none of it reaches Loreto. The National Water Commission has two monitoring sites in the Loreto area: one near Isla Coronados and one a few miles south. Those stations report the cleanest water in the entire Sea of Cortez. As the mayor finished his ice tea and rose to leave, pumping Benito's hand and my own, Benito repeated these key points emphatically, urging the mayor to discuss water quality and what it could mean for Baja with other regional leaders at an upcoming conference. Even in my presence, he squeezed the political opportunity from every moment.

I was impressed, as heartened by Benito's quick tongue and political acumen as I had been by Pepe Murrieta's grassroots passion. But as always, questions remained. Benito's generally rosy picture didn't jibe with the apocalyptic environmental reports I'd encountered elsewhere. Was this a man who would confide real concerns about corruption, overfishing, or political compromise? And if so, why should he confide them to me—a heat-addled, overeager gringa, leafing through her note-book with pale, sweaty fingers?

But I did like him. And I wished him well in his monumental endeavors. "*Amigos,*" I would have liked to say, as the Indian said to Ricketts, after their borrego hunt proved fruitless. It's easier to become fast friends when you have no agenda—no pressing desire to acquire an object or data or immediate insight. It's easier to know someone when you're not desperately trying to figure them out; when you are simply accepting "what is," and enjoying the view of a sparkling gulf.

MUY DURO

We boarded a northbound bus. We planned to resume our explorations of the coast in the Midriffs. But no good road led there directly. Instead, Highway 1 climbed up and over the Baja's mountainous spine and then rolled northwest along the Pacific coast, past the gray-whale lagoons near Guerrero Negro. This took us into an altogether different climate—foggy and cool—and well out of our way. *Zuiva* was far behind us now, but this tacking business would follow us up onto dry land and all over Western Mexico.

When, at 11:00 P.M., the bus reached a small fork in the road leading back to Baja's eastern coast, we asked the driver to drop us off. "Here?" he asked, pulling the bus off onto the desert's soft shoulder. "You sure?"

We unloaded our backbreaking piles of luggage and erected our tent within view of the highway, on the thin-soiled desert floor, next to a crackling communication tower. In the morning, we packed quickly and stuck out our thumbs. The sun rose, a dim orb masked by woolly clouds, but little traffic materialized. Usually, on Baja's Highway 1, a vehicle passes every five minutes or so. Today, the silence between cars was two or three or five times as long. "Where is everyone?" we asked each other. Then we remembered. Today was a holiday. Not a good time to be thumbing it.

The side road we wished to travel was even more deserted. The minutes dragged on, and not a single vehicle turned east. We paraded Aryeh and Tziporah up and down the dusty shoulder, ready to look charming should any vehicle appear. Our children didn't ask why we were spending a whole day pacing a ditch, and for this we loved them even more.

We moved our mountain of gear around—making it more visible, less visible, easier to grab the moment a ride materialized. Then we gave up and turned it into a windbreak. We dug through backpacks, shivering and grumpy, to retrieve thicker clothes. We ate cereal and brewed tea. "Happy Mother's Day," Brian mumbled, handing me a warm mug. Aryeh took out his journal and drew pictures of beetles ambling between meager desert succulents, their black, scent-spraying rear ends tilted toward the sky. We saw no other signs of life. Finally we decided to try a slightly larger side road farther north.

The day proceeded slowly: a short lift to the next town, a taxi ride two hours north to a junction with a road leading east to Bahía de los Angeles (no buses plied this or any other side roads heading toward the Cortez coast). And then pacing the ditches again, thumbs extended. At each place we waited, the desert had a different character. Near the Bahía de los Angeles junction it was an entirely different world from the desert just a few hours south. This landscape was crowded with cardón cacti and also boojums, the scruffy, candle-shaped trees named after an imaginary creature in Lewis Carroll's *Hunting of the Snark*. Except for one small patch in Sonora, the boojums grow in a 500-mile-wide band on the peninsula—and nowhere else. Strange, small, hard melons nestled in a tangle of vines on the desert floor. We juggled these and snapped cactus photos and petted two balding stray dogs that looked like coyotes with mange. We strolled along-side the road, picking up an amazing assortment of small gears and springs and bolts that had shaken free from a thousand passing beaters. It wasn't a bad afternoon, actually. The kids played with the gears for hours, making us wonder why we'd ever invested so much money in Legos at home.

Watching Aryeh entertaining himself amidst so much detritus reminded me that in all the Baja fish camps we'd visited, I'd never seen a child with a conventional, commercially produced toy. Once, when Brian and I were paddling the coast, we met a toddler on the beach at Calamujué, not far from this junction. He was three years old, with dirty, salt-stained cheeks, shredded clothes, and chestnut hair streaked golden by the sun. We first spotted him perched astride the bow of an incoming panga. His father, a fisherman, grunted a greeting at us and proceeded to unload a toothy hammerhead shark from his boat. The toddler, beaming, played with the shark on the sand. I'd heard of "dead" sharks snapping unexpectedly to life and watched with morbid fascination as the young boy's chubby fingers traced the inside of the hammerhead's mouth.

Finally the father shooed him away. The toddler turned his attentions toward the shells on the beach, which he began to sort into piles. He selected a few and showed them to us, "his favorites," chattering in a slow, simple Spanish. I was happy to meet someone who spoke at my level.

"Do you like them?" I asked.

"Oh yes."

"Do you collect them?"

"Of course."

"Do you have many?"

"Oh, yes, very many."

"Where do you keep them?"

The toddler looked at me and smiled patiently, as if I were daft, or else pulling his leg. Then he gestured broadly, his chubby arms encompassing the whole beach.

"Here," he said. "All these are mine."

We reached our coastal destination just before dusk. The town of Bahía de los Angeles, set against a bay of the same name, had a postapocalyptic, Mad Max look—blowing litter, shacks and shanties, exposed rebar, dust devils dancing on unpaved corners. Expatriates lived here too, many of them in unfinished houses that looked like concrete bunkers. A guidebook said that telephone service had arrived recently, though I never saw a phone. There was no mail service, and no way to cash a check or use a credit card. Money seemed beyond the point here, as did beauty. In town, boojum and cactus forests gave way to wilted, parsley-thin trees plastered by the wind against chain-link fences. Everything looked brown.

But Guillermo's Restaurant had pink cloth napkins. And in a town this ugly, that was enough. We ordered breakfast from a waitress who didn't seem to understand English or Spanish. I asked for a spinach omelet.

"*Espinaca?*" she asked. I said it again, in both languages. I pointed to the word in the menu. I hadn't eaten a green vegetable in days.

"Right there," I said. "It's in the menu."

"I don't think so," she said, and went to consult the cook.

Next to our table was a large glass terrarium housing a reptile the size of my arm. It lethargically nosed an old, pale piece of cabbage. On the other side of the terrarium, a large balding customer with a pinkish red pate—a gringo—noticed us studying the creature. With the casual manner of a regular, he slid back his chair and lifted the reptile out of the terrarium so that Aryeh and Tziporah could see it better.

"They call it an iguana, but it's not," he said. "It's a member of the chuckwalla family."

The American said that he'd worked as a docent in the United States and knew the Mexican family who had imprisoned this reptile. A boy and his father had taken it from Isla Angel de la Guarda, the massive desert isle far offshore, beyond the cluster of fifteen rocky islets that guards the inner bay of Bahía de Los Angeles.

"I take it out and let it run in the desert," he said, lifting the chuckwalla onto his own meaty shoulder. "Keep tellin' 'em to bring it back. I knew they'd just give it iceberg lettuce. Without the sun or vitamins or insects, it'll just die." The man seemed aggravated, but resigned, too. He could have set the chuckwalla free on his own, but he did not. And maybe that was the only kind of expatriate who lived in this small, clannish town happily—the kind who knew better than to interfere too much in the locals' lives.

I admired this man's candor and asked him about "the accident." Five men affiliated with the University of California at Davis (two Americans and three visiting Japanese researchers) had died here only six weeks earlier. One of the Americans, Gary Polis, had been a renowned scorpion expert. An obituary said that Polis considered the arachnid-rich isles off Baja "heaven on earth."

We hadn't been able to knit together the whole story in the United States, when it happened, and we knew too much about Baja to trust the news fragments we had heard. One newspaper stated that several scientists had died at Bahía de los Angeles after flipping their Zodiac boat. But this was Baja. We knew it was probably a fiberglass panga. Most of the published stories said the windstorm had taken the researchers by surprise. But that's the nature of local windstorms in Bahía de los Angeles— they whip up quickly, but with such regularity that they can't be considered "surprises" at all, only unfortunate occurrences. (Also, the cloud patterns frequently serve as predictors. Over the mountains, wispy clouds shaped like elephant trunks sometimes signal the onslaught of an *elefante,* as these local howlers are called.) But maybe something more complicated had happened. All this mattered greatly to us, because we had our own boat trip to plan, and our own risks to evaluate.

"Cheapness, that's what did it," the man told us. "Nine people in one boat. They didn't want to hire the second panga." And about those "surprise" winds, he added: "The locals had predicted them. That morning, they had warned the scientists not to go."

We would ask a dozen more people but never get a more succinct explanation. The accident seemed to be just another in a long series of mistakes and misunderstandings that seem to plague this bedeviling, enchanting place.

Americans have been coming here, sometimes to study but mainly to fish, since before Steinbeck's day. By sea, it's not an easy place to reach. The tides north of Mulegé get higher and higher the farther north one goes; the currents are stronger. The winds blow and stir—usually from the north, sometimes from the west. Cold upwellings are drawn from the gulf's deepest, darkest submarine canyons, turbocharging the food chain; thus the distinctly nontropical water despite a fair number of tropical species, and the riot of sea life—whales, fish, and what turtles remain—plying the plankton-rich channels between sun-blasted island rock.

Captain Tony Berry of the *Western Flyer* navigated these waters nervously, fighting the tides all the way. He looked forward to the day when he would turn back south. The Midriffs—as the whole island-choked region, from here to Isla Tiburón, is called—aren't the best or safest place to steer a large boat.

So when the *Western Flyer* arrived at Bahía de Los Angeles, the crew probably felt like they deserved a dose of explorer's glee. Given the chance, they might have done a little Hernán Cortés dance right there on the sand. But then they spotted some fellow gringos, and their egos deflated. Steinbeck's sulkiness mutated quickly into suspicion. He thought that the Americans, who had arrived by small plane, were engaged in something illegal. Like rum-running. Or gun-running. I think he was just aggravated that someone else foreign had gotten here first. With Ricketts, he wrote:

"The fishermen did not look like fishermen, and Mexicans and Americans were *too* interested in us until they discovered what we were doing and too uninterested after they had found out." This was said without a trace of irony. Good old Steinbeck and Ricketts. They, like me and Brian and a great many invertebratologists, were slow to realize that some people will never be interested in sponges and sea cucumbers.

Later they added: "We have little doubt that we were entirely wrong about this, but the place breathed suspicion, and no other place had been like that."

Steinbeck's suspicions were unfounded, but Bahía de los Angeles did have a strange quality to it. There was a stubbornness here—a bedrock density. A fair share of the populace seemed dim, like the waitress; or slow to learn, like the chuckwalla captors and every tourist or researcher who heads into a windstorm despite precautions. Bright, friendly people lived here, too. A good many of them volunteered at the local one-room museum or at a sea-turtle conservation facility. But these capable people seemed like renegades.

Maybe it was unfair to categorize the people at all, when the environment was the source of the town's balefulness. But one could be forgiven for confusing the two. Once, when Brian and I came here to paddle, we were forced to hole up in the Casa Díaz motel, waiting for the weather to settle. Every night, blasts of wind shook the windows. Unable to sleep, we threw open the windows. Airborne sand and dirt showered us, turning our floor into a small Sahara. We waited for three days, sleeping in sandy motel sheets, and watching the cockroaches climb the ancient, heavily soiled curtains as westerlies screamed through town. Finally, frustrated, I asked one of the Díaz men when this damn wind was going to go away. "Go away?" he snorted. "That wind *lives* here." He said this with a hint of resentment, as if I had insulted a member of his own family.

Baja is a transient place that preserves little of its recent history. But Bahía de los Angeles is different. The Díaz clan still runs the show here. And in many ways, the town still seems like the rustic, World War II–era, fly-in fishing hub that Antero Díaz made it, if a little worse for modern wear.

Señor Díaz brought his family here in 1934 or 1935. He was a self-made man from the mainland who spent his early teen years working in the mines. The young Díaz carried ore in a sack held on his back by a wide band that crossed his forehead. Years later, after he'd pulled himself up by his *guarache* straps, Antero Díaz invited American sportfishermen, his customers, to touch the indented ridge in his skull left by the tight band at an age when the bone was still growing.

"*Muy duro,*" Díaz said about his early life. "Very hard." Steinbeck would have loved that. If the author hadn't been so damned suspicious and determined to stay aboard his boat, he might have tipped some tequila with Antero (who was already settled in Bahía de los Angeles when the *Western Flyer* arrived) and spun an entire novella from Díaz's rag-to-riches story. It was Steinbeck's loss. And ours.

For Antero Díaz, Bahía de los Angeles was not sun- and sand-blasted purgatory, it was the lush life. In Baja, he became Señor Díaz, a patriarch and a boss. He built an empire in the desert: a motel, grocery store, restaurant, and gas station; everything that visiting game-fishermen needed.

John Hilton, who captured that time period in a memoir, *Hardly Any Fences*, recalled this story from Cruz Díaz, Antero's wife:

"When little Chubasco [their son Antero, Jr.; nicknamed, appropriately, for a windstorm] was born four years ago, he came at a very embarrassing time for Mr. Díaz. 'We had thirty fishermans eating at the Casa Díaz that week,' she told me. 'I was working in the kitchen making a new pot of beans when the pains came. I told Mr. Díaz to finish the beans and call a woman to help me. Then I went into the bedroom and had Chubasco while the thirty Americanos were eating dinner. When Mr. Díaz came out and told everyone it was a boy, I could hear everybody cheer and drink lemonade toast to the new baby and the mother. I no make noise when it happen, just bite my lip hard because I not want to upset the customers' supper.'"

Talk about catering stoically to Americans' desires. In return, the visiting fishermen respected Díaz and his wife to a fault. When Antero claimed that he could predict the weather or when the next plane would arrive according to the way a certain sleeping dog's legs sprawled, they believed him.

Antero proved less omniscient about the environment. His sons and neighbors were no wiser. In their time, many local marine species were decimated, including the sea turtles that once thrived here. In the 1950s and '60s, local fishermen caught ten times more turtles in Bahía de los Angeles than anywhere else on the peninsula. The peak came in 1962, when 185 tons of turtle meat were harvested. By 1972, the population had crashed. Now, all five species present in Baja—green, hawksbill, loggerhead, leatherback, and western ridley—are listed as endangered.

For the most part, Mexico protects its sea turtles now. Japan, one of the primary markets for eggs, meat, leather, and tortoiseshell, banned importation of turtle products in 1991. Occasionally, Bajacalifornios still boil up turtle soup on the sly. It's a hard habit to kick. The *Western Flyer's* crew prepared a sea turtle the wrong way and ended up with an "evil-smelling mess" that they threw overboard. Prepared correctly, sea turtle is reputed to be savory.

But not all fishermen sneak turtles home. Some carefully extract turtles from their gill nets and deliver them to a local researcher, Antonio Resendiz, who tags and nurtures them in large beachfront tanks and ultimately lets them go. Resendiz's conservation and research station, Programa Tortuga Marina, is located on the beach north of town. Resendiz is world-famous for his turtle-tagging and tracking studies. A loggerhead he marked and released was found, a year later, in Japan—not as a purse or eyeglass rims, but alive and kicking, having migrated across the Pacific.

Just an hour's boat ride south in San Francisquito, fishermen repeated the sea-turtle mistake when they started harvesting sharks for export, in 1985. They started small: one family, three pangas, a four-month season. They sold the shark fins—an Asian delicacy—and dried meat. The next year the fleet grew to seven pangas. Fishermen from La Paz came to help. By the early 1990s, this was no small-scale fishery. Two shrimping vessels from Guaymas were used to haul the fresh shark to the mainland for processing. Dolphins and seals were killed for bait. According to Seawatch, the organization that chronicled the birth and death of this short-term and shortsighted industry, seal carcasses washed onto beaches forty miles away at the slaughter's peak. In a decade, two hundred thousand sharks were killed. The bay ran red with blood. It became, according to a Seawatch report, "almost uninhabitable from the smell and the millions of flies the pollution attracted."

The local industry's last year, 1994, coincided with a boom in shark fishing worldwide. All over the Pacific, northwestern Atlantic, and Indian Oceans, fishermen were rushing to develop this "underutilized" fishery—a "savior fishery" in management parlance, meaning sharks and other cartilaginous fishes might substitute for other fisheries that had already been depleted. Everyone was doing it. Then, in San Francisquito as in some other small villages around the world, the fishery collapsed. Sharks live a long time and reproduce only slowly. The fact that San Francisquito fishermen were able to pull thousands from the water only proves how unbelievably fertile the Midriffs are.

I read about this tragedy recently, with horror and an appropriate degree of mild skepticism. ("Bays running red" always does that to me, as does the mention of cute dolphins and seals as bait.) Then I remembered a kayaking trip Brian and I made in this region in the summer of 1992. We'd seen one seal carcass washed onto a beach, and paddling around a point we'd surprised some men gathered around another seal carcass. The men had turned their backs to us, to hide the thing they were dragging. At the time, we didn't understand what they could be doing.

I knew what the *Log*'s authors would have said: "Good men doing a bad thing." I judged them to be Steinbeck's words.

Ricketts, less judgmental, would have said not "good," not "bad," but simply: "Men."

SEA OF SPIRITS

Antero Díaz had passed on to that great gill net in the sky, but on our Bahía de los Angeles visit, his earthly empire still stood: motel rooms around a stone courtyard with a small church off to one side, and a grocery store stocked with overpriced instant foods. I procured our room key, towels, and toilet paper from one of his grown sons.

Most of the Mexicans we met on this trip were so recently planted here that it made no sense to ask them about the long-ago days of the mid-twentieth century. But in Bahía de los Angeles, a town of small-engine planes and Spam, 1940 didn't seem so remote.

I asked Antero's son, "Have you ever heard about an American writer—*muy famoso*—visiting here, in 1940? *Se llama* John Steinbeck."

"No."

My quickest interview ever.

"Well, do you have some Ramen noodles, then?"

"Over here."

One Díaz led to another, and the next morning I rapped on Alfredo's screen door. Alfredo was Antero's son, brother of both the motel owner who had handed me my key and the restaurant owner who had overseen our breakfast. Alfredo didn't remember anyone named John Steinbeck either, but that's not why I was bothering him. I asked him to arrange a one-way panga charter for us. Brian, the children, and I had already spent a morning tidepooling along the town shoreline, and wanted to go farther now, south toward San Francisquito. We planned to paddle back, over three or four days, stopping at good tidepooling spots along the way.

"You heard about the accident," he said. It was more of an antiliability statement than an offer of candid information.

"Yes, the wind. *Muy fuerte*. But don't worry. When it's windy, we stay on the beach."

We talked about the weather a while. Unlike his father, he refused to offer any firm predictions, dog or no dog. But he did hazard some guesses. Tomorrow was supposed to be a good day. After that, who knows. He told us he'd pick us up on the beach in front of our motel room at 8:00 A.M.

Alfredo was only a little late, but I'd been up since dawn, nervously studying the sky and repacking our clothes and books and food into waterproof dry-sacks. A breeze blew my sink-washed bra off the porch railing, where it had been drying, and this faintest hint of wind almost made me vomit. Early mornings and pretrip anxiety always curdle my stomach. We'd kayaked here before, but never with young children, and never within weeks of human fatalities. I couldn't wait to be on the water, with no options for turning back.

An hour later, Alfredo dropped us at a remote sandy beach spilling out of a fold in the rust-colored mountains. It was called Ensenada Alacrán, Scorpion Inlet. Aryeh was tickled by the name. He said it again and again, rolling his r's: "Alacrrrrrán, alacrrrrrán."

I quizzed Alfredo on the names of local landmarks as we unloaded our gear from his boat. Many of them were curious. To the north of us lay Punta Quemado, Burnt Point. Changing a single letter, one of my less reliable maps reported this place as Punta Que Malo—roughly, Really Bad Point.

To the south, farther than we intended to paddle, was a point called Las Ánimas—The Souls, or The Spirits.

"They found human skulls there," Alfredo said. "Many of them."

When our bags were all above the high-tide line, Alfredo looked at us and our children. He squinted up the beach. "When are you coming back?"

On paddling trips, this was always hard to answer. If you run into trouble, you want someone to know you are missing before you run out of water and food. But you don't want people worrying too soon. Kayakers too often risk bad weather out of embarrassment that they might keep someone waiting or out of undue obedience to an itinerary. Inevitably that's when tragedy strikes. Even before the scientists went down in their panga, an American teen paddler had died in Bahía de los Angeles. Many years earlier, several Outward Bound Students had died kayaking between Mulegé and Loreto. Compared to any other sport or transportation method, the accident rate wasn't alarming, but the causes were worth noting. Every Baja kayaking fatality I knew of involved kayakers paddling when they should have stayed beached.

"We have enough food and water for seven days," I told Alfredo, paying him nearly all our remaining cash. "Don't worry about us until then."

He nodded and stepped back into his panga. I was grateful for his concern. We'd chartered panga rides before and no one had ever asked us where we were heading or when we'd return.

"If you need help, there's a fisherman," he added, and gestured up the coast. "He has a radio."

"Bueno, bueno. Gracias. Está bien."

"And watch out for the *víboras*. Don't let the kids play there," he said, gesturing to the scrubby desert that sprawled just above the high-tide line.

"Víboras?" Aryeh asked a few minutes later. He knew *serpiente* and *cobra,* but not this latest word for poisonous snake.

Alfredo gazed inland and scowled. An involuntary shiver shook his head and shoulders. Then he turned his panga around and roared away.

Brian spent several hours assembling our kayak, which hadn't seen water since La Paz. It was a long, slow process: laying out a skeleton of aluminum tubes, fitting them together following the assembly crib sheets, stretching the rubbery skin onto the frame, adding seat backs and arranging foot pedals. For the kids, it was too sunny to be outside. So I kept them in our tent, where it was darker—albeit a good twenty or thirty degrees hotter. Eventually they realized escape was futile and we were all able to take a siesta.

Circus sounds invaded our dreams: the relentless *awrooo, awrooo* of perhaps fifty or more barking sea lions. The racket was incessant. The seals seemed no more than ten or fifteen feet away. It was a strange and mind-bending auditory illusion. From our tent, we couldn't see them at all.

Late in the day, we left most of our gear on shore and paddled east from Ensenada Alacrán. Shadows crept down the inlet's bluffs. The water was cold and black. Low waves rolled toward us, even and oily smooth. The kayak lifted soundlessly up and over each wave. After one and a half miles of steady paddling, we came to an exposed rock reef in the center of the inlet.

This was the source of the din, and up close it was deafening. The boulders were covered with black and mocha bodies—impressive piles of fat, with wrinkled necks and noses tipped toward the sky. The largest bulls burped, growled, and coughed almost continuously. From one side of the reef to the other, sea lions stretched and pushed and complained. They reminded me of kids trying to share a bed. The youngest sea lions, pushed off the end, splashed into the water and cruised around the reef.

These sea lions seemed less "playful" than the ones at Los Islotes. No doubt they'd seen fewer humans. We stayed at least eighty feet offshore, back-paddling any time a juvenile entered the water. Occasionally a bowling-ball head would part the water, fix on us, then sink down again, swallowed by the black water. Our kayak felt tippier than usual despite the sea's smoothness. For once, Aryeh was a little nervous to be in it. But I think we all perceived our own unsteadiness in contrast to the sea lions' innate grace. Or maybe it was the water's opaque darkness. Every approaching wave, no matter how gentle and rounded, suggested the shape of some living creature scurrying under a black satin sheet.

We pulled ashore that evening, hungry and tired, at Ensenada Alacrán. Halfway to our tent, we spotted a few white flecks and Styrofoam bits on the sand. Our eyes adjusted to the darkening beach. Smiles fading, we noticed that garbage was strewn all the way to our tent.

What was this? Brian and I took a few more steps; the children ran ahead. When the realization struck, it struck hard.

"Dumb, dumb, dumb!" I cursed, pounding my forehead with the heel of my palm.

An animal had pecked or gnawed through several thick plastic dry-sack layers and gotten into our food bags. The Styrofoam bits were all that was left of several Ramen instant-noodle cups. The white flecks were scattered rice. Popcorn kernels were mixed into the sand. Pasta had been dragged across our campsite. Other small food packages had disappeared altogether, leaving a trail of plastic-baggie shreds. Even Tziporah's diaper supply had been violated. As we studied these relics, a raven danced and squawked—laughed, it seemed—at the far end of the beach. To be outdone by a more notorious and charismatic Baja animal, such as a mountain lion or hammerhead shark, would be one thing. But no. A black bird had bested us.

"Our food!" Ayreh yelled.

"Only some," I rushed to reassure him.

But the damage was, in fact, worse than that. The raven, with or without the assistance of corvoid friends, had also poked into two of our six double-layered water bags. Once the shape of overstuffed throw pillows, these comforting three-gallon bags were now limp squares, maybe a quarter-full. The sand underneath them was damp, but quickly drying.

"This," I whispered to Brian, "is a little more serious."

There was only one thing to do: plan to paddle a little faster. We still had enough water for five thirsty paddling days, if not a safe and comfortable seven.

Make that four paddling days. The next morning, just as we were planning to break camp, a wind kicked in. It wasn't an *elefante,* but it was brisk enough to make kayaking impossible. The inlet's surface glittered navy and gray and finally white, a confusion of small whitecaps.

It was a typical late-spring wind day: too breezy to paddle, but too sunny and hot to spend outside the tent except in half-hour spurts. Inside the tent, we drank warm water and nibbled our snacks. We read books, and ventured out now and again to stretch and pee and poke along the shore. But we quickly returned to shelter. Even with hats and sun lotion, we were all badly burnt. The entire white-hot beach was a reflector.

Every time we returned to the tent, we tracked a little more sand inside. We soon grew sick and tired of the feeling of coarse grains stuck to sweaty thighs. The tent grew smaller by the hour. The kids got crazy and we yelled at them. Aryeh flailed around and accidentally kicked Tziporah in the jaw. Without thinking, I spanked him—one terrible slap, just to make him stop thrashing—and felt guilty about it for three hours. Finally, when the midday sun had passed its evil zenith, Brian and I shouted, "Out! Out! Out!" and we all headed down to the waterline to tidepool.

The water washed it all away: the bad feelings, the hot crankiness, the coarse grains on our sweaty body parts. It was shockingly cold—again, so different from the tepid water at Pulmo. If the water from Mulegé south felt like a seductive tropical caress, this northern gulf water felt like a baptism. Wading into it, you couldn't help but gasp and sputter and maybe question just a little if you really wanted to see God's face. But wading out, you felt reborn.

The tide had fallen and kept falling. For once we were in no rush. No Doug. No *Zuiva*. No tour guide. No fellow tourists. No panga lifting anchor. We scoured the coastline from one side of the bay to the other, lifting rocks, sifting through seaweed garlands, poking into crevices, following the sea as it retreated. We shared our discoveries. We snapped photos. Then we doubled back and tidepooled again, seeing a whole new zone revealed by the still-ebbing tide.

Tziporah found brittlestars—the skinny, active sea stars that look like five thrashing millipedes joined by a black button. Aryeh found pale, translucent shrimp. Both these invertebrates displayed a high and disturbing degree of autotomy—which is to say, they started committing harakiri as soon as we lifted them from the water. The brittlestar humped up one leg until there was a barely audible snap and the leg broke off, revealing white goo inside. "Hold it carefully. Carefully!" we cautioned. But even cradled gingerly on Tziporah's still palm, the brittlestar would not settle. It flicked another leg up and broke it off with a forceful matchstick snap. The two separated legs continued to thrash, independent of the central body. This seemed to bother us more than it. "Put it down!" we yelped to Tziporah. Lips parted with incredulity, she let the alien thing slide off her hand and back into the water.

A few minutes later, Aryeh's shrimp got the same sacrificial notions. As soon as he lifted it to show us, it dropped a pincer. "Don't!" I called out, uselessly, to the shrimp. And then to Aryeh, because this creature had only two front limbs, not five: "Quickly—put it back."

Autotomy is a defensive reaction—a sacrifice of a leg or pincer or two, which will regenerate, in hopes of saving the whole organism. It's common among sea stars, crabs, and shrimp. While collecting, Steinbeck and Ricketts learned to drop those organisms quickly into fresh water, to kill them before they curled up into hopeless balls or "went all to pieces." But we'd never seen autotomy like this. Why it should be more developed on this beach than others, we did not know. If this had been a surfy area, it might have made sense, since autotomy is often seen in animals living where breaking water traps them behind or under rocks. The self-severing process sets them free. This bay, despite the wind, was fairly calm. All science aside, this self-injuring trait matched the spirit of the area. Everything about Bahía de los Angeles and the Midriffs region seemed more elemental and extreme.

We tidepooled into the evening. I had time, for once, to study each animal—to really look—even before I knew any species' given name. I found two different chitons: one I knew and one I did not. A chiton has a flattened, oval body, about the size of a thumb. It is covered by eight armadillo-like plates. These symmetrical plates can be gray or tortoiseshell brown or opalescent. They'd make beautiful broaches, except for the fact that they, like nearly all marine animals, look most stunning wet and alive. Underneath the chiton, a snail-like foot and surrounding girdle anchor the creature to its rock. They're hard to dislodge, but if you do pry one free, it will curl into a ball, like a pill bug. Clamped in place, the chiton appears to be inert. But if you watch long enough, you'll see that the armored oval is in fact moving, mowing thin trails of edible algae off the rock.

The chiton I didn't recognize had fuzzy horizontal stripes over the armored plates—like the stitches on a pigskin. I dubbed this little mollusk the football chiton, never mind what the books called it. We were delayed by the weather, on a desert beach, with not enough water, so who the hell cared about Latin? Not that we were worried. Strangely, we were not.

My own name for the chiton might never help another tidepooler verify this species, but at Ensenada Alacrán, the outside world did not seem to exist. Next week did not exist. I was naming for myself. Just to see the thing more clearly. Just to remember.

What did Lao Tsu say? "Give up learning, and put an end to your troubles." Abandoning formal names, I felt like I wasn't learning so much as being: enjoying the chitons the way one might enjoy a well-arranged vase of flowers.

I felt the same way about the bay's limpets. We found many live ones, but these hardly compared to the thousands of dead limpet shells washed high on the beach. The most common shell was pink and mound-shaped, rising to a pearly point. No two were identical. Some of the mounds were rounder than others, and some were perkier, and the points were variously pale or flesh-colored. "Nipple limpets," I said to Brian and

Aryeh and Tziporah. Aryeh giggled. Brian shot me a worried glance, on the lookout for signs of sunstroke.

I loved my football chitons. And I loved my nipple limpets. And when the sun set and we were finally able to remove our hats and bring our camping chairs out onto the sand, I loved this beach. The wind died and the water calmed. We cooked dinner and let the kids run free, up and down the shore. Just surviving the day had seemed like a marvelous thing. The air-cooled water we drank at dusk with our dinner tasted exquisite.

The same northern gulf sun that had stewed our brains all day had beat down upon the heads of Steinbeck and Ricketts, inspiring them to marvel quietly and reverently about the region's harsh qualities. They observed, "As we ascended the Gulf it became more sparsely inhabited; there were fewer of the little heat-struck *rancherías,* fewer canoes of fishing Indians. Above Santa Rosalía very few trading boats travel. One would really be cut off up here." They continued, "Food is hard to get, and a man lives inward, closely related to time; a cousin of the sun, at feud with storm and sickness."

This adversity was, paradoxically, a calming thing. It reduced the world to essentials. It burned and cleaned and cured and pared away.

A little later, en route to San Francisquito—perhaps thirty miles south of the beach where we now camped—Steinbeck and Ricketts added, "One thing had impressed us deeply on this little voyage: the great world had dropped away very quickly. We lost the fear and fierceness and contagion of war and economic uncertainty. The matters of great importance we had left were not important. There must be an infective quality in these things. We had lost the virus, or it had been eaten by the anti-bodies of quiet. Our pace had slowed greatly; the hundred thousand small reactions of our daily world were reduced to very few."

Between Ensenada Alacrán and Bahía de los Angeles, a hand-shaped headland reached out into the water. We spent the next day tracing the shoreline, paddling in and around each stubby finger as we made our way north. In the *Zuiva,* we'd had to stay far offshore, separate from the world we most wished to know. But in a kayak we could travel in a few feet of water and land any time we pleased. Sea stars glowed on the sandy sea bottom underneath our bow. Crumbling bluffs loomed up alongside us, stippled with fossilized scallop shells from days long ago, when the sea reached higher and farther. A sea lion conducted espionage on us, surfacing silently here and there to track our position before vanishing into submarine depths. Pelicans eyed us from nearshore rocks as we passed.

We stopped for a midafternoon break. While Tziporah and Aryeh investigated cakes of white salt dried onto rocks ("This is where salt comes from? Really? You can eat it?"), Brian and I took turns summoning the courage to swim. The water in this cove was even colder than it had been at Alacrán, if that was possible. It looked different, too: deep green and milky. Summer upwelling was in full swing. Brian snorkeled for a few minutes and came back gasping, his face tightened with pain. "Really cold," he sputtered. "But there's clouds of life in there—plankton or something."

I tried to snorkel next, but couldn't last even as long as he had. The cold water bore so deeply into my bones it made me feel panicky, unable to inhale smoothly through the snorkel. The sound of my own hyperventilating pulsed in my ears. Ahead, in the dark green water, I saw the edge of a blizzard—white-flecked life riding an icy current. But then I had to surface, turn, and race back to shore. Coming ashore, I had to pour seawater over a sizzling ledge of rock until it was cool enough to lie down on. I sprawled in the sun until my body temperature climbed back to normal.

That night we camped on the perfect tidepooling beach—sand up high, a field of cobblestones down low, bluffs to either side. We found fleshy sun stars, hundreds of sulfur sea cucumbers, a sand dollar, and a heart urchin. Aryeh caught and identified a mole crab that we'd never seen. Not far away, two oystercatcher birds paced the cobbles, injecting their papaya-colored beaks between the rocks in search of their own tidepool dinners.

Before dark, Brian took Aryeh paddle-fishing from the kayak. I started a pot of rice boiling for Polynesian Spam, then headed down the shore to tidepool again with Tziporah. At one point I put on a snorkeling mask and set my face atop rippling water only two inches deep. It was hard to focus, but the effect was like looking through a microscope. Below me, a colony of baby sea anemones no bigger than a pinkie-nail flailed their translucent pink tentacles against a gently falling tide that must have seemed, to them, like a tempest. Living, speck-sized debris swirled around the anemones' tiny stinging tentacles. Whirlpools the size of pencil erasers formed and dissipated in front of my eyes. The shift in perspective was dizzying. For

Brian, Aryeh, Tziporah, and me this vesper hour was tranquil. Paradisiacal. But for the tidepool creatures, storm and struggle never ceased.

I watched the tide fall, grateful I had no sailboat or motel room to return to. Hurrying at previous stations, we had focused mainly on the tide's retreating edge. But now, traveling by kayak and camping on the shore, with more time to study the beach at all stages during the tidal cycle, we saw the tidepools in three dimensions.

"Species are only commas in a sentence," the *Log*'s authors wrote. It was one thing to believe that, another to see it, another to know it, and a whole thing yet again to feel it. The tidepool in front of me now, at sunset, was a whole sentence. Maybe more than that: A poem. An essay. The great cosmic novel. I still couldn't read it, but I knew it could be read.

The next day was even hotter. We couldn't sit bare-legged on any of the cobble niches where we took our midday paddling breaks. We spread bags and clothing on which to briefly perch, but our lungs still protested the saunalike air. It was too stifling to stay anywhere for long.

At a hidden cove called Puerto Don Juan, we landed for lunch. Extracting dry-sacks and bottles from the bowels of our boat, we added water to some dehydrated hummus. I mixed the paste while Brian dug into our food bags for some extra camping spoons. We arranged the children on their bag-covered cobbles and handed them bowls and crackers. I reached for the metal spoons, which had been set, just a few minutes earlier, on a boulder. I yowled. Left in the sun, the spoons had become too hot to handle.

We had considered camping at Puerto Don Juan, but decided to press on. Dusk, that delicious hour that made all the day's heat and effort worthwhile, seemed an eternity away. It was better to be on—or in—the water.

Steinbeck and Ricketts had started the Cortez part of their trip on March 18. They left the gulf on April 13. We had arrived on the shores of the Cortez on April 1. Today was Sunday, May 14, and we still had nearly two weeks of our trip to go. In other words, we had started later, and traveled many more days, and we found ourselves now a month deeper into the hot season than Steinbeck and Ricketts had experienced. I thought of Ricketts's nightmares about fire, and his daydreams about the cool, life-filled sea, and marveled again that here, both the fear and the fantasy come together, mingling on that intertidal edge where desert and ocean overlap.

And I thought again about heat as a curative force. Our trip was both longer and steamier than the *Western Flyer*'s had been. Maybe we needed that extra dose of fever. Perhaps it would burn away the remaining virus—the contagion of worldly worries—that Steinbeck and Ricketts had described. Perhaps it would even burn away the immodest strivings that still lurked in our hearts. Brian and I still thought that—just maybe—we would figure this sea out.

"The habitat's still here," Brian thought out loud as we paddled. "That's the difference. Even if they've removed top predators, even if they've overfished, the tidepools are still rich. The water is still rich."

We paddled around burnt outcroppings, over and around rocks. The sun blazed: Huitzilopochtli, the Aztec god of war, shook his fist with pleasure against the memories of Spanish conquest.

Whether Brian and I sang to the children or talked or soaked up the silence, our arms never stopped moving—a steady rhythm, muscling our way through hot, still air. The calm water became increasingly opaque, almost sticky. Grebes paddle-kicked across this tacky surface. Their triangle-shaped heads looked like dark sails—the cut-out props of a child's theater production—moving across a cardboard-calm sea.

In places, a greasy coat of guano coated the water, like skin atop warmed milk. The slightest breeze would have churned the seabird excrement into the blue-green depths, but there was no breeze. It was stinky stuff, part of the great web that makes the Cortez so fertile. Guano from islets and rocky outcroppings rains down onto the sea—food for plankton, which is food for fish and crustaceans, which is food for larger fish, and so on, and so on.

"My hands are getting numb. I'm falling asleep paddling," I said to Brian, mesmerized by the repetitive motions, and thoughts, of a long day on still water. "I don't know how much farther I can go."

"Should we stop for the night?"

I looked down at Tziporah, asleep in my lap, and at Aryeh, contentedly sprawled in the middle cockpit seat, his eyes glazed, a hair away from closing. "No. As long as they're not complaining, let's get as far as we can. Tomorrow could be windy."

To the west, five miles away across open water, was the town of Bahía de los Angeles, but we'd never risked such long crossings with children aboard. We hugged the land closer, dipping south to follow the southern shore of the bay of the same name, looking for a place to make camp. We'd already paddled eight miles.

Ahead of us, in the far distance, small waterspouts rose from the bay's surface. They looked like splash-plumes sent up by dive-bombing pelicans. But it was hard to tell in this land of mirage. We set a diagonal course, cutting off the southeast corner of this large bay, and paddled toward the spouts. One mile, then two. The spouts grew larger. We could see spray hanging in the air after each splash, but we could not see the birds themselves. Calm conditions prevailed, and the water became not only greasy, but clotted. A different kind of scum, more frothy-looking—some natural bloom or residue, we guessed—covered the water in patches.

Another half-mile. Now we neared the center of this large bay, a bay we hadn't even planned to cross. Another spout, but this time we could hear it: it wasn't just water moving, it was air, too. A deep, steamy bellow.

A gray hump split the surface. My jaw dropped. "Aryeh," I whispered hoarsely. Then louder, "Aryeh! Whales!" He peeled one eye open. Tziporah didn't stir. Brian and I paddled harder, lured by the hopes of getting at least one good, clear look.

Ahead of us, a speckled gray tail slapped the water. Off to our right, a rounded back emerged—a temporary island—and vanished just as quickly. Behind us, the huffing sound of breath again. Ahead and to our left, now, a barnacle-covered head with downturned mouth.

"We're surrounded!" I called out, giddy.

"Is that okay?" Aryeh asked, shaking off his sleepiness.

"I think so, as long as they know where we are." I rapped three times on the kayak's gunwale.

When the huffing breath behind us seemed too close, we paddled harder. The whale ahead and its partner to the side disappeared, then reappeared several thousand feet away. This bay was shallow, and the whales seemed to be rolling around, unperturbed. More scum on the water. Were they exhaling it? Feeding on it? Scraping their mouths against the sea bottom? Eliminating their bowels after a feeding frenzy? Were they gray whales (our best guess) or another species? Lots of ideas. No conclusions.

All this time, we might have been paddling through whale food, spit, or poop. It didn't matter. The magnificent beasts continued to surface and sigh around us, sending up little clouds of moist air. A breeze had begun to stir, dissipating the blowhole spray more quickly, but we hardly noticed it, because we were zigzagging among whales—away, then closer, then away again.

Sometime that hour the breezes began to gust harder and faster, until they had mutated into a rowdy westerly wind. At last, a respite from the sauna! But the timing couldn't have been worse. We were forced to finish our bay crossing against powerful gusts. Our biceps felt like lead. We'd overpaddled, lured by sirens, and had kept crossing open water when we should have hugged the shore. For an hour more, we paid for our indiscretion—heads down, shoulders screaming, counting off paddle strokes in sets of fifty.

"Shouldn't have done it," I mumbled to myself, truly worried now about our distance from the shore and the caustic exhaustion dribbling into my back and arms. A surreal set of images reeled through my mind, a sunstroke-induced slide show that flashed by in seconds: giant chuckwallas, soup turtles, thirsty ravens, bloody water, empty pangas, drowned bodies, nipple limpets, whale-breath, whale-breath, whale-breath . . .

Tziporah woke. "Almost there," I said. Her only response—an anxious *thuck-thuck-thuck,* the sound of a well-worked pacifier. When at last we reached the bay's far shore it was hard even to stand. We lifted the children from the kayak, grunting with pain. On a five-mile day, we'd accidentally paddled thirteen miles.

The place we'd landed was perfect: a gorgeous sandy beach, fronted by black rocks and backed by dunes. The town of Bahía de los Angeles was only two miles up the shore. Even in bad weather, we'd make town the next day before lunch. No worries about freshwater now, though the wind would get its chance to razz us. Where the water had been greasy calm, whitecaps started to build. The wind howled. Temperatures had dropped from one-hundred-plus to a steamy ninety or so.

"That was risky," I said to Brian as we lifted the kayak past the intertidal boulders. "We shouldn't have tried crossing."

"It was great," Brian said.

"It *was* great. And that's how people die here."

All evening there was a little symphony outside our tent door: a bass roar of wind, the high tinkle of a rising tide edging up the rocks, and the percussive exhalations of the whales. The next morning, we could still see them in the center of the bay, rolling and huffing. At breakfast, just for fun, Aryeh and I timed the whales' breaths: about three per minute. And our own: about twenty per minute. But it was a hard thing to do. Our observation of the phenomenon changed it. Just concentrating on breathing for the sake of measurement, we began to inhale deeper and more rapidly, and the easiest of all human actions began to seem labored.

It occurred to me that much about our trip had become labored, too. The harder we tried to know, the harder the knowing became, except perhaps for a short while at Ensenada Alacrán, when I had temporarily renounced scientific naming. But the most self-conscious and frustrating aspect of our quest was not simply naming. It was judging.

We had begun our trip simply wanting to see and know some small and rather strange invertebrates. But the more we traveled, the more we began to think as environmentalists instead of as naturalists, and as epidemiologists instead of as adventurers. Sometime in the last few weeks, our simple fascination for tidal life had turned into a missionary zeal for diagnosing the gulf's health and predicting its prospects. The gulf's future had never been Steinbeck's and Ricketts's concern—they'd known their hands were full simply trying to understand the gulf's present.

But we couldn't help it. We wanted to know whether the sea was truly "ruined," whether Pepe Murrieta and Benito Bermudez had any chance of stewarding their local resources, why terrible things had happened in the gulf, and whether the same mistakes that had been made (the slaughter of turtles and sharks, and even the self-destructive habits of researchers and travel writers) would keep happening again and again. Perhaps we even saw a role for ourselves in helping set things right. Steinbeck had been an activist and a reformer when it suited him. Even Ricketts had spoken up about Monterey's overharvested sardine fishery, accurately predicting its collapse. When an issue hit close to home, both men shed the cloak of philosophical detachment and decided, quite quickly, how they felt and what should be done. When it came to Okies or sardines, they kept Lao Tsu in the closet.

And yet, we sniffed around the few conclusions *we* had indulged, and even to us, these judgments smelled fishy. Part of the problem was our limited time and knowledge—it was impossible to know the gulf intimately in two months, or even in ten years. But part of the problem was the nature of judgment itself. It was one thing to know true from false, another to know good from bad. Steinbeck's preacher Casy said, in *The Grapes of Wrath*, "There ain't no sin and there ain't no virtue. There's just stuff people do."

The twelfth-century Jewish scholar Moses Maimonides put it another way. Before Adam ate the apple, Maimonides wrote, he possessed intellect. He was guided by reason and reflection. He was innocent, but he was also wise. He could distinguish between necessary objective truths. In other words, before the fall from grace, Adam was a scientist.

After the fall, Maimonides wrote, Adam suddenly knew right from wrong—"apparent truths," Maimonides called them, instead of "necessary" ones. This was not a flowering of the intellect, but a wilting of it. Adam became a lesser being: instead of a scientist, a moralist. He began to worry and preach about overfishing and litter, about chuckwallas in cages, about wearing life jackets and respecting the weather.

In one sense, his blinders had been removed. But in another sense, this new faculty blinded him even more. He could no longer see life's pure, simple truths—the beauty of a sea cucumber, say. And he rushed to cover himself, feeling shame.

Ricketts had his Easter Sunday sermon, all twenty-four pages of it in the *Log,* and that was ours, a good bit shorter.

Adam never found his way back into the garden, and we wouldn't either. Casy said there wasn't sin, but Steinbeck knew how to point a finger or pick a fight when he had to. The same went for Ed, whether he was standing up for sardines, dogs, or men. A pillar of peace and introspection, he once witnessed a policeman pistol-whipping a drunk, and set upon the cop with his own bare hands. Even Ricketts couldn't always be Ricketts. That thought made us feel a little better.

PART THREE

A
Terrible
Thirst

THE DELTA

The *Log* is conspicuously silent about the Sea of Cortez north of the Midriffs. Steinbeck and Ricketts took a hard right at Bahía de los Angeles, heading across the gulf to Isla Angel de la Guarda and then Isla Tiburón, and missing the entire northern Cortez (about a quarter of the gulf's length) in the process. Regardless of the *Western Flyer's* abbreviated route, we couldn't imagine understanding the gulf without seeing its sandy northern stretches and freshwater source. Our lack of a boat, troublesome at times, was now a boon. By road, with no worry about thirty-five-foot-high northern gulf tides, Brian and I could choose to see hundreds of miles that Steinbeck and Ricketts missed.

For a guide, we turned to Aldo Leopold, the nature writer who was Steinbeck's contemporary. Brian had introduced me to *A Sand County Almanac* years after we first paddled the Sea of Cortez. The landscape Leopold described—green lagoons, mesquite jungles, wild melon-covered mudflats—was so unfamiliar to me that I filed those descriptions in some other part of my brain, away from the "Cortez files."

"It's Baja," Brian said, pushing the book under my nose.

"No," I countered, fixed on the black-and-white illustration of a jaguar, and a paragraph opposite, which listed "avocets, willet, and yellow-legs; . . . mallards, widgeons, and teal." This was no place I recognized.

Leopold wrote about a canoeing and hunting trip he made with his brother to the gulf's northernmost reaches—a trip he would make once, and never repeat, because as he cautioned, "To return not only spoils a trip, but tarnishes a memory." That philosophy saved Leopold a lot of heartache. If he had returned, he would have found an unrecognizably thirsty country: an orphan, cut off from its great mother river.

But in 1922, the land was still green, wet, and loud with birds:

"Dawn on the Delta was whistled in by the Gambel quail, which roosted in the mesquites overhanging camp. When the sun peeped over the Sierra Madre, it slanted across a hundred miles of lovely desolation, a vast flat bowl of wilderness rimmed by jagged peaks. On the map the Delta was bisected by the river, but in fact the river was nowhere and everywhere, for he could not decide which of a hundred green lagoons offered the most pleasant and least speedy path to the Gulf. So he traveled them all, and so did we. He divided and rejoined, he twisted and turned, he meandered in awesome jungles, he all but ran in circles, he dallied with lovely groves, he got lost and was glad of it, and so were we. For the last word in procrastination, go travel with a river reluctant to lose his freedom in the sea."

That last sentence seems prophetic now, albeit with a twist. The meandering river that resisted surrender to the sea ultimately lost its sovereignty many miles north. Engineers' first attempts to harness the Colorado failed catastrophically, when floods sent the river rushing down a canal without a headgate, turning the Salton Sink—a remnant of the Sea of Cortez—into today's Salton Sea. But men, no less persistent than barnacles, tried again.

In 1936, fourteen years after Leopold's visit and four years before the *Western Flyer's* Baja cruise, the river was finally tamed, held back by Hoover Dam, a concrete wall 726 feet high. The Colorado River from the dam south to the gulf became a three-hundred-mile irrigation ditch. Mexico has treaty rights to a dribble-share of U.S. Water, but this too is dammed and channeled. The last of the Colorado's current is diverted at Mexico's own little Hoover, called Morelos Dam, just across the border south of Yuma, Arizona. In wet years, surplus flow that might quench the delta's long-suffering thirst finds itself diverted into one aqueduct after another, aimed toward Sonoran farm fields, where wheat, cotton, onions, and fruit grow.

On scorching afternoons, it's hard to imagine large steamers once plied this route, chugging all the way from the Sea of Cortez to Yuma. Now, a traveler would be hard-pressed to float a canoe in it. Some years, the ditch is bone dry. The Colorado River Delta, once a wetlands the size of Rhode Island, is now a tenth its original size.

Leopold remembered the earlier delta with a melancholy resignation—mellow acceptance—that sounded positively Rickettsian. Reading Leopold's classic work, I felt like I was hearing one naturalist's thoughts echo through another naturalist's words, both softened by the smoky haze of years. The fact that both men died only months apart added another ghostly layer of coincidence. I don't know if Aldo knew Ed (or John, for that matter), or if they all simply shared a generational acquaintance with progress's intractable hand. All three men had seen, in their formative years, the rise of the automobile, the spread of cities, the final taming of the West.

"Man always kills the thing he loves," Leopold wrote about the Colorado River Delta, "and so we the pioneers have killed our wilderness. Some say we had to."

The Colorado's harnessed waters now support electric power, daily water use, and crop irrigation for over 23 million people. Agriculture takes the biggest share and is to blame, more than anything else, for the death of Leopold's lovely green lagoons. Writing half a century after Leopold for *The Atlantic Monthly,* William Langewiesche observed about the Imperial Valley, "The desert is never far from view, a reminder of the consequences if the water stopped flowing or became too expensive. The Irrigation District encourages this understanding in publications that juxtapose color photographs of sand dunes and crops. You have to admire the gall of the farmers: their biggest crop is alfalfa, a cow food that is notoriously wasteful of water. They farm in hell and thumb their noses at the devil."

Steinbeck did not see the delta from the Baja side, but his Okies came close. The Joad family, fleeing the Oklahoma dust bowl of the late 1930s, found a moist Eden in California's Imperial Valley, which is just a graffiti-stained international wall away from the Valle de Mexicali, the Valley of Mexicali.

It had not occurred to Brian and me, until we stood along the delta's sediment-rich shores, that *The Grapes of Wrath* and *The Log from the Sea of Cortez* were connected by the Colorado River. The green farmland setting of the 1938 novel seems a world away from the wilderness desert setting of the 1941 travelogue. But the Imperial Valley would be a wilderness setting, too, if not for the irrigation that has reduced the Colorado River to a muddy leak, and the northern Cortez would look less desolate if more freshwater managed to trickle through, greening its shores. The river lured the Okies west. The river, before it was dammed and diverted, created the delta, a sediment-rich nursery for fish, shrimp, and innumerable other invertebrates—the place upon which many of the upper gulf's species still depend. A political border divides both settings. But it's all one ecosystem—far larger and more complex than Steinbeck recognized when he set two stories along its radiating lines of influence.

Even before Brian and I arrived at the Valle de Mexicali, a mere border-hop from the Okies' promised land, migrants were on our mind. We hitchhiked out of Bahía de los Angeles, first with a kindhearted policeman named Martin (plastic-encased scorpion on his dashboard, wide belly rubbing the steering wheel) and then with a clothing vendor and his family, headed north to Tijuana (numerous stops along the way to walk their dog, to drink Coke from Styrofoam cups, to check the malfunctioning carburetor, and to pay respects at a Virgin de Guadalupe shrine in the desert near Cataviña). These were our fourth and fifth thumbed rides in Baja. No American, rich or poor, ever offered us a lift, but Mexicans seemed to understand our plight. Mexicans did not question why we traveled this way with young children, or the fact that everything we seemed to own was on our backs. Only once in five times did a driver accept some gas money in return for helping us.

The main road headed toward the cool Pacific again—our only choice, though our ultimate destination was the upper Cortez. Within a half-day's drive of the border, we saw the Okies' modern counterparts in the faces of Mexican farm laborers, all working their way north. Few of them looked Baja-born. In busy San Quintín, where football-field-sized plastic tarps covered the spring strawberry fields, we saw hundreds of young men with copper-colored high cheekbones: laborers from the southern mainland states of Oaxaca and Chiapas. They rode old black bicycles or crowded onto pickup trucks or walked the busy shoulders of the highway, hunched into the dusty wind, faces covered with bandannas. Sometimes they wore rag turbans over their heads.

We stayed overnight in San Quintín, then endured an all-day bus ride to Ensenada—more migrants, this time from all corners of Mexico. We connected with another bus heading east, just below the border, all the way to Mexicali, the biggest Baja city within striking range of the Río Colorado.

Here, we encountered the face of immigration again, but with yet a different slant—not Okies, not even Oaxacans, but Chinese. Mexicali is home to Mexico's highest concentrations of Chinese residents. Their story—like that of the Okies, and that of modern Mexican farm migrants—has always been braided with the flow of water. The region's first "coolie" laborers built the irrigation system used in the Valle de Mexicali. Chinese who stayed on after the system was built concentrated in Mexicali's downtown, called Chinesca. By 1920, Chinese outnumbered Mexicans by a ratio of fourteen to one.

Times have changed, Mexicali has grown, and the ethnic balance has tipped. Ethnic Chinese are now a minority here, but a highly visible one. Most of Mexicali is a modern border-town sprawl, a little rough around the edges. Closest to the border wall, motels stand next to girly bars. On the outskirts of town, literally hundreds of *maquiladoras* (multinational industrial plants) line well-tended boulevards. Sandwiched between these worlds is downtown Chinesca: several city blocks overlaid with pagoda accents, moon-shaped doorways sheltering Mexican panhandlers, neon restaurant signs advertising both shrimp tacos and Szechwan chicken, jewelry shops, money-changing *casas de cambio,* and Chinese clan houses.

We ate our best dinner in weeks at a large, family-style Chinese restaurant. It was so good we came back the next night, greeted like old friends by the trilingual owner, who brought our children lollipops and fortune cookies with English messages.

After the owner walked away, I wondered aloud about the contrast between China and Baja, and how strange it would be to migrate to this irrigated desert from Shanghai or Harbin. But it would have been weirder still for earlier settlers, who came here with a naive hope for high wages that never materialized, and little understanding of the geography or climate.

The delta's most tragic story happened a century ago. The year was 1902; the month was August—perilously hot. A group of Chinese immigrants traveled by boat up the Sea of Cortez and were dropped at a fork in the Río Colorado. Their Mexican guide informed them that Mexicali was a short hike inland. In truth, it was eighty miles away. All but six of the Chinese laborers perished in the desert. A small peak on the delta's western edge is named Cerro El Chinero, Chinaman Peak, in memory of those misled wanderers.

It sounded like something so awful it couldn't happen again. But in fact, during the spring and summer of the year we traveled the Cortez, it was happening every week. In cities near the border—first Mexicali, later Golfo de Santa Clara and Bahía Kino—we heard news stories about undocumented immigrants dying in the desert. The border patrol had cracked down hard, forcing *coyotes* (the human guides who smuggle illegal aliens into the United States) to cross farther east, in the driest and most dangerous parts of the borderlands. By year's end, more than five hundred migrants would die trying to enter the United States, a 60 percent jump from the year before.

Newspaper headlines announced one tragedy after another: Mexicans or Central Americans led astray by unscrupulous or simply incompetent *coyotes,* men and women and children found dead on the parched desert floor next to empty one-gallon jugs.

The worst incident happened in May. It involved a Oaxacan woman named Yolanda Gonzalez. We were in Baja when it happened, but we wouldn't read all the details until after our trip, when we crossed into Arizona and got our hands on English-language newspapers. At first it seemed like a tragic tangent. Then it sank in and seemed something more: a piece of the upper-gulf puzzle, of which Steinbeck's Okies and the Colorado River and the Chinese-built irrigation channels and the hope of all migrants were also a part.

Yolanda Gonzalez came from a family that was used to traveling far in search of agricultural work. When she was three, her parents had traveled to Baja to pick strawberries and tomatoes for six dollars a day. They were just like the high-cheekboned laborers we'd seen in San Quintín, saving scant wages to build a house back in their southern, rural homeland.

A generation later, Yolanda had her own baby daughter to feed, and a husband who had gone even farther—all the way to Oregon—in search of work. In a year, he sent home less than one thousand dollars. It wasn't enough. Her brothers gave Yolanda enough money—twenty-five hundred dollars—to pay a *coyote* to smuggle her and her baby across the border. She hoped to reunite with her husband in Portland. She expected to cross near Tijuana. Instead, a *coyote* brought her farther east, to the border near the Tohono O'odham Reservation, southwest of Tucson.

Until about one hundred years ago, the O'odham made periodic multiday pilgrimages from their desert homelands to the gulf's edge. They prayed and made offerings and raked salt from coastal deposits. Other tribes traveled the route, too, trading shells and obsidian. Now, the trade is mostly illicit: drugs and human cargo. The seventy-mile walk is a difficult one, even for those who know the way.

Yolanda didn't make it. The coyote abandoned her and her baby on a cow trail, in 110-degree heat. The desert floor would have been closer to 180 degrees.

I could not help but think of the controversial ending of *The Grapes of Wrath,* when Rose of Sharon, a young mother whose baby has just died, lends her breast to a starving man. In the case of Yolanda Gonzalez, it was the mother who perished, her breasts dry and her tongue swollen in her throat. It was her eighteen-month-old daughter, Elizama, who lived. When the border patrol found them, the baby was nursing the single ounce of water left in her bottle, sheltered from the sun by her dead mother's arms.

In Mexicali, we rented a car. Though riding in a silver Japanese compact didn't seem particularly Steinbeckian, we buckled in with gratitude. This was the only way we knew to see our final coastal tidepooling stops, short of hitching. And as May temperatures climbed into the 110s, waiting roadside had lost its road-warrior allure.

It was a relief to be in charge of our transportation again. At last we could give our thumbs a rest, and dig deep into backpacks for the cassette tapes we hadn't listened to all trip. We headed to the northernmost community of the gulf, the tiny town of El Golfo de Santa Clara: south and east, past *ejido* (collective farming) communities, around the head of the gulf. Our map showed it dashed and dotted with little marsh symbols that looked like a stick-figure's punk hairdo. But in reality, there was no marsh. The surrounding land looked alternately Mars-dry or grassy-green, depending on the presence of concrete-lined irrigation ditches. We passed a watermelon vendor selling his fruits roadside. It was worth buying one just to see him cleave it in two with a fearsome rusty machete. The roads got smaller and dustier; we stopped often to ask directions. We drove through the middle of a dump—paper plates and tin cans in heaps on either side of the road—and asked a boy at the side of the road, "*Estás seguro?* This way to Golfo

de Santa Clara?" He gestured ahead. We cranked the air-conditioning
and kept going.

Just when we spotted signs for Río Colorado, the road ended. At the
foot of a bridge, a new road was under construction, parallel to a line of
railroad tracks. We pulled to the road's shoulder and wandered down an
embankment to talk with construction workers.

"Golfo de Santa Clara," I said. "Is this the only way?"

"Go ahead," one of the men told me. "You can drive."

"Where?" I said, seeing only the dead-end road where the new bridge
crossing would be.

The man pointed again.

"The railroad tracks?"

"No train coming now," he said.

I got back in the car, drinking the air-conditioned air like lemonade,
cold and sweet. Then I told Brian and the kids to buckle up and hold on.
We headed onto the tracks. For a hundredth of a second as we neared the
bridge's midpoint, I allowed myself to look down at the Río Colorado
below. Considering everything we'd read and heard, we were surprised
to see it was flowing. Not a torrent, but at least a riffling stream, contained by the canal's concrete walls. Deep enough to have floated
Leopold's canoe. This seemed like a good sign. We made it over the
bridge and back onto the road beyond the construction zone, cheering.

Nearing Golfo de Santa Clara, we passed a large lagoon that ran parallel to the highway: Ciénaga de Santa Clara. It looked lush and green and
perfect for birds, or maybe I was just taking my cue from a billboard that
announced ecotourism opportunities at this place, the northern boundary of a biosphere reserve. Based on our millisecond-long sighting of the
flowing Colorado, and now this view of the Ciénaga's glittering surface, I
might have misconstrued as bunk all that we had read about the delta's
demise. But looking up the landmark in *A Natural History of the Sonoran
Desert*, I found this sobering entry: "The Colorado River Delta was once
a stellar example of ecosystem diversity, displaying a breath-taking mixture of riparian gallery forests, closed-canopy mesquite bosques, saltgrass
flats, backwater sloughs, rivers, ponds, and Indian fields. Much of it is
now dead, except for the hypersaline wetlands known as Ciénaga de
Santa Clara." So, this salty pond was just a relic, the geographical equivalent of a panda in a breeding zoo.

An optimist would say it was more like the California condor: something that, with care, might rebound. A 1998 study suggested that even though the Colorado's outflow has been reduced from 5 trillion gallons a year to nearly none, the delta still can be mended, if only California and Arizona will give up a fraction of their water share. A "One Percent" campaign is under way in the Southwest, urging states to do just that, though U.S. Water officials—too busy fighting among themselves—have scoffed at its feasibility.

The Sea of Cortez came into view around dinnertime and we cheered again. We set up our tent on a private beachfront campground, between a contingent of happily drunk Mexican weekend partyers and a quieter man from Ensenada, camping with his wife. We played soccer on the beach with the first group, shared coffee with Juan and Carmen, and passed watermelon slices all around. When more urban campers arrived, fumbling with the snap-together poles of their new tents, Juan quietly but persistently directed Brian to take charge, while flattering him with compliments about his outdoorsman's prowess. Considering all the noise and the crowds and the social demands, this beach could have been hell. But everyone, drunk or sober, seemed knitted together with gratitude for having survived the desert's worst and having made it to this refreshing, breeze-stirred shore.

The tide had receded, and low steel-gray waves broke against sand in the far distance. From our campsite, near the high-tide line, it was a ten-minute walk to the water's edge. At spring tides on the shallowest of upper-delta mudflat slopes, the water can withdraw for three miles. These were the northern tides at their most extreme, among the highest in the world. The sea was too turbid for snorkeling (in fact, 80 percent of that turbidity is organic, a muddy plume of plankton and other suspended miracle-sea stuff.) But it was warm. We dug under the wet, exposed sand and found several species of clams. In the flyblown palapa restaurant behind our campsite, steamer-type clams were sold for a dime apiece. To the weekend partyer, happy on beer and watermelon and seafood cocktails, this might have seemed like bottomless plenty. But once, the clams were so numerous they formed entire islands in the northern gulf.

In the 1930s, about five clams could be found every square foot. Now, one clam is found every three square feet, and some areas have no clams at all. These numbers come from an article in the December 2000 issue of the journal *Geology*. Researchers described the steep decline of delta shellfish and suggested that less easily documented species—fish and shrimp—have suffered similar fates. The investigation's informal title: "Silence of the Clams."

You wouldn't find that kind of black humor in an article about the Amazon rainforest. At least I'd picked the right dying ecosystem to grieve.

In 1993 the upper gulf and Colorado River Delta to north of Ciénaga de Santa Clara were declared a biosphere reserve. The core zone, where most human activities (including commercial fishing) are restricted, extends from the river's mouth to El Golfo de Santa Clara. From El Golfo south, a less strictly managed buffer zone extends nearly to San Felipe on the western Cortez coast, and Puerto Peñasco on the mainland side.

Our campsite sat on the dividing line between core zone and buffer zone. And yet we saw local pangas head out near sunset into the sparkling waters, and motor north. Only sightseeing, perhaps. But we doubted it.

For dinner, we drove into the village—gritty, a little urine-scented around the edges, with lots of ATVs. We ate fish tacos at an open-air corner restaurant. Four men and women kept the tortillas and fish chunks frying, while Mexican families crowded around picnic tables, eating from plastic baskets. A playpen was next to our table. Inside, a one-year-old in T-shirt and diaper fussed and clung to the sides of her padded prison. Occasionally, a waitress or one of the cooks would pick up the child for a minute or two, and then set her back down. I expected them to move her away from our table or at least acknowledge—perhaps with a joke, or at least a smile—that it was a little strange to have an unhappy baby parked next to a customer's table. But no such comments were forthcoming. I liked having the baby there. I thought of all the times our own children have fussed in restaurants, and how embarrassed I was about it and still am. I envied these fish taco vendors their unbending faith in the collective spirit—the idea that it was everyone's responsibility to keep little Maria Jesús away from the deep fryer.

The tacos were tough and, well, a little fishy. "Cajón," one of the cooks explained. "A small shark." Tender fish—corvina and other fish from the croaker family—are abundant in the northern gulf, or used to be. Brian liked the cajón, but I judged it a second-class substitute.

Long ago, we might have come to this town to eat totoaba, the grand-daddy of all croakers. At one time, this fish, which grows to four hundred pounds, supported important sport and commercial fisheries. Its range parallels the southern boundary of the biosphere reserve. Great schools of the basslike, big-lipped giants once migrated to the mouth of the Colorado each year to breed in the brackish shallows. But changing habitat walloped the species, and overfishing gave it a final pounding. Protected in Mexico since 1975, and listed in the United States as an endangered species, the occasional totoaba still turns up, as incidental by-catch, in gill nets. Sometimes it is caught on purpose: an icthyologist I talked to recently reported his graduate students' sightings of illegal totoaba for sale in an Arizona fishmarket.

Illegal totoaba fishing has brought an even rarer endangered species to the brink of extinction. The vaquita, a kind of harbor porpoise, is snagged incidentally by both shark and totoaba gill netters. Found exclusively in the shallow waters off the extreme northern gulf, this "little cow," as the Mexicans call it, has the most limited range of any marine cetacean (a group that includes whales, dolphins, and porpoise). Some call it the rarest cetacean in the world, period. It is small. At four and a half feet long, it is a foot and a half shorter than a good-sized totoaba, with whom its destiny is linked. The vaquita has black eye-patches and upturned, coal-colored mouth. Even dead in a gill net, it appears to be smiling.

From our campsite, we regularly scanned the choppy gulf surface, hoping to glimpse a vaquita's fin or rounded dolphinlike head. But that was dreaming. Even though up to thirty vaquitas drown each year in gill nets, few people ever see them alive and swimming.

Just outside Golfo de Santa Clara, there was a modest visitors center, a series of cone-shaped buildings modeled on an indigenous design. The center was three years old. It had already been hit once by a hurricane and looked a little unstable. Inside, we lucked into meeting José Campoy, a young biologist who is the biosphere reserve's director. I asked him how many vaquitas there were.

"Less than a thousand, but they can't be counted," he said.

Not true: numerous aerial surveys have been done, and abundance estimates usually range from three hundred to seven hundred. But I didn't think Campoy was trying to obfuscate. I think he was trying to be critical, to admit how much we don't know for sure. About other matters, he was frank.

"The gill nets are a problem. They're left overnight in place. We have rangers at about four places around the perimeter. But we have trouble patrolling the uppermost delta."

I scribbled that down, as I'd scribbled frantically during all my interviews. Campoy paused patiently. He knew that Americans needed to know, that here at the upper gulf, we were half—maybe more than half—of the problem.

Even delivering bad news, Campoy expressed an eager and youthful optimism. He was the perfect border straddler—in appearance both Mexican and American, wearing fashionable, square-shaped eyeglasses, a denim baseball cap, and white T-shirt. He was literate and bilingual, recommending favorite books and magazine articles about the Colorado River. He spoke fondly about the college students who use the visitor center as a base for exploring the delta.

José Campoy was approachable and collegiate—the right man to work with the Arizona and Sonora professors, graduate students, and conservationists who tend to the delta's dying gasps. He complemented his southern Baja colleagues well. Grassroots Pepe Murrieta was a self-made man among ranchers and fisherman; Benito Bermudez had survived a working stint in Mexico City, and seemed at home with bureaucracy. Each of the three Cortez guardians had their own style, well-suited to the regions in which they worked. But they also seemed to share a common vision, and a tone of cautious optimism.

I had tried to avoid placing too much faith in any of these individual men. The force of their personalities and the strength of their own convictions seemed no match for such an extensive desert coastline and such a long history of exploitation, ignorance, and fraud. But meeting Campoy broke my resolve. I couldn't keep writing off these individuals as lone rangers. Maybe these three men were more than three men—maybe they were a vanguard. And behind them, each one hastened to remind me, was a strong and respected woman: Julia Carabias, Mexico's secretary of environment. Nearly all the recent changes, including the creation of the marine park at Loreto, had happened under her watch.

Not that political change could do everything. Maybe it couldn't do *anything,* in light of continuing corruption. As Artemisa Castro, the former head of Mexico's national shrimp research program in Sonora, was quoted saying in *The Arizona Republic,* "There are lots of laws in the country to protect the environment, but there's no law enforcement at all."

The fact that I was sifting desperately through all these thoughts and quotes and brief meetings, searching for a reason to be optimistic, suggested that I was both simpleminded and perfectly human.

About hope, the *Log's* authors observed cynically, "Probably when our species developed the trick of memory and with it the counterbalancing projection called 'the future,' this shock-absorber, hope, had to be included in the species, else the species would have destroyed itself in despair. For if ever any man were deeply and unconsciously sure that his future would be no better than his past, he might deeply wish to cease to live. And out of this therapeutic poultice we build our iron teleologies and twist the tide pools and the stars into the pattern."

Is that what I was doing? Twisting the tidepools and stars into the pattern that I wanted to see? Instead of seeing simply, in Steinbeck and Ricketts's oft-repeated words, "what is"?

Everything at the northern gulf was more extreme: the tides, the threats to particular species, the sense of past or impending loss. Elsewhere in Baja, marine problems had been hidden under the surface: fewer fish, fewer sharks, fewer sea cucumbers, and even those facts were suspect. Here, no one questioned the imperiled status of totoaba and vaquita. And those species-specific problems were minuscule compared to the overall problem of habitat loss.

The vaquita, the totoaba, the clams and the shrimp, the fish (which require just enough freshwater), and the seabirds (which eat the juvenile fish) had all evolved to fit the extreme characteristics of this environment: shallow sun-warmed water, saltier than any river, one of the most productive estuarine environments in the world. Their species strategy included no contingency plan for the creation of a Hoover Dam. Bottom-scraping trawlers and gill nets just added insult to injury.

Some of the local people still fished for corvina, a fish that relied on freshwater trickling into the gulf. But others had switched from catching quality food fish to second-class shark. At least they had a living, for now, and that was good, because the long, hot walk north from the delta to find work elsewhere often ended in tragedy. Consider the Chinese. Consider Yolanda Gonzalez. Anyone who survived the hike might end up working on some farm that siphoned water from the Colorado, further reducing the flow, so that the northern gulf, with its endangered totoaba and its endangered vaquita, might become saltier and drier still.

It boggled my mind. I wasn't sure what to do. I wasn't sure what anyone could do. I wanted to know more. But I wasn't sure what knowing more would accomplish. I couldn't turn to Steinbeck for advice. I already smelled his hand in the writing of that fancy "hope" passage from a few paragraphs back. I couldn't turn to Ricketts for advice, but I knew to whom *he* would have turned: Lao Tsu.

The Chinese scholar observed, "In the pursuit of learning, every day something is acquired. In the pursuit of Tao, every day something is dropped. Less and less is done until non-action is achieved. When nothing is done, nothing is left undone. The world is ruled by letting things take their course. It cannot be ruled by interfering."

But of course, I'm not Taoist. The only time all trip I'd experienced true nonaction was in Loreto, after quaffing two double margaritas poolside with some drunk marlin fishermen. And that had felt good, especially after all those long hot days looking for Benito. But it hadn't felt like wisdom.

At Púlpito, during the first week of our trip, we had thought ourselves clever for being able to see a tidepool creature—for learning to spot shiny gobs on the sand that were really small anemones, or for turning a rock and finding stinging worms underneath. At Isla Coronados, I had been proud for continuing to search even when my eyes were tired, and I had been rewarded with the discovery of a moon snail's sand collar. At Puerto Escondido and Isla San José and many other places, we had learned the scientific names for things. And at Ensenada Alacrán I had learned, at least for one sun-broiled afternoon, that species can be seen even when they have no names except for the ones we give them.

Kayaking from Ensenada Alacrán to Bahía de los Angeles, we had slowed our pace and stayed at beaches long enough to see the full cycle of tides rise and fall, fall and rise, so that for once we saw not only species, or a tidal frontline, but an entire tidal range exposed—a whole community, the poem instead of the comma, the novel instead of the sentence. And that had been a reprise of Cabo Pulmo, where in the strobe-lit world of the coral reef, we had seen species intermingling, if only for brief disco-bright flashes.

And both those glimpses had been only a prelude to larger connections, moving toward what Steinbeck and Ricketts described reverently as "the time when what we know as life meets and enters what we think of as non-life: barnacle and rock, rock and earth, earth and tree, tree and rain and air. And the units nestle into the whole and are inseparable from it." James Lovelock hadn't even elucidated his Gaia hypothesis yet, and these two 1940 Cannery Row wisecrackers were rambling about it like the whole organic-inorganic-world-biosphere thing was old hat. Pass the wine.

We had stared at reefs and into tidepools. And finally we had begun to move from the small to the large, panning wider and wider, opening the aperture of the mind's eye, trying to hold the mind's camera still enough to tolerate a long exposure. But as any photographer knows, you can't have it all: wide-angle and close-up lens, low f-stop and slow shutter-speed. You can see a lot crowded into the frame, or a little shot close. As for light *and* time: Let them both in, all at once, and all you get is an overexposed blur.

But the sense of a large, sharp picture—the potential—was there. We had seen the universe in a tidepool. But here at the northern gulf, a single tidepool seemed like nothing. This upper-gulf delta ecosystem was larger than any I'd ever pondered. It extended from above the Midriffs where the cold currents raced; up and around the gulf's head encompassing ancient clam beds and totoaba and corvina and vaquita breeding grounds; and into the broad, lower delta, where lagoons once stood; and up the Colorado River for some fifteen hundred miles, to places where no one had ever heard of cajón tacos.

And it encompassed invertebrates and vertebrates, animals and people, ecology and economy (the fishermen had to make a living, too, even the ones who killed smiling vaquitas; and the farmers; and the watermelon man with his rusty cleaver; and María Jesús's father selling shark tacos). It encompassed nature and also ideas, science and also literature: a *Log from the Sea of Cortez*, and a *Grapes of Wrath,* and all the books and movies and labor movements and songs that the more famous, latter book inspired.

Big. Too big.

We drove away from El Golfo de Santa Clara, tired and quiet, air-conditioner cranked, pavement shimmering, Bruce Springsteen again on the tape player:

The highway is alive tonight
Where it's headed everybody knows.
I'm sittin' down here in the campfire light
Waitin' on the ghost of Tom Joad.

COMFORTING SOUNDS

We were almost done. The empty wallet had said so long ago. The journals assented: I had run out of pages in my primary diary and had started to write tiny without breaking for paragraphs, the way Steinbeck wrote his novels even after he could afford paper; except that my handwriting was much worse, and I let it crawl like sand fleas all along the edges and upside down in smeary saltwater-curled corners.

Even the map was almost ready to agree. So far on this trip in Mexico, we had traveled three thousand miles by land and water. On the mainland side, we had four of the original twenty-three official tidepooling stations left.

Of these, the best and most frightening was our next stop: Isla Tiburón, Shark Island. The name alone had lured Brian and me for ten years. But the island's formidable reputation had just as surely kept us away. As long as there has been a Tiburón, it seems, travelers have feared it.

A *National Geographic* magazine article from 1896 (only one grainy photograph in black and white) described Tiburón and its adjacent coast as the "fatherland of a fierce tribe, the terror of explorers since Coronado, the dread of Sonora today, the nightmare of the few local settlers. . . ."

In 1919, another *National Geographic* article about the Seri people appeared. And though twenty-five years had passed, the hyperbolic, awestruck tone remained the same. This is just the sort of popular magazine article that might have been laying around the Steinbeck household in Salinas, California, when John Steinbeck was an impressionable seventeen years old. It tickled me to imagine the rangy teenager who might have read:

"The Seris, these strange lonely people are called, and they inhabit a lonely, evil rock called Tiburón (Shark) Island that lifts its hostile head from the hot, empty waters of the Gulf of Cortez. . . . And all down this coast the name of Tiburón is spoken with a shrug of the shoulders, for these Seris are thieves and killers. It is even whispered that long ago they were cannibals. However, they did not try to eat us or even hint at it while I was visiting them."

Steinbeck and Ricketts tidepooled at the southwest corner of Tiburón for one evening, and anchored there overnight before heading south to Guaymas. In fine form, they continued the tradition of speculating on the Seris' uncivilized habits: "We searched the shore for Seris and saw none. In our usual condition of hunger, it would have been a toss-up whether Seris ate us or we ate Seris. The one who got in the first bite would have had the dinner, but we never did see a Seri."

All talk of fierce tribes aside, it wasn't cannibalism that worried Brian and me; it was the currents. As kayakers, we'd eyed maps of Tiburón many times, but fear of fast-moving, unpredictable water was the real reason we hadn't visited the Sonoran coast until now. This square-shaped island, the gulf's largest, sits nearly flush against the mainland. Every six hours, the tides must work hard and fast to squeeze by—imagine Tokyo crowds spilling in and out of subway-train doors twice each day—creating even more dastardly currents and wave patterns than found at the other Midriff islands to the west. Canal de Infiernillo, Hellish Channel, is the local name for the narrow strait separating Tiburón from the mainland.

Plenty of geographic features in Baja have frightening names. My favorite was a strait just south of Bahía de los Angeles, the Canal de Salsipuedes: Get Out If You Can Channel. Our cruising guide, which included pleasant information about the anchoring possibilities at Salsipuedes, was emphatic about Infiernillo: "Heavy tidal action, strong currents, & shoal areas. Avoid traveling here."

We commended ourselves for our prudence: We would not kayak at Isla Tiburón. Instead we drove to the coastal town nearest Isla Tiburón and set about hiring a panga and guide. We soon discovered that we needed official permission, too.

"You'll need this signed by the governor," a secretary informed me inside the modern tribal government office in Bahía Kino, after I'd explained what we wished to see and do. By this she meant the tribal governor, since management of Seriland—Isla Tiburón and adjacent coastland—had been ceded to the Seris by presidential decree.

Around the tribal office, clusters of men were standing and chatting— mestizo-looking men wearing straw hats, and Indians with long plaits of jet-black hair. Most indigenous Mexicans are small, round people, but these Indians had a northern lankiness, with sharply carved features.

A tall, lean man had been listening to our conversation and stepped toward us. His skin was as shiny and dark as a Teflon pan. His cheekbones were high polished ridges, mounted over cheeks so hollow they looked like they'd catch water. There was a quick intelligence in his eyes. Even with brown-stained teeth, he was strikingly handsome.

"Humberto," he introduced himself, and took the permit form from the secretary's hand. "I will do it."

More confusion: He would be our guide? Or he would obtain the governor's permission?

The secretary had listed the names of several marine organisms we wished to see while tidepooling. We'd never specified *jaiba,* the local word for crab, as our quarry, but that word had somehow made it onto the form. Humberto underlined this word emphatically. Twice. Glancing around the room, I saw a poster that showed the recent development of jaiba commercial-fishing locations near Tiburón. Either Humberto perceived our interest as ultimately commercial, or he was simply savvy and knew that the governor would spot and sign a form that said "jaiba" long before he'd sign something that said "barnacle."

"We go tomorrow," Humberto said. "Eight o'clock. Meet me in Punta Chueca."

That was one of two Seri villages up the coast, a world apart from Bahía Kino, the newer side of which had blossomed into a modest seaside resort of Mediterranean-style houses and golden-sand public beaches. Many prominent and wealthy Mexicans owned vacation homes in New Kino. But only the occasional anthropology-minded gringo or curio trader continued on, via gravel road, to Punta Chueca.

"We're staying at a motel in Kino," I explained. "Is the road between Kino and Punta Chueca bad?"

"Not too good."

"Would it be better to camp in Punta Chueca so that we can wake there and get an earlier start?"

"No. There are no good places to camp."

That was strange, because Punta Chueca is on a beach surrounded by scrub desert—both easy places to erect a tent. But I admired the Seris for keeping tourists at arm's length.

"Well, how will we find you?"

"Don't worry," he said. "I'll find *you*."

In ten years of traveling through Baja, we'd had no experience with indigenous peoples. All the fishermen we'd ever met, all the tourism guides and taco vendors and missionaries and college students and locally trained biologists had been *mestizo*—mixed blood, the race born of Spanish-Aztec union. Occasionally we met someone who had been born in Baja, but usually, their parents or grandparents had come from the urban mainland. A Mexican family in Mulegé or La Paz might have a trace of Baja Indian blood, but they were just as likely to have Chinese, Russian, German, or French blood, added to the mix by the peninsula's early Asian and European immigrants. For centuries the peninsula has been a favorite place to jump ship or start again, and so it has become a melting pot.

Baja's true indigenous peoples are an invisible minority. When the conquistadors arrived, there were perhaps thirty thousand to fifty thousand peninsular Indians. During the missionary period of the 1700s most of the natives were killed in colonial skirmishes or wiped out by disease. But not all: Several distinct tribes of no more than three hundred individuals, including the Cochimi and the Yumano, still populate the peninsula. They tend to live away from the tourist path, in the high sierras of Baja California Norte, on ranches and farms. Traveling along the coast, we had never encountered indigenous people, or even multi-generational mestizos with a long and intimate knowledge of their environment.

The Sonoran Seris, on the other hand, still relied on the sea. They lived next to it, ate from it, protected it from the incursions of mestizo poachers, told stories about it, and—so I had read—sang sacred songs or canticles keyed to certain coastal and oceanic landmarks. These songs, like the songs of the Australian aborigines, were lyrical maps, but they were also prayers: a way to soothe the cantankerous sea or wind spirits that made ocean passages so dangerous.

Writing for *Sierra* magazine, Gary Paul Nabhan, an Arizona naturalist and writer, described traveling with a Seri guide who sang this canticle: *Wind, don't come/ Wind don't come/ Keep the male hill in sight/ Keep the female hill in sight/ The ones (that could be) shrouded in clouds. / You who are going asleep: wake up!/ You who are going asleep: wake up!/ Don't sleep anymore, for the sea is making its foaming sound/ Hear the sound of the sea foam.*

We hoped our guide, Humberto, would know such songs.

As promised, he located us within minutes of our arrival in Punta Chueca. I suppose our silver rental car was easy to spot, pulled up next to the wall of decrepit shacks and shanties that ran parallel to the beach. The Seris have shifted from a nomadic lifestyle to a village-based one only in the last generation; there is a devil-may-care look to their houses—some corrugated tin, some concrete, many unfinished. Garbage was everywhere, and the beach reeked of fish. But the people were beautiful: Teenage girls promenaded past us, chins held high, long skirts grazing the ground.

While Humberto wandered off to procure gas for our panga trip, an old woman sidled up to me. She began to show me her snail-shell necklaces, while making pleasant conversation. The shells were tiny—it took perhaps seventy to one hundred shells to fill a necklace. They had been tinted various colors: green, purple, or red. I did like them. All trip, I had gathered only a handful of common shells, and on island shores even that was prohibited by Mexican law. But now, to please the old woman and to remember her, I made up for all the glossy shells I'd bypassed and bought several strands. I had the correct change in pesos, but within a minute or two it became clear that the old woman couldn't do simple math. Nor did she want to admit this. She guided me to a one-room grocery store and asked the woman at the counter to handle the transaction. The young woman took my pesos and handed them to the old woman, and took the old woman's necklaces and handed them to me; then we all smiled, and both women told me to have a safe trip.

When the panga was ready, Brian, the children, and I pulled on life jackets and heaved our dry-sacks full of snacks and snorkeling gear into the boat. Humberto wore a high-domed red baseball cap, jeans, a T-shirt, and black rubber boots. Other than that, he came empty-handed: no emergency gear, dry clothes, tool kit, or food.

The morning air was surprisingly cool, and a soft but steady breeze blew. We motored northward, up the Canal de Infiernillo, discussing where we should stop to look for marine organisms.

Steinbeck and Ricketts saw ample life at Tiburón's southwest corner. I described the location, but Humberto clucked his tongue authoritatively and said he'd take us somewhere better. We were in his hands, happily so. I had no desire to choose our route through the Hellish Channel.

Tiburón, a jagged red-rock island, rose on our left; the mainland was a smoother, tawny apron on our right, fringed with electric-green mangroves. The panga sped and slowed, sped and slowed, the motor alternately whining and gurgling, clearing its metal throat each time Humberto brought the panga to an idling drift so that he could stand high in the stern and scan ahead for the next sandbar. Sometimes he pushed past us, hurdling one panga bench and then the next, so that he could stand in the bow. We tried to keep lookout, too. But we weren't any real help to him—he wasn't searching for anything as simple as an exposed rock, but instead studying a more intricate underwater geometry of hues and textures.

We could see, by the colors of this water, that this shallow channel was more complicated than it appeared on any map. There were shoals and reefs and curlicues of sand that unfurled from the mainland shore, like a reef feather-duster unrolling to sweep up edible plankton—or like a beckoning finger tempting boats to wreck. Ribbons of color—olive, brown, or brilliant turquoise—hinted at the water's changing depth. The waves were never large, but they were confused, slapping against our hull from several directions. The sun-dappled channel flowed against the wind—fast tide against light breeze—and became a glinting confusion of sparkling ripples and triangles.

After a while, we stopped at a shoal in the middle of the breeze-stirred channel, off Tiburón's eastern shore, and Humberto put down anchor. "There," he said. "You snorkel?"

We thought he'd take us to a beach. But Brian and I pulled on our fins and soon forgot about expectations. Taking turns—one in the boat with the kids, the other kicking furiously around the panga—we tried to survey the channel bottom.

The water felt warmer than the air, and was only five feet deep—though we didn't dare stand. The current was strong. Visibility was no more than one foot. Masks down, we felt like we were watching an underwater hurricane: particles whirling furiously over a brilliant, densely carpeted seafloor. Many of the organisms were completely unfamiliar, or at least unidentifiable in the fraction of a second we stared at them, before we were swept to another snorkeling spot by the current.

Underwater, the theme was carpet shag in 1970s colors: burnt orange, tan, a little plum. The motifs were pore, siphon, or feathery tentacle. The primary textures were wispy or rubbery. Everything here seemed suited to straining the fast-moving water for nutrients. Among the pulpy invertebrates were tunicates, barrel sponges, sulfur sponges, tubelike sponges, webby bryozoans, and globs of neon-orange sea pork that looked like its name—gelatinous and fatty. Encrusting sponges clung to rocks and old shells. Mucous webs spun by snails hung in the water, like snotty parachutes. Mossy material fluttered in the current. Altogether, it looked like a messy kid's bedroom floor, complete with unidentifiable and possibly toxic food residues.

Or like an enchanted garden, wildly overgrown. Between the fatty blobs and tufts were all kinds of feathery things: sea feathers and sea plumes and tiny sea anemones. A feather duster polychaete, frightened by my shadow, snapped into its chalk-colored tube; but while I struggled to maintain my position, I saw it emerge again, slowly spreading its brilliant purple feeding plumes into the particle-dense water. It was like watching one of those high-speed documentary sequences of a flower blooming.

Adding to the cluttered, chaotic nature of the channel floor were mounds of shell rubble. Some of the bivalves were still alive: With one scoop, we could have gone home with a handful of campfire-ready clams and scallops. But more impressive than these were the dead and vacated shells, because they had become the home to new forms of life. I picked up one empty hacha shell, bigger than my hand, and held it above the water's surface. A crab was crawling around inside it. Some lacy, lavender-hued material was growing on top of it. A colony of small anemones had attached near its hinge. It had become a small reef.

Back in the panga, Brian and I babbled about the alien world we'd just seen, trading guesses about the names and natures of things. Humberto became more talkative, too, asking us as many questions as we asked him, a trait we hadn't yet observed in any guide. But he seemed puzzled, perhaps a little disappointed, about how little we truly knew. Just as we expected him to be a *National Geographic* Seri—fierce and "primitive"—he expected us to be *Scientific American* biologists—rigorous, precise, detail-oriented, professional, all-knowing. We might have fooled him if we'd kept our mouths closed. Instead, we gasped and jabbered and grabbed each other's sunburnt shoulders: *What the hell was that? Incredible.*

One thing Brian and I did know: Appearances could be deceiving. Sponges looked like blobs, and so did tunicates (also called sea squirts). But sponges were among the simplest multicellular invertebrates, while tunicates are not invertebrates at all. They are chordates—animals with a backbone or backbone precursor—in the same phylum as humans and fish. The spinal chord (technically, a notochord) isn't visible except in larval stage, when the tunicate looks like a small tadpole.

A tunicate does not yield its secrets easily. It refuses to play a role in traveler's epiphanies. Never mind that the tunicate's evolutionary path bears similarity to our own. Holding the gelatinous adult form in her hand, a snorkeler could not guess that she was eyeing a distant cousin; no matter how long she looked, no matter how carefully she observed, no matter how open her heart and soul to cross-species connections. Neither time nor intention would open that door of perception. To understand, a snorkeler would have to take off the mask, sit down, narrow her focus, take out the microscope and the formaldehyde and nowadays the gene splicer, become a "real" scientist, watch the tunicate at all its life stages, devote years.

Ricketts had praised this act of devotion to the particular. Scrawling notes to himself (as he often did, sometimes in late-night insomniac bursts), he once reflected, "If you could know everything about any thing, almost any one single smallest object, you'd know it about everything. Because lines of reference go in every direction, from every thing to every other thing. . . ."

But wait. Hadn't Steinbeck and Ricketts, in the *Log*, praised just the opposite strategy? Hadn't they poked fun at "dry-ball" specialists studying pale specimens ad infinitum, out of context? (Remember the sierra fish and the lab scientist, removing his specimens from evil-smelling jars, and counting their spines? "*There you have recorded a reality which cannot be assailed—probably the least important reality concerning either the fish or yourself.*") And yet that's what it would take to know one creature intimately.

Hadn't they suggested moving, rather quickly, beyond simple species, to the ecosystem, even into space? "It is advisable to look from the tide pool to the stars," the *Log*'s authors wrote, "and then back to the tide pool again."

And then back to the tidepool. Back, perhaps, even to the microscope and the formaldehyde—once the beer is drunk, the trip is done, the Indians and funny deckhands and brothel girls all gone home. From the small to the large and back again, from the part to the whole and back again. It's easy to say "Do both." Most of us don't. Most of us can't even manage to do one part well.

At some point, whether the view is micro or macro, the mind tires. Information overload. Experience overload. A kind of intellectual sea-sickness: too much movement, and no steady horizon.

Aryeh had not been able to take part in the midchannel snorkel, and Tziporah wanted to run on the beach, so we chose as our next stop a rocky tidepool farther north on the mainland channel shore. Along the way, I tried to listen to Humberto over the panga's roar. Leaving the snorkeling spot, a switch had been turned. In us: Brian and I had gone from garrulous to pensive. And in our guide: Before, he had been mono-syllabic, but now he lectured precisely and passionately (albeit softly) about changes in Seriland.

In Spanish, he told me about the overharvest of sea turtles, and the competition between Seri and Mexican fishermen, who use the area with or without permission. I translated as fast as I could for Brian—again, over the wind and the motor's roar—and missed half of Humberto's subsequent statements. But he kept going, warming to the subject: "disturbed" areas, and the things "we must care for." He waxed eloquent about the turtle (*caguama* here in Seriland, instead of *tortuga*). He talked at length about Isla Tiburón's population of bighorn sheep—the same species Steinbeck and Ricketts unsuccessfully sought, which white trophy hunters now pay thousands to bag.

I'm no good at translating and it exhausts me. For the hundredth time, I wished I spoke better Spanish. But it might not have helped. Humberto, as intelligent as I'd imagined when we first met in the tribal office, linguistically tap-danced all over me, using Spanish words for some things and Seri words for others, and throwing in the Latin he'd picked up from visiting biologists (*real* biologists) to describe fish or plants or land animals that didn't ring a bell in the other two tongues.

The waves steepened and Humberto finally paused his enthusiastic lecture. I filled the silence with a question—one I had wanted to ask all day. We knew, of course, not to trust most of what we'd read about the Seris. But there was one thing I desperately wanted to be true.

"Do the Seris really have canticles about the sea?"

"Yes," he said.

"Do fishermen know the songs?"

"Yes."

"Do you know the songs?"

"Yes."

Back to the monosyllabic answers. But I pried no further. A silent minute passed. I did not want to be a cultural tourist. I did not want Humberto to think he had to perform for us simply because we had paid him; didn't want him to feel pressured to sing or chant something potentially sacred out of context.

Then again, maybe this wasn't out of context. The wind and waves were strong.

"Here is one," Humberto finally said, and he started singing, so softly I had to strain to listen. Aryeh loves songs, especially native songs, especially sea songs, and I wanted him to hear this most of all, but he was seated behind me. Five thousand miles of travel and a foot too far away to hear. But what could a parent do? This wasn't Disneyland or an IMAX movie. I couldn't talk to the manager or push the volume button on the remote. This was life: a brief moment, a dry land, a quiet song nearly drowned out by the wind.

Humberto's voice lifted and dropped, just a rhythmic and hypnotic little song, a tuneful little chant. It was all in Seri, so despite its lilting loveliness, I could not understand the words.

"To calm the waters," he said, by way of explanation, when the song was done.

"And to calm us?" I asked.

Humberto smiled—the most relaxed and hearty grin he'd let loose all day.

"Yes. That too."

We zigzagged up the channel, braking for sandbars and also for dolphins. Then we beached the boat on the mainland shore. This spot was more sheltered, with less current and clearer water. Brian and I took turns here, too, both tidepooling and snorkeling, seeing more of the same wonders that had enthralled us midchannel: bivalve and sponge life, if not quite so dense and chaotic as before.

Humberto spent some time teaching me the Seri names for things, or trying to. He'd lift an organism from the tidepool and exhale the word at me. I can't pretend that I managed to accurately mimic or memorize even one.

K'pah'hicktp'kah he would say while holding up a clam shell.

I'd say *Aaaaaah . . . K'pah'pahpahpah.* And try to nod my head sagely. But my mind felt ready to burst—I was still stewing about what I'd seen or hadn't seen and understood or not understood about species and habitats at the midchannel snorkeling spot. And I hated to hear myself say a foreign word all wrong, with the syllables broken all to pieces like a poorly sectioned orange.

He'd point to something else in the water. He'd name it in Seri— sometimes in Spanish and Latin, too, but always in Seri. I'd try to repeat it. A marble-mouthed mess. A guttural insult.

At one point, when Brian had come ashore for a rest, Humberto walked down the beach and came back with two kinds of seaweed that looked like dark, slippery vermicelli. "Maruchan," he said.

"Maruchan," Brian and I both repeated earnestly—at least this was a word I could say. Then Humberto's smile widened and I saw the empty noodle cup in his hand. He'd brought the Styrofoam container to collect more of those tiny snail shells for the necklace lady.

"Maruchan," Brian explained to me, pointing to the labeled cup. It was a brand of instant Japanese noodles. And the seaweed *looked* like noodles. If Humberto hadn't grinned, I would have spent the rest of my life proudly repeating this one "indigenous" word. But thanks to Brian, I got it.

"Seri humor," I said.

But then Brian went snorkeling again, and Humberto and I got serious. He told me more about Seri problems with Mexican fishermen. Surrounding us, on the beach, were hundreds of empty hacha shells.

"Mexicans did this," he said.

"How can you tell it was them?"

"Seri wouldn't take so much. And they wouldn't leave the shells here. Too dangerous. We would go to the middle of the channel and put the shells there."

The Mexicans had overused an important local resource. But what angered Humberto more than the pillage was the poachers' lack of common sense. He lifted one of the ax-head-shaped hachas to show me its razor-sharp edge. "Someone could get hurt on this beach."

Not morality, not outrage, just fact. I thought of Ricketts's non-teleology: not good, not bad, only "what is."

Murmuring assent, I opened our dry-sacks and offered Humberto some of our peanut butter and jelly sandwiches. He frowned at these, but accepted some plain flour tortillas. Then he turned away from me to eat.

The food reminded me of another pressing but problematic question. If I *did* ask, I risked disrupting the friendly candor we'd established. If I *didn't,* I knew I'd rue my own timidity. I summoned my courage for the second time this day. I waited until he'd finished his tortilla. Then I plunged.

"Humberto, this is a stupid question. I have read these books, I know they're all wrong," I stumbled, stuttered, kept going. "I'm not saying I believe this, but, but . . . *Did the Seris ever eat people?*"

The corners of his mouth dropped. He squinted into the far distance, disgust and anger clouding his face. Then he gestured toward Tiburón. "All this food, the turtle, the fish, the seafood, the sheep. Eat people? When there is meat, when there is fish?"

He wasn't finished and already, I was backpedaling, apologizing, blaming other peoples' books, blaming *National Geographic*. "You're right," I said. "It makes no sense, it's stupid . . ."

"This is not a hungry country," he said. It was more than an observation, more than a statement; it was a sovereign declaration.

"Of course. I'm sorry," I babbled again.

"Now," he grunted, and waited for my undivided attention before continuing. "We Seri did not eat the people who came here without our permission. However," and here he paused briefly—"we *did* kill them."

The naming again. Humberto and me, side by side. He'd point to something in the water and enunciate its name. I'd repeat, with the "Aaaaaah" before the unfamiliar word and the reverent nod afterward.

After a while, I left out the Seri word and just said "Aaaaaah."

A while after that, I left out the "Aaaaaah" and just nodded. A little less reverently. I didn't want to do this anymore. It had been a long, full day. But he kept trying.

Humberto looked so disappointed. Here he was, creating the world in front of my eyes—Adam in the garden all over again. And unlike the boys in Loreto, I wasn't even naming back to him. I just stared and smiled vacantly.

"You're not taking notes?" he finally asked.

This comment should have been an arrow in my heart. Back home, in Alaska, in another life, I worked as a journalist. Even now, I was hoping—planning—to write a book. Even when nothing is happening, I take notes.

Tziporah had wandered down the beach; Aryeh was swimming with Brian. Humberto and I were sitting side by side, on the beach, almost knee to knee. A stranger watching from afar could have been forgiven for thinking this was an intimate moment.

"I have a notebook, but I'm not taking notes," I answered him.

The disappointed look again.

I continued, "No. This is only the beginning, I'm just trying to . . . I would have to return . . . It's just better . . . Not right now . . ."

Why not now? Steinbeck, Ricketts, help me out here—why not now?

I'd never agreed with Lao Tsu before. But now, his words found their way into my heart: "Once the whole is divided, the parts need names. There are already enough names. One must know when to stop. Knowing when to stop averts trouble. Tao in the world is like a river flowing home to the sea."

I didn't try to say it in Spanish or—god forbid—Seri. But the thought was in my heart. *Ricketts, you would have been proud! I agreed with Lao Tsu!*

Then a funny thing happened: "A crazy literary thing," Steinbeck would have called it.

Humberto picked up a handful of sand and I realized it wasn't sand at all. It was all shells—tiny shells, as small as buttons, as small as pencil erasers, and some even smaller, small as the period at the end of this sentence. Most Cortez sand beaches are really tiny-shell beaches. Biologic beaches, they're called. Graveyards, actually. Graveyards for millions and billions of once-living invertebrates. Species that lived millions of years before us, and species that may live millions of years after us.

Humberto started to pick one shell at a time out of his hand and name it. And then drop it. And name the next one. And drop it. I'd done my share of repeating and cooing and nodding. Now I just stared ahead. He kept going—for himself, for me, a way to pass the time, a mantra, I don't know. It was a little strange.

And I let the Seri words wash over me. Just listened to each one and let it go. There was another invertebrate I didn't recognize. And there was another species name I didn't know. And there was another one that Ricketts would have known, that Xantus would have known, that Brusca surely would know. And there was one I might have known before but I'd forgotten. And there were thousands of years of Seri wisdom that made our two months in Baja seem like a joke.

I just listened to each word, each shell, and let it go. Like waves crashing against the beach, spending their energy, and cycling under, preparing to crash again. And pretty soon, Humberto's words didn't sound like Seri. They became white noise. They became my own mantra. They sounded like, "I know nothing." Another dropped shell. "I know nothing." Another shell. "I know nothing."

And they were comforting sounds.

CADENZA

Then, another thing happened.

Steinbeck and Ricketts had heard a thunder clap on their way south out of the Sea of Cortez—that was their "crazy literary thing"—and they knew to end their story there. The rest would just be anticlimax: wheel-watch and Sparky's spaghetti and Pacific seasickness and arguments with invisible Carol and thinking about all the laundry to be done back in California. We'd already had our share of things happening, but our story wasn't done.

As we were preparing to leave the beach—the afternoon wind was really rising now, and Humberto's face was a tight mask of apprehension—Tziporah screamed. We ran to her. She had tripped. Bracing her fall, she had spread out one hand and caught the razor edge of a discarded hacha shell. Her palm poured blood, a deep wound. She stood bravely, not crying after that one yelp, a shocked look on her small face. Humberto's face was worse. First, worried; now, appalled.

"Dangerous," he muttered, and chucked the shell, hard, into the sea.

Brian, who'd been quiet and a little passive all day, sprang into action. He shined at moments like these. Out came the first-aid kit that he packs for every day-trip even when I complain about the weight—a bag big enough to serve the needs of most Everest expeditions. Out came the disinfectant, the antibiotic cream, the butterfly strips, the sterile gauze.

I watched the blood drip and felt close to losing my lunch. Humberto looked both furious—cursing those dimwitted shellfish-poachers again—and quite afraid, as if he expected little Tziporah's hand to fall right off. But it wasn't that bad. Brian comforted and mended while the rest of us watched. For once, Humberto looked impressed.

"Did you study medicine?" he asked Brian.

"No. Just first aid."

We hadn't proved ourselves as biologists or linguists, but at least my spouse had proven himself handy with a pair of surgical scissors. Maybe also Humberto was awed by the first-aid kit's bountiful contents. I felt the gap between First and Second Worlds yawn wide—all the medical supplies we took for granted would be much appreciated here.

By procedure's end, Tziporah looked shaken but stoic, with a mummy-wrapped hand. One crisis averted, we had only the weather to worry about now. The channel, glinting and breeze-stirred this morning, was roiling. The wind lifted particles of moisture into the air, a spindrift that soon overlay the water like a lace tablecloth. The eastern shore of Isla Tiburón, seen through this gauze of spray, looked hazy and unreal.

"Did you hear about the accident in Bahía de los Angeles?" Humberto asked as we loaded the panga. Yes, I said, and added that I was surprised to hear the story had traveled across the gulf.

"Biologists and their adventures," he sighed.

I waited to hear more, but he tipped his face to the sky. "Nothing in life is certain. Do you understand? *Nada es cierto.* It's like a *nube*—a cloud. It appears and disappears. That's why we must take care of each other."

He looked at Tziporah's hand. "God is strong. But sometimes the devil sneaks in."

Then he nodded at all of us: *Vamos.* We climbed into the panga and prepared for one hell of a ride.

The hardest part was just holding on. Every time we slammed over a wave, we all bounced an inch or two off our seats. It would have been easier to grip the underside of the panga bench if we hadn't been so intent on squeezing each other. I held Tziporah in a football cradle, pressed into my chest, until the claustrophobia became too much and she pushed away from me. She insisted on sitting on the bench between Aryeh and me, making it even harder for me to keep her from launching skyward. On the biggest bumps, both Aryeh and Tziporah shrieked, and then burst into maniacal laughter. Better than crying, I thought. "It's a roller-coaster!" Aryeh screamed with glee, barely closing his mouth before a curling wave showered us. But I could see from his face that he was a little scared, too. The waves were big. The foam was white. The panga danced and skipped and slammed.

I was grateful when I heard Aryeh start singing: the way we'd always dealt with long or anxious crossings in the kayak. It was a Cherokee song, from a kids' compact disc at home: *Ah-yah, Ay-yah-ayyy Yo Hi-yah* . . . His voice rose louder and louder, until it was stronger than the wind. I wondered if Humberto could hear this, and whether he would recognize this as a cultural kind of convergent evolution—different peoples developing the same behaviors to deal with the same geography, the same anxiety.

Then a smaller voice joined Aryeh's. I leaned close, questioning my own hearing.

It *was* Tziporah! I couldn't believe it; she had turned two years old just weeks earlier. She spoke only twenty or thirty words clearly (*sea star* and *crab* were among the few) but she'd never sung until this moment. Her full Hebrew name translates as Little Bird, and this English pet-name has always matched her quiet disposition. But now she howled over the wind and waves, too, mimicking her brother, mimicking—without even knowing it—all the people who had sung away their fears around these shoal-clotted bends: *Ay-yah, Ay-yah-ayyy Yo Hi-yah.*

And that's where the personal part of this book should have ended. Oh, there'd have to be some biographical wrap-up: what happened to the *Western Flyer*'s crew at Guaymas, until they, too, closed out their story and headed home.

But our family narrative should have been complete. For the rest of our Mexico trip, I would never see my children so ecstatic and full of life, even in the face of danger. True, Tziporah had been mildly wounded, but her slashed hand only confirmed our ultimate competence: All trip we had avoided injury, and now when something did happen, we were prepared. Tziporah, so much more mature and resilient than she had been at trip's beginning, had responded to the incident bravely. And a small injury could not overshadow the pleasure of our time with Humberto.

I would never feel more content in my absolute ignorance than I had while sitting next to our Seri guide—a brief and ephemeral moment of Rickettsian grace, when I had stopped trying to figure and know and judge. I had "broken through." Which is not to say that, when that veil of blissful acceptance lifted, I did not begin all over again to scratch and claw, to figure and analyze, to impose my own judgments on the world. But that moment of letting go had been a blessing. It had felt simultaneously like a numbness and a tingle, like pleasure and pain.

It reminded me of my first Cortez experience at San Nicolás, years ago, when I wandered with my sister Eliza out of the desert and into the sea, and saw mysterious alien life all around me—sequins and sparks and ciliated blobs—and I had not known enough about marine life even to know that these things were alive. But the not-knowing had been fundamental to my awe. And then my legs had begun to burn, stung by those beautiful creatures: *agua mala*.

It reminded me also of an elemental Jewish story which says that before humans are born they know everything. Then, at the moment of birth, an angel comes and puts a finger to their lips. That light brush—I imagined it as both tingling and numbing—causes babies to forget all. Gone is the wisdom of the ages, the possibility of mind and heart united in complete understanding. But this intellectual plummet is not a punishment. It is a blessing: an electric zap of ignorance, so that the newborn person may enjoy, their whole life, the process of learning.

Was it a coincidence that these stories twined so easily: that both ended with a light brush against something both awesome and irksome? Was it a coincidence that both stories ended with a sting?

Steinbeck and Ricketts motored from Isla Tiburón into Guaymas and immediately began to feel their Cortez experience slip away from them. Guaymas was different. It was bustling. It was modern. It was connected. It was mainland—not Baja at all, not really desert either, since the mainland coast from this point south begins to change into a moister, tropical, estuarine environment.

Captain Tony Berry was ready to go home. Normally taciturn, he finally let a trace of personality drip into his colorless captain's log. "Dropped anchor for the night," he wrote at Puerto San Carlos. "Mosquitoes galore. They can give this country back to the Indians."

For Sparky and Tiny, Guaymas was a highlight. Tiny was invited to take part in an exhibition boxing match and lost. The next day he and Sparky went on a whorehouse spree, visiting six or seven brothels in town. The price of a girl in a room was eighteen cents. Then the boys returned to the *Western Flyer* to find another party in full swing—complete with pretty girls and some guitarists picked up in a restaurant. "We really loved Guaymas and were talking about living there," Sparky recalled.

Ed and Carol had their share of booze and song and spirited confusion, too. But Steinbeck became instantly morose. Mosquitoes or no mosquitoes, girls or no girls, the real world was flooding back in, and he didn't care for it. He picked up his mail and posted his own letters. He began to think of writing again, of agents and publishers, of the war brewing, of the future of his marriage, of everything he'd left behind. Back on board the *Flyer,* he picked a brief fight with Tony over a comment the captain had made about Carol.

Ricketts recorded in his personal journal, "John very low." A few nights later, still anchored near Guaymas, Ricketts himself slept poorly, dreaming forlornly about a woman. He got up, thinking it was time to lift anchor, though really dawn was still four hours away. And he heard Carol call out—also having a nightmare. He called back, trying to reassure her. They had all lived so closely over the last weeks that even their moods were bound together, even their dreams.

Among the deckhands at Guaymas, there was a feeling of violent and lascivious frivolity. But among the more reflective crew members—John, Ed, perhaps Tony, too—there was an anticipatory air of discontent. They would hit another few tidepools on the way back to California. They would continue to absorb and reflect upon and be changed by their Baja experiences: the competition and predation and commensalism of the tidepools, the ferocity and richness of the open sea, the subtle humor and mellow wisdom of the Mexican people.

But the desert dreamtime was over. It was time to go home.

In Guaymas, we too reconnected with the world. And not for the better. We'd arranged for Alaska friends to pick up our mail and deposit any monies received. Our finances were so perilously low that every check mattered. When some of the monies appeared to be missing, we were forced to cloister ourselves inside Mexican long-distance phone booths, trying to reach employers, trying to reach publishers, trying to make our bank balance perk up. It was the worst kind of end-of-trip nail-biting: I would have preferred getting slugged in a four-round boxing match.

Just days before leaving Alaska (an eternity ago, it seemed) I'd finished writing a slim guidebook. With a joyful sense of deadline accomplishment, I'd express-mailed it. Then we'd boarded a plane and disappeared into Baja. Picking up month-old phone messages, I now discovered the manuscript had never arrived. Which explained one of the missing checks. More cramped phone booths, more phone calls across time zones. The peace of mind sculpted from weeks of oceanic immersion began to crumble.

"Already?" I asked Brian as we sat in a full-blown urban Guaymas traffic jam, pawing through ATM slips and ferry schedules, while also trying to spot, through the stream of honking cars, a *zapatería*. Aryeh needed a new pair of sandals: That would cost ten bucks. Ferry: It sailed across the gulf, to Santa Rosalía, on Tuesday only; today was Wednesday, plus the ticket price had climbed. Rental car: Overdue back in Mexicali, payment on delivery. Publisher: Still can't find the missing manuscript, even with a tracking code. Friends: Sorry, no more checks.

"Already," Brian said. "The world returns."

We visited the *Western Flyer*'s next tidepooling area. Called Puerto San Carlos, it had been obliterated by the development of a huge marina-condo complex (Cabo San Carlos, Brian called it). To get a sense of what Steinbeck and Ricketts would have seen, we made our own substitution, tidepooling a few miles south, just outside Guaymas. This less-developed spot was still rich. We saw crabs, slate pencil urchins, rock oysters, chitons, and a new kind of sea cucumber—elephant gray with pinkish warts. Within sight of downtown Guaymas, we saw a Mexican man snorkeling far offshore, harvesting some kind of shellfish.

We had only two official stations left: Estero de la Luna, south of Guaymas, and Agiabampo, a murky lagoon another hundred miles beyond that. Both meant long hours of driving and several more days of camping and peso-pinching. Neither tidepool station, as described in the *Log,* seemed particularly enchanting.

As for Agiabampo, it had been gray, muddy, and relatively sterile in 1940. There was no reason to expect that the passage of years had improved it. We wondered aloud: Wouldn't it be so much easier, so much more pleasant, so much more economical simply to end things at Guaymas, and take the ferry back across the gulf? Except that the ferry wouldn't run for another week. So either way, the mainland coast held us in its muggy grasp.

There was one silver lining: In Guaymas, there was an elegant, old-fashioned resort, the Hotel Cortez. Brian and I had stayed there six years earlier, when I was pregnant with Aryeh. It had been our first taste of the Cortez after weeks of tramping around inland Mexico. We had woken next to the blue sea, invigorated by the clear morning air and boundless horizon. We had been served breakfast in an ornate dining room facing the gulf. Scooping the last spoonfuls of melon into our mouths, we had spotted dolphins through the restaurant's French doors. It had been a magical moment, during which my first-trimester nausea had lifted and cleared, if only briefly. We'd always dreamed of returning.

Of course, we were flat broke this time around. But no matter: During our first stay, the hotel (which also hosted RVs) had allowed us to pitch a tent in their extensive parking lot. We had been able to sleep cheaply while enjoying the hotel's fine dining, showers, and pool.

We remembered the dolphins and the view, but not the hotel's exact location or even its name. We spent hours searching, certain only that the Hotel Cortez was sequestered away from town, off a dirt road, behind an immense screen of palm trees. At every dead end we reassured the children that we were on the trail to paradise. Once we located this phantom hotel, we promised, all pleasures would follow: food and plumbing and the best view in Mexico.

When we finally arrived at the hotel, around 9:00 P.M., Aryeh and Tziporah were woozy with hunger and exhaustion, but Brian and I were triumphant. We babbled to the night guard (*"Years ago, before the children ..."*). We paused in the parking lot, paralyzed by our wistful memories (*"The bougainvillea—do you remember?"*). Finally, we charged toward the front desk (*"You check us in and I'll see if the restaurant is still open—I can't wait to see the view in the morning!"*).

But then nostalgia met its demise, shattered like a clay-pot piñata. The front-desk lady would not allow us to pitch our tent in the RV lot. We told her about our previous stay, but the romantic simplicity of it did not impress her. Even though the parking lot was empty, even though ancient bellhops haunted the hotel's dark hallways in desperate search of some suitcase to lift, she would not cut us a deal. We shrugged in defeat and asked about regular rooms. But this, too, had changed—the rates were much higher than any we remembered. Time had passed; the dollar had weakened. In any case, we could not afford to stay.

"What do we do now?" Brian asked.

"I don't know," I said. "I can't think. Let's go outside." The front-desk lady, and all the bellhops too, looked relieved to see us go.

Beyond the grand hotel's front doors, on the way to the parking lot, we passed a fountain. A warm, soothing wind blew. A soft light illuminated our path. We could smell the bougainvillea. The moon, a pale orb above us, worked its tidal magic on the sparkling gulf.

"Here," I said. "Perfect. Let's sit. The kids can play while we compare our options."

Aryeh chased Tziporah around the bubbling fountain for a minute or so, until the strap on his sandal broke. "See? I need a new pair," he griped. But Brian and I were already crunching numbers—how much left on our credit card, how much a typical Guaymas motel might cost. We did not want to discuss shoe shopping.

"Just take the sandal off and keep playing," I said. "The concrete's fine. We're not tidepooling."

He shrugged and removed the sandal. Brian and I returned to arithmetic. "Even if we can find a cheaper place, I just don't want to drive anymore. And to find a good camping beach this late . . ."

That's when Aryeh shrieked. His mouth formed a great gaping hole. Sound gushed forth—a primal banshee wail. I'd never heard so much pain and panic in his voice. It made Tziporah's earlier scream (was it only earlier today that she'd gotten hurt?) seem like a muffled whine by comparison.

Aryeh's scream seemed never-ending, but it was really time that slowed down. I stared at him. He was balanced on one foot, with mouth still agape. Then my eyes tracked to the concrete walk around the fountain. And there on the well-lit walk was the thing: honey-colored body, arched tail, pincers brandished, every arthropod segment glowing. I hold

244 SEARCHING FOR STEINBECK'S SEA OF CORTEZ

that image in my mind even now, framed by horror, and perhaps I have embellished it, just as I have reviewed a dozen times the steps that led to the moment. (Financial distraction, broken sandal, my own bad advice, and then that evil thing. . . .) At some point, Brian ran to Aryeh and scooped him up, and Tziporah found her way into my arms. At some point, too, Brian had the sense to run after the scorpion and get a good look at it, to try to identify its species and estimate its toxicity, though—to my regret—he did not kill it.

Then, somehow, Tziporah was in Brian's arms and Aryeh was in mine, yelling about his foot, and we were hurrying into the same hotel lobby we'd just departed. The front-desk lady rolled her eyes and the bellhop looked away, as if embarrassed to watch us petition again about camping options or a discount. But I shouted at them both, "We're not here for a room. It's my son. *Un alacrán.* From out there, by the fountain. He's really hurt. You have to help us!"

All cynicism drained from the woman's face. She shuffled behind the desk and produced a white pill—an antihistamine, we were later told. I should have cared more about medical specifics—what dosage was this, and would it even help—but I was too distraught to think clearly. "Swallow," I ordered Aryeh.

The bellhop vanished and reappeared with several garlic cloves, a folk remedy. We made Aryeh chew the garlic, though he cried while he did so, the pungent pieces a sobby mush in his half-open mouth. Tears splashed down his cheek. The garlic made him gag. He said he might throw up. I begged someone to bring a glass of milk, and after a few minutes, one appeared. We propped him on a lobby couch, swollen foot stabilized on a pillow.

"Is it okay?" I asked Aryeh. "How do you feel?"

"It's in my leg now. All the way to here," he said, voice shaking, while he pointed to his groin. "It kinda hurts. But it's numb, too." And this was worse than pain, because we knew that the numbness meant the poison was traveling toward his heart, and was already halfway there.

I begged the front-desk lady to call a doctor, the paramedics, anyone. "You have to help us!"

Aryeh looked to Brian. "It was a small one, wasn't it?"

"Yes," Brian said. "The small kind."

Aryeh knew too much. He knew the most dangerous scorpions are the little ones, not the more visually frightening larger kind. He knew that adults aren't really endangered by scorpion stings, but that babies and young children under thirty pounds sometimes die. Aryeh weighed about thirty-eight pounds. He remembered *The Pearl,* of course. And he couldn't feel his leg.

"Keep chewing," I told him while the bellhop rubbed his toe with a garlic clove. "Crackers? Anyone have crackers?"

Meanwhile, the bellhop mused nonchalantly in Spanish to the front-desk lady, "I've seen it many times. Children die. I wouldn't be surprised."

The front-desk lady looked to me with wide eyes, checking my face for signs of comprehension, and then to the bellhop, whom she tried to shush with a glowering look. But he didn't notice. "Thirty-eight years I've worked here," he continued. "This is serious. Wouldn't be surprised at all . . ."

"Stop that!" I yelled at him. "I understand what you're saying. You stop saying that!"

Sweeping Tziporah into my arms, I raced outside the hotel and across the parking lot, to our car, and started digging in the backseat for some snack food to take away the bad garlic taste in Aryeh's mouth. It was a futile search, with Tziporah crying fearfully for her brother, clinging to me with her one good and one mummy-wrapped hand; and me burrowing in the half-dark, blinded by my own tears, trying to be helpful while I pictured Aryeh back inside the hotel, convulsing from a heart attack. And some of this horror seemed somehow linked to our earlier hubris: We had patched Tziporah's hand and patted our own backs while doing so, praising our preparedness, our competence, and our luck. But this was a different matter. "God is strong," Humberto had said. "But sometimes the devil sneaks in."

I heard an ambulance pull up and saw the night watchman rush out to greet the paramedics. "It's my son," I shouted. "Inside!"

By the time I joined the three young paramedics in the hotel lobby, the ambiance had changed from fright to frivolity. They checked Aryeh's blood pressure and heart rate, and then stood around, ogling the hotel's ornate lobby. Aryeh was still sniffling and wincing, but the paramedics looked cheerful, as if they'd raced here just to enjoy a bit of drama on a dull night.

"Whatever could happen would have happened by now—a reaction, an attack, whatever," one of them told me, smiling. "The worst is over. He is alive, he is breathing. There will be some pain, but there is nothing for us to do."

It took forty-eight hours for us to recover. Aryeh was fine after twelve hours, but the rest of us needed a few days in the Hotel Cortez before we could summon enough energy to leave Guaymas. *("I don't care; just run the credit card, if it'll work.")* After a piña colada, a good night's sleep, and a long morning by the pool, I still caught myself trembling. I had no urge to camp, turn over rocks, or feel awe for God's humbler creatures.

The first night, Aryeh and Tziporah were terrified of any shadow moving on the floor, but they got over it quickly. In fact, by the time we were ready to check out of the Hotel Cortez, Aryeh was actively hunting scorpions, eager for a chance to see the creature that had tried to kill him. Even now, he calls himself *Saguaro Alacrán.* He maintains a collection of scorpion toys and images, and seems to draw some kind of totemic strength from them.

The daily cost of the rental car haunted us, the ferry wouldn't leave for several more days, and we didn't want to wait. So we changed plans yet again. We decided to skip Estero de la Luna. We decided to skip Agiabampo. And we decided to finish our trip entirely by road, up and around the head of the gulf and down into Baja all the way to Mulegé (where we'd clean the safely arrived *Zuiva* and sell her motor for enough cash to pay the rental car bill) and back up to Mexicali to return the car. Hundreds more miles, many more nights, even some more time in tide-pools—but really, the trip was over.

It was over as soon as the scorpion stung, because at that moment, Steinbeck had his last say: "People don't take trips—trips take people," a line from *Travels with Charley.* And then he and Ricketts and the *Western Flyer* vanished from our minds. Even when we tried to summon their spirits, for one last spot of advice or a more formal goodbye, they refused to come.

The two men had provided us with inspiration, a question, and a design. Only we could find our own ending. The taut string between

1940 and the present, which had quivered and hummed and occasion-ally cut into our hands, now snapped. The oscillation between past and present, science and philosophy, what should be and "what is," simply collapsed. It became a single point in time—*now*—and a single entity—*us*. And we knew that we weren't traveling any more, but only going from place to place, trying to get home.

ACKNOWLEDGMENTS

This trip couldn't have been made and this book couldn't have been written without the help and support of many, all of whom understood that Mexican saying, *El que no se aventura no cruza la mar.* Biggest thanks to Eliza, whose loyalty and joie de vivre have made many journeys possible. A hearty thank-you to sponsor Lyle Hancock at Folding Kayak Adventures, who loaned us one of his fantastic, family-sized Feathercraft kayaks. Our boat captain took a risk with us and endured to the best of his—and our—abilities. For this we thank him and hope his future passages are trouble-free. Even before Roy loaned us the *Zuiva,* he was a good friend to us and to many Baja travelers. We hope he continues to find peace and satisfaction south of the border.

At Sasquatch Books, Kate Rogers took a big chance on our little expedition. Her trust and flexibility were essential to this project. Several other kind people at Sasquatch added their capable expertise to this book, including Laura Gronewold, Sarah Smith, and Karen Schober, as well as copy editor Don Graydon (olé) and proofreader Sharon Vonasch. Thank you to the members of my Anchorage writing group who endured rough early drafts: Nancy, Jim, Jon, Bill, Ellen, Dan, and George.

I am grateful for the existence of the Stanford University Libraries Department of Special Collections, the Center for Steinbeck Studies at San Jose State University, and the National Steinbeck Center in Salinas—all inspiring places to visit, and all staffed by considerate and competent devotees of California literature. I'm indebted to literary scholars, scientists, government officials, and tour guides who answered my questions and directed me to additional sources in both "Alta" and Baja California. In addition to those already named in the book, I thank Katie Rodger (Center for Steinbeck Studies), Peter Brueggeman (Scripps Institution of Oceanography Library), and seabird expert Daniel W. Anderson.

I am fortunate that I have a family that supports my writing efforts. The Arizona hospitality of Elizabeth Sweet, Ariel Sweet, and Dorothy

Clausen helped us recover from our Sea of Cortez trip. Thanks to Aryeh and Tziporah, the best travel partners a tidepooler could ever want. And thank-you, finally, to Honorée Romano and Catherine Romano, whose responses to this story, in its prepublished form, meant more to me than they could ever know.

SOURCES

As background for this book, I relied on many books by John Steinbeck, including *The Log from the Sea of Cortez, The Pearl, The Grapes of Wrath, Cannery Row,* and *Travels with Charley.* I have quoted him frequently in this book (with permission), and paraphrased him (as in this book's prologue, where he and Ricketts describe being watched, as they are tidepooling, by Mexican boys). I also tried to capture the flavor of his outlook and writing style in some aspects of my own retelling and recreation of the *Western Flyer* expedition.

Obviously, this book would not exist had the *Log* not been written first. It is my hope that readers who are not familiar with the *Log* or its unabridged predecessor, *Sea of Cortez,* will be intrigued enough to head to their favorite bookstore and look for this less-known Steinbeck classic. Originally published the same week that Japan bombed Pearl Harbor, *Sea of Cortez* was underappreciated for many years and has become a cult classic in recent times because so many modern scientists and Baja travelers continue to find its descriptions, reflections, and irreverent tone astonishingly timeless.

Of the many biographical sources I consulted, the most definitive and essential to my research was *John Steinbeck, Writer: A Biography* by Jackson J. Benson. This exhaustive study provides key insights on Steinbeck's childhood, first marriage, and early writing career. Benson describes Steinbeck's mindset during—and the public response to—the publication of *The Grapes of Wrath,* which set the stage for the author's 1940 escape to the Sea of Cortez. What Benson is to Steinbeck, Richard Astro is to Ed Ricketts. Astro deserves credit for being the first biographer to examine in detail (in his 1973 book, *John Steinbeck and Edward F. Ricketts: The Shaping of a Novelist*) the influence "Doc" had on his famous neighbor.

To understand more about the Steinbeck-Ricketts friendship, as well as tensions between *Western Flyer* crewmembers, I drew from unpublished letters and published sources including the slim but humorous

With Steinbeck in the Sea of Cortez by Sparky Enea as told to Audry Lynch; *Inside Cannery Row* by Bruce Ariss; and *The Outer Shores* by Joel Hedgpeth. This latter book, published in two parts and currently out of print, pulls together many otherwise difficult-to-acquire sources, such as Ed Ricketts's Sea of Cortez trip journal, several of Ricketts's otherwise unpublished philosophical essays, and Tony Berry's captain's log. Hedgpeth's insights into the personalities and philosophies of John Steinbeck and Ed Ricketts are important to anyone interested in either man. I enjoyed many of Hedgpeth's anecdotes and borrowed two of them: his description of the Cannery Row fire (also described in the essay "About Ed Ricketts" by John Steinbeck), and Steinbeck's offhand description of himself as a "sort of biologist," which Hedgpeth himself credits to Willard Bascom. The epigraph by Ed Ricketts that opens this book's prologue was also quoted from Hedgpeth's *The Outer Shores.*

Several writers, including John Steinbeck himself, have reflected on the author's interest in Charles Darwin, and his passion for natural history in general. I owe my awareness of that topic to a scholarly anthology called *Steinbeck and the Environment: Interdisciplinary Approaches,* edited by Susan F. Beegel, Susan Shillinglaw, and Wesley N. Tiffney, Jr. Two essays in that book stand out: "Searching for 'What Is': Charles Darwin and John Steinbeck" by Brian Railsback, and "The Poetry of Scientific Thinking: Steinbeck's *Log from the Sea of Cortez* and Scientific Travel Narrative" by Stanley Brodwin.

I take full responsibility for any scientific errors made in naming or describing tidepool animals. For anything I got *right,* I would like to credit *Animals Without Backbones* by Ralph Buchsbaum, Mildred Buchsbaum, John Pearse, and Vicki Pearse; *Between Pacific Tides* by Ed Ricketts and Jack Calvin with revisions by Joel Hedgpeth; *Common Intertidal Invertebrates of the Gulf of California* by Richard C. Brusca, et al.; *Marine Animals of Baja California* by Daniel W. Gotshall; *A Field Guide to Pacific Coast Fishes of North America* (from the Peterson field guide series) by William N. Eschmeyer, et al.; *The Sea-Beach at Ebb-Tide* by Augusta Foote Arnold; *Animals of the Seashore* by Muriel Lewin Guberlet; and *The Ocean Almanac* by Robert Hendrickson. Though it contains only a few mentions of the Sea of Cortez, I enjoyed and quoted from Cindy Lee Van Dover's *The Octopus's Garden: Hydrothermal Vents and Other Mysteries of the Deep Sea.* For information on desert ecology, I relied on *A Natural*

History of the Sonoran Desert, edited by Steven J. Phillips and Patricia Wentworth Comus.

I thank David Quammen for being one of the first popular writers to muse in depth about sea cucumbers for a popular audience (in *Outside* magazine, later anthologized in his *Natural Acts: A Sidelong View of Science and Nature*). In my own reflection on sea cucumbers, I relied on other (mostly technical) sources and my own encounters with echinoderms, but his playfulness and curiosity were an inspiration for this and other facets of our Cortez trip.

For background on Baja California and the Sea of Cortez from journalistic sources, I drew from archives at the *Arizona Republic, Sacramento Bee,* and *Los Angeles Times.* In particular, I appreciate the reports filed by journalists Steve Yozwiak, Usha Lee McFarling, Tony Perry, Kathleen Ingley, and David Madrid. For details about the Yolanda Gonzalez tragedy, I relied upon the reporting of Mark Shaffer *(Arizona Republic/Associated Press).* William Langewiesche's coverage of the border region for the *Atlantic Monthly* is both reliable and poetic, and I enjoyed its concise depiction of Colorado River water conservation issues.

Tom Knudson's *Sacramento Bee* series, "The Dying Gulf" (available from that newspaper's online archives), is required reading for anyone interested in Gulf of California environmental issues. Knudson has been one of the few reporters willing to tackle the "big picture" of the gulf, even while challenged by a dearth of scientific data. In book format, another important "big picture" work, written by scientists but accessible to most lay-readers, is *Island Biogeography in the Sea of Cortez* edited by Ted Case. In particular, I appreciated the chapter about early scientific expeditions to the gulf. A second edition of this book is rumored to be in the works.

For those readers wanting to look back to the years before Steinbeck's and Ricketts's expedition, I recommend *Travels in Southern California* by John Xantus, the nineteenth-century naturalist. For an eighteenth-century perspective, I relied on Miguel del Barco's *The Natural History of Baja California,* which is a translation of part one of the original *Historia Natural y Crónica de la Antigua California.* For an understanding of Baja during and just following Steinbeck's visit, I relied on *The Forgotten Peninsula* by Joseph Krutch; *Hardly Any Fences: Baja California in 1933–1959* by John W. Hilton; *A Sand County Almanac and Sketches Here and There* by Aldo Leopold; and old newspaper columns by Ray Cannon, collected by

Gene Kira in *The Unforgettable Sea of Cortez: Baja California's Golden Age, 1947–1977: The Life and Writings of Ray Cannon*.

Plenty of guidebooks and charts have led us astray during our years traveling Baja, but one that delivered was *Baja Handbook: Tijuana to Cabo San Lucas* by Joe Cummings, from the Moon Travel Handbooks series. From his description of Mexicali Chinese settlement to his recommendations for where to find a good taco, I appreciate this guidebook and recommend it to others.

Photo: Kristen Kemerling

ABOUT THE AUTHOR

Award-winning writer Andromeda Romano-Lax is the author of four guidebooks and has been a staff writer for the *Anchorage Daily News* and the *Homer News*. Her travel essays, sportswriting, and features have appeared in numerous publications, including *Sea Kayaker, Writer's Digest, Steinbeck Studies,* and *Alaska* magazines, and she recently contributed to an anthology of women's travel writing.

Romano-Lax has a degree in Political Science and a Master's of Marine Management; her studies included specialization in the history, politics, and environment of Mexico, especially the Sea of Cortez. She also recently completed a science journalism fellowship at the Marine Biological Laboratory (M.B.L.) in Woods Hole, Massachusetts, and is a member of the adjunct faculty of the University of Alaska Anchorage. She has traveled extensively in Mexico over the last decade and now lives in Anchorage with her husband and two children. You can visit her online at www.booksbyandromeda.com.